Ambassador Extraordinary

*

Ambassador

Extraordinary

Clare Boothe Luce

*

By

ALDEN HATCH

Illustrated with Photographs

HENRY HOLT AND COMPANY · NEW YORK

83502-0516

Printed in the United States of America

ACKNOWLEDGMENTS

FIRST I want to acknowledge that I never had as much fun writing a book as I did with *Ambassador Extraordinary*. You cannot spend five minutes with my beautiful protagonist without being vastly amused by her wit and excited by her brilliant comments on world affairs—and people. Not only that, but her numerous friends with whom I spent many pleasant hours are as stimulating a group of people as you could find on five continents. The story itself was so crammed with variety of scene and subject, and so vitally connected with the history of our era that it was a tremendous challenge and a sheer delight to write it. Clare Luce could not be the subject of a work of fiction. Nobody would believe it.

I am most grateful to Mrs. Luce for fitting me into her crowded schedule for so many hours of good talk, and for her thoughtfulness and consideration in helping me with technical difficulties. It is a rare pleasure to work with a subject who has been both a top editor and a writer, and who therefore understands and sympathizes with one's problems.

Others who helped in every possible way and contributed a great deal to this book include Henry Robinson Luce, Mrs. Dorothy Farmer, Miss Letitia Baldrige, Bernard M. Baruch, Buckminster Fuller, Bishop Fulton J. Sheen, Senator W. Stuart Symington, Congressman Joseph W. Martin, Congressman Albert P. Morano, Minister Counselor Elbridge Durbrow, Counselor Francis Williamson, Ambassador Alberico Casardi, Minister Remigio Grillo, West German Ambassador von Brentano, Indro Montanelli (*Corriere della Sera*), Mr. and Mrs. Landon Thorne, Miss Dorothy Thompson, Miss Elsa Maxwell, Brigadier General Emmet Cassady, Attaché John Deneen, Mr. and Mrs. Arthur Menkin, Mrs. Raymond Clapper, Eric Severied, William B. Sale, Mrs. Allen Grover, Duchessa Lante della Rovere, Mrs. Edna Woolman Chase, Miss Ilka Chase, Mrs. Buff Cobb Rogers, Mrs. Irvin Cobb, William M.

Chadbourne, Miss Margaret Case, Mrs. Margaret Thompson Biddle, Miss Mary Holbrook Russell (Principal of St. Mary's Cathedral School), Mrs. Helen Brown Lawrenson, Mrs. Reginald Benson (formerly Mrs. Condé Nast), Lady Malcolm Douglas-Hamilton, Miss Tere Pascone, Mrs. Dorothy Burns Holloran, Miss Ruth Burns, Mrs. Isabel Hill, Miss Gladys Freeman, James L. Barry, and Robert A. Hug, of the New York Public Library.

Books and articles that I have consulted include all the published books of Mrs. Luce, "The Real Reason," published by *McCall's,* and various articles by Mrs. Luce which have appeared in *Vogue, Vanity Fair, Time,* and *Life,* as well as "The Candor Kid," by Margaret Case Harriman, published in the *New Yorker,* The Profile in *Newsweek,* and "Au Clare de Luce" by Faye Henle published by Stephen Daye.

CONTENTS

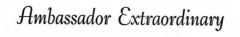

Ambassador Extraordinary

CHAPTER ONE

APPOINTMENT AT THE COMMODORE

IN THE WHOLE HISTORY OF DIPLOMACY SINCE THE FIRST CRO-Magnon chieftain sent his fastest talker to negotiate with the foreigners in the caves across the valley—for fifty thousand years or more—no woman has held so important a diplomatic post as Clare Boothe Luce, Ambassador Extraordinary and Plenipotentiary to the Republic of Italy. For Rome, always the center of the Mediterranean world, has become the court of courts at a crisis of history, since it is there that communism comes closest to tipping the hairline balance of power between the East and the West. A slip on the part of the American Ambassador sends tremors through the fragile fabric of the alliance of free nations. Complete failure on her part could lose the world.

What sort of woman holds such power and carries, like Atlas, the heavens of democracy on her slight shoulders? Practically no one agrees about that.

Brilliant, yet often foolish; idealistic, yet realistic to the verge of cynicism; tough as a marine sergeant, but almost quixotically kind to unfortunates; with the mind and courage of a man and exceedingly feminine instincts; the complexities of her character are as numerous as the facets of her career. She was born in comparative poverty, was a child actress at ten, and was educated in a fashionable girls' school. In turn she has been a society matron, magazine editor, wit among wits, social reformer among starry-eyed liberals; playwright, war correspondent, congresswoman, lecturer and student of theology, wife of America's leading publisher, and, now, Ambassador. No wonder Tere Pascone, her political associate and friend, wrote beneath her picture, "And one man in his time plays many parts." She might have added, "And thinks many things," for Clare Luce has been everything from a theoretical Communist to a practicing Catholic.

There is really only one point of agreement in the controversy that has raged around her most of her life; and that is the irrefutable fact that at fifty-two she is one of the most beautiful women in the world.

Meanwhile she apparently walks her diplomatic tightrope with the airy grace of the Daring Young Man. Actually, the intensity of her inner dedication is like that of a young acolyte swinging his first censer. Possibly the reason no one understands her completely is because she does not even understand herself.

First Clare Luce's own story of how she came to be appointed to her difficult post.

In the campaign of 1952 the Luces went down the line for Eisenhower, all the way from the first glint in his eye that indicated he might try for the Republican nomination to that final roaring night at the Commodore Hotel when they watched the flood tide of votes pour in to make him President.

Clare had thrown herself into the campaign with a single-purpose, all-consuming drive that absorbed every moment of every day and most of every night. She had no time to think of herself. But the day after victory she took stock of her position.

It seemed highly probable that the President-elect would ask her to take some post in the government. She recalled what he had said to her the first time they talked politics together, three years before. Eisenhower was president of Columbia then, apparently determined on disassociating himself from politics. President Truman had scored his surprise smash victory in the election of 1948, and the Republican party was groggily trying to pull itself together. Thinking realistically about the state of the party, Clare reached a conclusion. She announced it to her husband one evening: "Harry, if it isn't Ike, we're not going to win next time either. I think I'll go to see him."

"Why don't you?" said Harry Luce.

Clare had met General Eisenhower on a trip to the battle fronts in 1944 and had seen him often after that in Washington. But their first real talk was in his office off the rotunda of Columbia's Low Library. He was evasive but indubitably interested. She gathered that the strong current of his patriotism was beginning to erode his adamantine determination to stay out of politics.

Just as she was leaving she asked lightly, "How many politicians give you advice, General?"

Grinning broadly, Eisenhower answered, "Nobody can come through that door without giving me advice."

"I'm no exception," Clare said. "If you take my advice you will be President. My advice is this: Don't take any advice."

The general's laugh boomed out through the waiting room and echoed in the marble rotunda. "I tell you, if I do get to be President," he said, "you're one of the people I want on my team."

Of course Clare did not take that seriously. But during the campaign she had come to know Eisenhower well. He had shown appreciation of her ability and real liking for her. Take it all together, she thought she had better decide what she wanted to do.

Her first conclusion was that she wanted nothing more to do with politics. As she usually told herself in moments of reaction like this, her real career was writing. In order to take part in the campaign she had closed her play, *Child of the Morning*, on the road—the fact that the out-of-town notices had been terrible had had something to do with that. But another play, *Love Is a Verb*, was in rough form in her notes, and Hollywood was waiting for her final script of *Pilate's Wife*. She certainly did not want "to go back to the maelstrom of Washington in a minor post." One thing was plain: If she could do as she liked, she would stay home and write.

On the other hand there was an obligation. As she put it, "I had played some small part in electing Ike, and my husband had played a great part. It would seem strange if I did nothing. I felt I should go on the team."

She talked it over with her husband. As usual Harry Luce made sense. "Don't go near Ike," he advised. "If he wants you, he'll offer you something, and you can make up your mind whether to take it or not. If he doesn't send for you, you can do what you really want to do."

That took the weight of decision off her mind, and she settled down to writing. At least she tried to. . . .

The author of *The Women* is certainly a leading expert on feminine foibles. By mid-December Clare Luce considered herself practically a case history. She was doing exactly what she wanted to do. She lived in a beautiful triplex overlooking the East River, in the apartment house that Alexander Woollcott had named "Wits End" because it was at the end of the street and so many wits lived there. Each afternoon when her husband came home from the magazine, they sat together in their lovely pink and crystal drawing room, looking through a picture window at the marine traffic on the East River and the map of Long Island spread at their feet. On clear evenings you could see the green and white flash of the beacon at Idlewild and the purple darkness beyond the lights at the edge of the ocean. It was wonderful and warm to sit sipping a cocktail and talking of great events with Harry, who knew so much and was so wise and stimulating.

But she was not really happy. In fact she was perilously close to being in what one of her characters in a play described as "a snit."

The trouble was that the papers kept announcing Presidential appointments: Foster Dulles to State, that was foregone; Charlie Wilson to Defense; and, much harder to take, Mrs. Hobby to the newly created Department of Health, Education, and Welfare. Ambassadors were named to England, France, and other countries. Many lesser appointments were announced. Still there was no request for her services. "I did not want a post, but I did want to be asked," she admits.

When she finally broke down and confessed hurt feelings to Harry, he was roughly comforting. "You're being absurd," he said. "Ike will send for you and offer you a job."

Then he went off to look at the war in Korea for his magazines.

That was a lonely week. Ilka Chase recalls that she asked Clare to tea to help her mother, Edna Woolman Chase of *Vogue*, with her book of reminiscences. Clare came early, talked brilliantly, and stayed until Ilka thought she would never leave.

When she finally departed, Ilka found her purse lying on the sofa. She telephoned to leave word. To her amazement Clare herself answered.

"What are you doing home?" Ilka demanded.

"Eating dinner alone," Clare answered. "I hoped you would ask me, that's why I stayed so long."

"Of course I would have, if I'd known. But I thought you'd be off to some brilliant function. Where's Harry?"

"Tonight he's in Tokyo."

"Why didn't you tell me?" Ilka asked.

"I guess I'm sort of shy," said Clare.

The call came at last. It was Arthur Vandenberg: "Mr. Eisenhower wants to see you, Clare. Can you come down to the Commodore about three this afternoon?"

She answered in the slow, soft, controlled voice which she uses when her emotions are most stirred. "Of course, Arthur, I'll be there."

She replaced the telephone in its cradle as casually as though this were just another call. But anyone who knew her as well as did her secretary, Mrs. Dorothy Farmer, could tell by the intense blue fire in her eyes and the stain of rushing blood in her transparent skin that she was tremendously excited.

Elation soon gave way to second-thought sobriety. She sent Dorothy Farmer off to lunch and sat alone in the office of her apartment. This was the room that really expressed her personality. The walls were muted salmon pink relieved by some fine modern paintings. The north end was like a luxurious sitting room with sleek blonde furniture, slip-covered in coral, turquoise-green, and beige, grouped around a glass-topped coffee table. The other part, with a plain businesslike desk and overflowing bookshelves, looked like a magazine editor's office. Thus the room was slightly schizophrenic. But Clare had made many hard decisions there. This one, she felt, was the most important of all.

If the President-elect offered her a post, she could take it or not, as Harry said. But what if he asked her what she wanted? Ever since her visit to Europe in the terrible blitzkrieg spring of 1940, her main interest had been in foreign affairs. She was dedicated to do all in her power that America should never find herself bankrupt of virtue, bereft of friends, and prostrate before a conqueror as France had been.

The most natural thing, Clare thought, would be a foreign post, but she rejected the idea. She had no wish to spend the next four years in some far-off country—to be separated from Harry for an indefinite period. She was a great deal closer to her husband than anybody knew, since their dissimilar careers gave the public an impression of separateness. All day she looked forward to their precious moments together in the late afternoon. Definitely she would not take a job that would keep her away from Harry for years.

Looking out the window to her left, she idly watched the luncheon crowd streaming out of the geometrical fantasy of the United Nations buildings. That's it, she thought. I'll ask to be a delegate. Home for lunch every day!

The gopher warren that was Eisenhower's Headquarters at the Commodore was seething when Clare arrived at exactly 2.59. It seemed that all the selfless, idealistic workers of the campaign had been transmuted by the alchemy of victory into job-hunters. The pressure on Ike must be terrific!

She sent in her name and Arthur Vandenberg came out to greet her. His round face looked oddly drawn and tired. Clare thought that Ike, too, would show signs of strain, but in his office the pressures seemed magically lifted. He greeted her with exuberant warmth, and they chatted for a while as though there were nothing in the world to worry about.

But when the President-elect got down to business, he fairly knocked her breath out. "Clare, how do you think you might fit on my team as Secretary of ——?* There's a precedent for such an appointment."

Clare had not even speculated on the possibility of this par-

---

* At the request of Mrs. Luce the name of the cabinet post is omitted.

ticular post. But even in the few seconds Eisenhower was talking, she realized that there were others who could handle it better. "I'm not your man," she said decisively.

Ike leaned back, grinning gratefully. "Well, I'm relieved," he said ingenuously.

Then serious again, he asked, "Where do you see yourself fitting on the team?"

"I'd like to be a delegate to the UN," she answered.

Ike shook his head. "I've already given that job to Mary Lord."

Clare had a sudden, unexpected feeling of relief. "Well, that's that," she said smiling. "You offered me a job. It's the *offer* I really wanted."

"Hold your horses," Eisenhower ordered, smiling. "How about ambassador?"

"To what country?" Clare interrupted hurriedly. "If it's a long way off, I don't want it. Harry couldn't be with me. . . . A small country in Europe? You shouldn't really send a woman to Denmark or Luxembourg again. Small posts should not be thought of as the perquisites for a woman. That really would hurt the feelings of some of our allies. Besides, according to the newspaper rumors, all the big posts are gone—Paris, Rome, London. . . ."

"What makes you think Rome is gone?" Eisenhower asked speculatively. "As a matter of fact, it isn't."

"That would be a great honor," she said, slowly giving herself time to think. "But most difficult. Especially for me."

"Why especially for you?"

Her mind saw it with realistic clarity, and she answered still slowly but definitely. "Because there will be sharp criticism of my appointment for at least four good reasons. The first is that I am a woman and it will be said that the Italians will not like dealing with a woman—that it will hurt their pride.

"Second, I am a Catholic, and there will be many good, uninformed people who will therefore worry for fear that I might get too close to the Vatican or be too influenced by Vatican opinions.

"Then, since my husband is an important publisher, people will feel that he will not report the news from Rome objectively if I am there.

"Finally, I am known to be so strongly anti-Communist that the

whole Italian left, nearly a third of the people, will hate and distrust me."

Eisenhower had listened attentively, his face very thoughtful. He
did not answer her objections but began to talk about the Italian
situation. He was amazed by the depth of her knowledge, the clarity
of her thinking. They discussed it for over an hour. Just at the end
he returned to the ambassadorship. "I'll think it over," he said, "and
you think about it too."

As soon as she got home, Clare wrote to Harry, telling him of the
"splendid offer" and adding, "but I shall refuse it unless you can
think of some plan that will permit us to be together much of the
time."

When she got his reply, Clare knew gratefully for the thousandth
time that he was certainly a remarkable husband. For Harry wrote
that if she decided to accept the ambassadorship, he would arrange
to spend alternate periods of six weeks in Italy. It was an astonish-
ing sacrifice for any man to make. Not only would he be subjecting
himself to great inconvenience and expense, and hampering somewhat his ability to run the magazines which were his very life, but
—as he was certainly well aware—in Rome he would be in the
anomalous position of being the Ambassador's husband—the tail of
her kite. Smaller men might balk at such apparent loss of dignity,
especially among the cynical Italian males, but Harry could take it
in his stride. After all, Clare thought fondly, no quirks of protocol
could make Harry the tail of anybody's kite!

Almost at the same time Eisenhower sent word that he had talked
her appointment over with many of his advisers. "All the criticisms
you foresaw have been made in that same order. If your judgment
is that good, I want you."

There it was: the way clear; the challenge pikestaff plain. Italy
represented all the difficulties that any other diplomatic post would
present, doubled in spades, because Italy, with the largest Communist party in Free Europe, was the focal point of Russian political pressure. Clare Luce knew that if she failed, she could expect
less charity from her countrymen and a harsher verdict in the court
of history than any man.

Not long ago Bernard Baruch said, "Clare's like a little game-cock. Ruffle her feathers and put her in that pit and she'll win every time."

This ambassadorship was a dare on a global scale; "it ruffled her feathers." She knew she could do a good job—all those years of intense study, concentrated thought about American foreign policy, gave her the necessary background. Her will to succeed would provide the drive. Pulling a piece of paper toward her, she wrote, "Dear Ike: I accept. . . ."

CHAPTER TWO

SINK OR SWIM

ANN CLARE BOOTHE WAS BORN ON APRIL 10, 1903, IN A DISMAL apartment house on Riverside Drive in New York City. Its small foyer hall, paved in imitation marble, was perpetually impregnated with the smell of stale cabbage. In a black iron cage a weary old man hauled on a wire cable to start the elevator creeping upward. Clashing gates opened on a narrow hall lined with uninviting doors. One of them, at the back, gave entrance to the three-room apartment transiently occupied by Mr. and Mrs. William F. Boothe and their infant son David.

Clare herself once succinctly pictured her unpropitious prospects as a baby. Shortly after her conversion to Catholicism, she was attacked by an ardent disciple of Mrs. Sanger for the Catholic stand against birth control. She wound up her tirade by saying, "I cannot understand anyone as enlightened as yourself subscribing to that doctrine."

"I think I appreciate your logic," said Clare. "Let's take the case of a young married woman, frail and ill, deserted by her husband, earning a precarious livelihood as a sales girl and about to become a mother for the second time. In due time the baby would arrive under circumstances that might be described as abject poverty—not even enough food in the house. No prospects of security for the child. Certainly no prospects of giving it even the ordinary opportunities for a happy home or a good education. Now I presume you would consider that those conditions would justify birth control?"

"Obviously," was the reply.

Clare snapped the trap. "That's just it. Now will you tell me why I did not have the right to be born? I, for one, am a pretty good argument against the birth controllers."

In actual fact, Clare telescoped time a bit in order to make her point. When she was born, Mr. Boothe had not deserted her mother—yet; and they probably still had enough to eat. But if truth need not be constricted too rigidly by time, her picture was accurate.

Billy Boothe, as he liked to be called, was a gentleman in the faded meaning of the term. He was descended from the Booth family who in early Colonial days arrived on the shores of the Chesapeake in the *Ark and Dove*. Since she was the *Mayflower* of Maryland, the Booths are just about as old a family as there is in America. The story about her family adding an "e" to the name when John Wilkes Booth shot Lincoln is apocryphal.

Mr. Boothe's father was Dr. William Boothe, a highly respectable Baptist minister who preached hellfire and salvation, first in Mount Holyoke, Massachusetts, and later in White Plains, New York. Clare's father was one of the eleven children he brought up in the ministerial tradition of simple living and godliness. But Billy Boothe was completely minus his family's strength of character. He was dreamily artistic. Educated in the classics and the great literature of the Bible, he loved music beyond everything, including his wife and children. His chosen instrument was the violin; but since his talent did not match his ambition, he had to be content always to play second fiddle.

In short, Billy Boothe was a singularly poor provider. Somehow he once acquired a little capital and tried to enter business. His daughter, who never forgave him for deserting her mother, sums up his business career caustically: "My father owned the first Coca-Cola bottling plant in the South. He sold it to buy a piano factory just as the talking machine was perfected."

Clare barely remembers her father. He disappeared from her life so long ago that his influence was purely negative. She saw him but once after she was grown up, and then only for a few minutes. He was running a music school in Los Angeles. There is a picture of him, white-bearded, dreamy-eyed, hanging in the back hall of the Luce home, Sugar Hill.

Clare's mother was the keystone of her arch of life. Everyone who knew her says that Ann Clare Snyder was even more beautiful than her famous daughter; just as Clare was more beautiful than *her* daughter, Ann Clare Brokaw. In fact, the third Ann Clare once remarked, "We seem to get uglier every generation." Yet Ann Brokaw was a remarkably pretty girl.

Mrs. Boothe, who was the daughter of Bavarian immigrants, was a dainty, golden-haired creature, whose eyes, they say, were the color of wet violets at sunrise. Her skin, which Clare inherited, had the delicate transparency that seems too fragile for daily wear and tear. But her tiny body was reinforced by a whipcord will.

When she was seventeen, Ann Snyder got a job in the chorus of a musical comedy. When she was eighteen, she met Billy Boothe and fell in love. Both families were against it. The old Baptist thundered traditionally about marriage with a chorus girl. The Catholic Snyders were even more violently agitated. For young Boothe had been divorced from his first wife, and if Ann married him, the Church would hold that she was living in sin.

Defying Baptist perdition and Catholic hell, the young couple got married anyhow. Both families promptly disowned them; and they left their respective churches. Thereby they allowed two psychological strikes against any children they might have. The third strike was poverty.

The two great rocks on which a child's world stands are faith and family. Clare never remembers her mother speaking of religion. From the time of her marriage Mrs. Boothe never entered a Catholic church except occasionally on Easter Sunday, when she would say to Clare, "Let's step inside and see all the beautiful flowers."

Clare says her mother loved to garden and would often say, "Flowers are my religion."

The rock of family was a broken shard indeed. Clare never saw her Baptist grandfather, and relations with her mother's family were almost equally distant. There was no sense of family continuity, no joyous returns home on Thanksgiving Day or Christmas. Home was where the Boothes happened to be boarding. So loneliness became an ingrained trait of character, and Clare is lonely still, though she hardly knows it.

All this does not mean that Clare's childhood was unhappy.

Quite the contrary. She only knew the good things she had missed by looking over her shoulder in later years. At the time she was fat and sassy and full of fun. A picture of her, aged three, shows a merry little girl with a hair ribbon askew on tousled golden curls, a dimpled, smiling mouth and eyes, not violet like her mother's, but crystal blue. Her happiness was due to her mother's gaiety which even peculiarly outrageous fortune could not quench.

Ann Snyder Boothe laughed a great deal and made others laugh. Mrs. Irvin Cobb, a connoisseur of humor, says that she had as quick a wit as ever bandied jokes with her famous husband. This wit Clare inherited, and honed it to a razor's edge.

Ann Boothe sang a great deal, too: never sad songs. Clare's first memory is of being tucked into bed and a light, lilting voice singing her to sleep with, "The sun and the stars and the angels . . ." In plain fact Clare's mother was the sun and the stars and the angels to her.

Clare's other memories of early childhood are kaleidoscopic, though they do not fall into neat geometrical patterns like the crystals in the mirrored tube. Rather they are a hodgepodge. This is because the Boothes were always on the move. Billy got a series of jobs playing in symphony orchestras, and in half a dozen years they lived in Nashville, Tennessee; Chicago; Memphis; Racine, Wisconsin; and Des Moines, Iowa. So the locations of the vignettes on Clare's memory are largely unidentified.

One is etched deep in bitterness. There was a dock extending over dark, deep water. Three-year-old Clare remembers walking down it in a bathing suit with her father. Suddenly he scooped her up and heaved her as far as he could. She came up sputtering to see him standing there shouting, "Come on, Baby, you can make it if you try! Daddy's waiting for you."

A little grimly she finishes the tale: "Howling and screaming, I made it somehow!"

From that time on Clare could swim. Though she has no record or recollection of formal swimming lessons, she eventually became so expert that in 1920 she was on the Connecticut swimming team that tried out for the Olympics. Her teammate, Eileen Regan, went on to Olympic laurels, but Clare did not quite make that.

However, they tell a tale of Burma when Clare was there as a war correspondent for *Life*. On a frying hot afternoon, while they waited for the Japs coming up to Mandalay, Clare and a group of officers and correspondents hired a native dhow for a sail on the Bay of Bengal. Among them was Merion Cooper, the Hollywood producer. In a nearly flat calm their boat waddled over the glassy swells. Reflected sunlight made it almost as hot as land.

It is physically impossible for Clare to stay still for long. Soon she felt impelled to photograph the picturesque group. Inspiration suggested an angle shot from the masthead. Wearing tight black slacks and a frilly white blouse, she went up the rigging like a cat up a tree, and, balancing against the roll, focused her camera with both hands. At the critical moment the one good gust of the afternoon hit the sails, flipping her neatly into the sea. Without a second thought Colonel Cooper went over after her.

Clare reared up out of the ocean like a blonde seal, shook her golden hair, and made sure the precious camera was still anchored to her neck. She saw the dhow clumsily trying to come about, and took off after it with the easy racing crawl that had once nearly carried her to Amsterdam.

As she raised her head to check her course, she saw that people in the boat were flapping and yelling in undue agitation. So she trod water and shouted, "I'm all right. The water's wonderful!"

A man's voice bellowed down at her, "You're all right, but Cooper's drowning."

Clare whirled like a whiting on its tail and saw Cooper's head in a lather of foam. In half a dozen strokes she reached him and circled, wary of his flailing arms. This called for the classic coup. She waited her moment and threw a beautifully timed right to the point of Cooper's jaw. He went limp as a mackerel, and she gathered his head in the crook of her arm and paddled gently on her back.

In due time the dhow came about and lumbered down to them. Cooper came to as they were hoisting him aboard. Regarding his rescuer malevolently, he foreswore chivalry with the bitter comment, "That dame didn't even lose her sun glasses!"

Other childish memories are gentler if less distinct than the first swimming lesson. Clare remembers the Ward-Belmont School in

Nashville, where she went to kindergarten; and she has a faint recollection of going to Sunday school somewhere in high-button shoes of white kid. Other places and other schools, and the succession of cheap apartments and boardinghouses, are a blur and of no consequence.

Only one other scene is significantly sharp. Clare thinks it was in Nashville when she was six years old that her mother was taken seriously ill. Her father was away on a concert tour so Clare was taken to a convent. She remembers the black-robed sisters bending over her, their white faces framed in starched white wimples. She liked the holy pictures in paper frills they gave her to play with. The memory, she says, remains a melancholy one, because nothing was fun if Mother was not there. Nevertheless, her subconscious could produce associations with a safe haven in a time of distress.

CHAPTER THREE

A STAR IS NOT BORN

CLARE WAS ABOUT TEN YEARS OLD, AND HER BROTHER DAVID eleven, when their father left for good. That was the time of real privation. There was, in truth, not enough food in the two-room apartment on Amsterdam Avenue, in New York, which they all shared with a woman friend of Mother's and a nest of mice. Mrs. Boothe was as close to desperation as she could get—which given her insouciant temperament was not very close, but near enough to make her willing to try anything. Her own hard life had slightly blurred her beauty and stiffened her muscles just enough to make a return to the theater impractical. So she eyed her daughter speculatively.

At that supposedly awkward age Clare was already an authentic beauty. Her long, softly curling hair was wheat-gold, framing a classically lovely face—fair, glowing skin, small coralline mouth, and clear blue eyes that were almost startling in their penetrating brilliance. Adults observing them had an uneasy feeling of being seen through, which was quite justified, since the precision instrument encased in that delicately modeled skull was already beginning to function with frightening clarity.

At ten Clare was a big girl. She could be called plump; rotund is more accurate. Despite this, she moved with the grace of perfect coordination. Studying her, Mrs. Boothe decided that her idea was worth a try.

Though Billy Boothe had abandoned her, no woman as lovely as Ann Boothe is ever long without beaux. One of them, with theatrical connections, gave her an introduction to Mary Pickford, who was rehearsing in *A Good Little Devil*, under the direction of David Belasco. Taking her daughter by the hand, Mrs. Boothe paid a call backstage with the intention of launching her on a career.

Clare towered half a head above America's littlest sweetheart, and no one knew whether the child could act or not, but Mrs. Boothe had artfully arranged her hair in the corkscrew curls that were Pickford's trade-mark, and her amazing beauty must have addled Mr. Belasco's brains. She was hired as Mary Pickford's understudy. Her stage name was Joyce Fair.

It is generally conceded that one of the best breaks Broadway ever got was the fact that Mary Pickford never missed a performance. For the one thing Clare can't do is to act—on stage. Why she can't is a psychological enigma. The likeliest answer lies in the extraordinary candor of her character, a quality that has gotten her into trouble in every sector of the globe from Boston, Massachusetts, to Burma, both ways around. She is no good at make-believe and cannot counterfeit an emotion which she does not feel. Nor can she fully communicate even those things she feels most deeply. Perhaps the stoic that was the child Clare, hiding hurts and even hunger, because the world must never know—most of all Mother must not know—perhaps that self-training formed a habit of repression through which the inner fires can never quite break through. Hence the legend of Clare's frigidity.

At any rate, she could not act.

Though she did not have the opportunity in *A Good Little Devil*, another engagement with Ernest Truex in *The Dummy* gave her a chance. Clare says, "I played the little girl who spends most of the play tied up in a chair. I was gagged. Perhaps that influenced my later character."

In that play, too, Clare suffered her only recorded attack of matinee idolatry. She fell in love with the star. Truex never forgot his intense embarrassment at Clare's too-palpable adoration, which she carried to the length of bestowing on him a moist good-night kiss at the end of every performance.

With checks coming in regularly, Mrs. Boothe looked around for new worlds for Clare to conquer. She found the newest world of all in an old barn at the Jersey end of the Fort Lee Ferry: the Biograph

Studio. She took her daughter there to make a screen test with Marie Doro for *Over the Hill to the Poorhouse*.

By now Clare was accustomed to the dust, disorder, and squalor on the reverse side of the enchanted land of theater. But she had never even imagined such a scene of compound confusion as that ramshackle building housed. Shreds and patches of scenery were scattered higgledy-piggledy throughout its dusty floor, which was strewn with tangled wires like monstrous viscera. Hanging from the ceiling, perched on beams, stalking on tripods, and lying in corners were hundreds of lights of all sizes from drum-shaped kliegs to baby spots. Scattered among them spiderlike cameras watched through Cyclopean eyes.

The whole place was seething with people. Stagehands were running about, tripping over wires, hauling on lights, carrying hunks of houses, pieces of furniture, or the front seat of an automobile. Carpenters were hammering; painters painting. Around them swirled the actors in all manner of costumes and the uniform brown pancake make-up. Everybody was gesticulating and shouting at the top of his lungs. It seemed that the one with the loudest voice was king—the directors were equipped with megaphones.

Clare was made up; the simple sequence was explained to her; and as the lights came on like a dazzling blow, Marie Doro stepped out of the crowd.

She was everything that Clare would like to have been, slender as a willow with a heart-shaped face, huge brown eyes, and dark hair piled on her small head. She made a magic circle of that arena of pitiless light. Watching her Clare was so bemused she scarcely heard the director shout, "Camera!" or noticed the rhythmic hands that cranked the film. She completely forgot to emote, and stood agape or moved like a zombie to follow directions bellowed through the megaphone. The result was less a screen test than a disaster.

Marie Doro had a gentle heart. She gave Clare a job anyhow— a walk-on part as an orphan. That was her final professional engagement.

Regrettably, it was not her final appearance on any stage. Twice more, not counting the Amateur Comedy Club, she braved the jinx that pursued her on the boards. The first time was when she was eighteen and intensely ambitious. For some months she had studied in Clare Tree Major's famous drama school. During that time she played a geisha girl and a Shakespearean extra. Came the last day of school, when each pupil was given a chance to demonstrate her virtuosity before an audience that contained some wary talent scouts. Miss Major's way of being fair to everyone was to write a series of scenes and put them in a hat. The girls then drew them out and read aloud the character they were to enact.

Clare by then was a rather statuesque blonde at the peak of her youthful, ice-queen beauty. She approached the fatal hat with apparent calm and a fierce hope that she would get something juicy. She almost fainted when she read the fatal words: "You are a cave man. You must go out and get dinner for your wife and child."

The audience began to laugh. Clare gamely went into a sort of crouch and swinging her arms below her knees uttered a horrible growl. The audience howled with glee.

Right there Clare lost her sense of humor. She straightened up and remarked, "This is perfectly ridiculous," and walked off the stage.

Miss Major bounded furiously after her. "Think what Fanny Brice would have done with that," she raged. "You just haven't got the stuff to make an actress!"

"She was right," says Clare.

She decided then and there that any future connection with the stage would be as a playwright, not an actress. Clare Luce's next personal stage appearance, which took place more than twenty years later, in August, 1945, when she was still a congresswoman, was even more frustrating. It began innocently enough when the star of the Stamford Theater, in which Clare was interested, quit during rehearsals of Bernard Shaw's *Candida*. Like most summer theaters, that one operated on the brink of bankruptcy. This looked like the shove that would send it over.

The manager begged Clare to save the day by playing the part herself.

"That seemed a fine idea to me," Clare says. "Now I could find out how the actors in my plays felt, a good thing for a playwright to know, certainly."

She only rehearsed for a week—on the front porch of her house.

Meanwhile the manager sent out a publicity release. The result both exhilarated and scared him. It horrified Clare.

"In spite of anything I could do," she says, "there was a perfect onrush of celebrities and critics seeking opening-night tickets. In vain I made statements that it was just an amateur effort. That I had no intention of becoming an actress. It did no good. The publicity was tremendous. People began to drop from trees looking for tickets. One woman said to the ticket seller, 'Two in the front row. I want to see Mrs. Luce act.' The ticket seller said, 'Listen, Ma'am, General Eisenhower himself couldn't get two front-row tickets for tonight!'

"That started the rumor that General Eisenhower was coming. On the opening night they had to call out the police."

Every major New York critic made the pilgrimage to Stamford. They had a Roman holiday with Clare as the Christian.

She herself was modestly pleased with her performance. She said, "I did the only thing I really wanted to do—remember my lines. And I found out how an actress feels facing an unfriendly audience." The only thing that went wrong was in the first act, when she was supposed to take off her picture hat. Anchored to a great false wig, the hatpin broke. People backstage kept whispering, "Take it off." Clare kept saying, "I can't," and played it out in a cartwheel of straw.

However, the lions of the aisles were out for her blood. They stacked her up—unfavorably, of course—against Katharine Cornell in the same part. They reached back in their memories for all the other Candidas and made odious comparisons. A fairly gentle critic simply called Clare "presumptuous."

Only the usually serpent-tongued Wolcott Gibbs was reasonable. He said, "Mrs. Luce is not a professional. My colleagues might at least have said that she looked pretty. I intend to be fair. She was very decorative."

Clare was very grateful for that faint praise. You might think that she would be used to critics, but no! She was hurt, bewildered, and thoroughly enraged: "When they attack me about politics or my plays, that's all right," she says. "But this was terribly unfair. Everyone knew I wasn't a professional actress and didn't want to be one—I was still in Congress." An amusing footnote to the whole affair, however, is that a number of theatrical agents offered Clare twenty-five hundred dollars a week if she would quit Congress and "go on the road" in Candida or any other show that appealed to her for a year. She couldn't act—but she could draw the crowds. And boxoffice is boxoffice. She refused. It can be stated definitely that Candida was her last, final, farewell performance on any stage.

In the spring of 1914 Mrs. Boothe came into a little money— very little. But one of her admirers gave her a tip on the stock market, and she made a profit of two thousand dollars. Figuring that she could live on that for a year in Paris, she put her son in a small military academy in Racine, Wisconsin, and took Clare on a cheap, slow liner to Europe.

Paris was wonderful. Clare and her mother lived in a cheap pension called the Hôtel Balzac, on the Rue de Balzac. Clare, who was used to much worse quarters than that, thought the Hôtel Balzac the height of luxury. Outside was the lovely city that seemed like one big spring garden to a little girl who had come from the concrete-bound ugliness of Amsterdam Avenue.

Mrs. Boothe saw to it that her daughter took full advantage of the bonanza of culture that Paris offered so inexpensively. They trudged through miles of corridors in the Louvre and studied the Gothic stone forest of Notre Dame. They heard good music at the two opera houses and the concert halls. Clare saw what theater could really be at the Comédie Française. Most important of all she learned to speak correct French with a beautifully clear accent and the proper trill to the "r"—an accomplishment beyond price in the unforeseeable future.

However, the Parisian idyl did not last the year which Mrs. Boothe had planned. In the last hot days of July, 1914, the board-ings and kiosks and the ancient walls suddenly burgeoned with red, white, and blue posters that proclaimed:

ORDRE DE MOBILISATION
Les Armées de Terre et de Mer

Then the black newspaper headlines read:

LA GUERRE!

It was tremendously exciting and rather beautiful. The wildly cheering crowds surged up and down the Champs Elysées and sang the Marseillaise in front of the Chamber of Deputies and the

Elysée Palace. Everybody seemed very happy and confident, except for a very few old women in black who remembered another war.

When the troops began to march through on the way to the front, it was even better. They wore gay uniforms—long-tailed dark blue coats and bright red pants. Cuirassiers, mounted on splendid horses with glittering horsetailed helmets and long lances, trotted splendidly by, their accouterments rattling like a Model-T Ford. Women and girls ran alongside the marching men laughing and cheering, and breaking into the lines to kiss them. And in the muzzles of the long, obsolete rifles with their glittering, knifelike bayonets were bunches of gay field flowers. This seemed a little odd to Clare.

Mrs. Boothe did not panic as did so many Americans in that strange false dawn of war. But when things turned out somewhat differently from the way the ebullient Parisians had expected, and the rumble of guns came through the earth from just beyond the Marne, she sensibly decided that a besieged city was no place for a woman alone with two young children. So she went to the American Embassy and succeeded in getting transportation home.

Clare had stayed just long enough to have indelibly printed on her brain the fact that war was not fun after all.

CHAPTER FOUR

THE PRINCESS OF THE CASTLE

B<small>Y THE AUTUMN OF</small> 1915 <small>MRS. BOOTHE SUCCEEDED IN ACCUMU-</small>lating enough money to send her daughter to the Cathedral School of St. Mary's at Garden City, Long Island. She had gotten a pleasant job as a Fifth Avenue saleswoman for a French firm that sold artificial or "Tecla" pearls, which were then coming into fashion. The school, which was High Episcopalian, was housed in a turreted Tudor building of rose-colored brick covered with ivy. The reception rooms on the ground floor were furnished in cluttered opulence of heavy Victorian furniture and glassed-in bookcases. What light the mullioned windows let in was lost in walls paneled in stained oak. Incidentally, the school motto was: *Let There Be Light.* Clare, who entered in the eighth grade, did not like it at all. Least of all she liked the headmistress.

Miss Miriam A. Bytel, B.A. of Radcliff, was an austere Latin scholar. Her idea of brisk entertainment was to go to the gymnasium in the cellar and hold spelling matches in Latin irregular verbs. The girls were so terrified of her that they would go up to the second floor and down another stairway to avoid passing the door of her office. Her favorite saying was: "Girls, remember your first inspiration comes from heaven; your second [pointing dramatically downward] from hell!"

However, the school had a group of extremely competent teachers, most of whom held college degrees, which was unusual for that time. Some of them remember Clare as an unhappy, fat little girl, who, when not in the school uniform, wore ruffled dresses that made her look almost square. She knew better, they say, but could not convince her mother that frills did not suit her.

Clare's room was a small cubicle on the fourth floor in a part of the long building that was ironically known as "Paradise." It had, in the early days of the school, been the chapel and its walls were still painted with angels and cherubs. Clare's own bed stood between two images of kneeling angels.

In St. Mary's, Clare got her first introduction to formal religion. According to her it made virtually no impression. She says that she enjoyed going to the beautiful little Episcopal cathedral in Garden City and listening to the fine singing. But morning and evening prayers in the new school chapel were a bore, to be enlivened by giggling and purposely flatting the hymns to tease George Sweet, who directed vocal studies. Clare, who could never carry a tune, frequently started the giggling by striking a flat note which she remembers being constantly reprimanded for.

Clare was confirmed in the Episcopal Church the following spring. All she remembers about it is that on the way to the cathedral her shirtwaist split in back. One of the teachers fixed it with safety pins. But Clare knew *that the pins showed*.

The best thing that happened to Clare at St. Mary's was Buff Cobb. The daughter of the famous humorist Irvin Cobb was also a fat little girl, but she had dark hair and a "puddin'" face. She tells the story of her first meeting with Clare:

"About three days after I got to St. Mary's, I was forced to play hockey, which I hated. The ball ran up my stick and hit me in the eye. It was all too much. I ran off the field and climbed an apple tree, just to get alone.

"Pretty soon there was a beautiful little girl standing under the tree. She was fat as butter, but she had long golden curls, clear blue eyes, and a lovely pink-and-white skin. She looked up and asked, 'Is that your private apple tree or may I come up?'

"I said, 'Sure you can.'

"Up she came and we introduced ourselves. Then Clare began to tell me a tremendously exciting story. It was Sherlock Holmes in *The Speckled Band,* where the murderer uses a snake—Clare called it a cobra—to do his killing. Just as we got to where the cobra was about to strike the heroine, Clare said, 'That will be all now. Good-by. See you tomorrow!'

"I never knew whether she had forgotten the end of it or did it deliberately to hold my interest. She certainly did that. I lay awake that night, homesickness forgotten, wondering what happened. When Clare did tell me the end, she made up a different one from Conan Doyle. But it was just as good."

That was the beginning of the first of Clare's lifelong feminine friendships which her myth does not allow her. She and Buff Cobb had a great deal in common. For one thing they both feared Miss Bytel's brand of heaven and hellfire, laced with Latin quotations. For another, they had been brought up in an adult atmosphere and were not used to other children. Buff, naturally gregarious, soon had many friends at school, but she remained closest to Clare, her first friend, not only through loyalty but because she found her by far the most interesting. Both girls liked books better than games.

At the first opportunity Buff brought her new friend home to lunch with her family. Irvin Cobb, gigantic and jolly, at the height of his fame, was amazed and delighted by Clare. Mrs. Cobb says that he had long talks on a completely adult plane with his daughter's twelve-year-old friend. Cobb himself said: "When I want to be absolutely sure about a point in history, I ask Buffy or Clare. These children can put me right."

The friendship between the girls was enlarged to their families. Buffy says, "Mrs. Boothe was very beautiful and funny, a really delightful wit. She went to call on my parents, and announced herself as Clare's mother. They became very friendly, even fascinated by her. I adored her—she was wonderful with kids."

However, Buff Cobb sometimes had to put up with quite a lot from her best friend. Mrs. Cobb tells of one Saturday lunch, when she was taking the girls to a matinee. Clare sat at the table very straight and neat, as she still does, with her long golden hair shining. Buff was slouching and giggling and talking so loud that her mother finally said, "Buffy, you must modulate your voice. No lady talks as loud as you do."

Clare asked rather airily, "Do you know what's wrong with Buff, Mrs. Cobb?"

Twinkling, Mrs. Cobb replied, "I know a lot of things that are wrong with her, but what do you think is?

"Why, she has no poise," Clare said.

She really did not mean to be priggish. She was just stating a helpful fact—a fatal habit of hers. Certainly she did not suffer from Buff's difficulty. Mrs. Cobb describes her as "the most startlingly poised child I ever knew."

Clare was in fact so poised that hardly anyone ever thought of cuddling or kissing her as they might an ordinary little girl. She seemed much too self-sufficient, too aloof, for that. Her manner made her unpopular with most of the girls at St. Mary's. Though she wanted their friendship desperately, she just could not unbend. For one thing she had too much to hide!

How much even she did not know at first. It was when she came back to New York for her Christmas vacation that she found the lengths to which her mother had gone to pay for her school. Mrs. Boothe had moved into one room in a cheap family hotel, on the west side of New York. As Clare describes it, the room was at the bottom of a dank court—there was almost always a fringe of gray snow on the window ledge because the sun never touched it. There was also "Lady Macbeth."

This was Mrs. Boothe's best and only friend in the hotel, a large, kindly Irish lady who lived with her traveling-salesman husband in the room next door. Her real name was Mrs. McClintock Bath, but as she always referred to her man as Mac Bath, that became her name. Only Clare, who had been studying Shakespeare, got a little mixed up.

At first she was terrified of Lady Macbeth, thinking of dark deeds in Scotland. She describes her standing over the sink in her narrow bathroom, bulging out of a petticoat and a pair of corsets, washing one of her husband's shirts. Clare pertly cracked, "Out, damned spot!"

But the Irishwoman was too amply affectionate to be put off by the child's superficial snootiness. She was one of the few people who dared to hug and cuddle Clare. As a result Clare came to love her dearly.

Lady Macbeth was a great help to Mrs. Boothe. She taught her all sorts of little economies such as how to seal a letter inside, but leave the envelope flap open to save a cent; how to leave the bottle of milk in a little draft just inside a window so it would neither go sour nor freeze on the sill. Most important of all, since cooking was illegal in the hotel, she taught Mrs. Boothe which foods were odoriferous, and how to connect a small stove by a rubber hose to the gas jet in the bathroom and to stuff towels in the cracks in the doors to keep the smell of cooking in. It was all very necessary.

Despite all the scrimping Clare was far happier there than at school. Even when she went on to a school where she was popular and gay, she could write in her diary: "I'm always so happy when I'm with Mother."

But it was not the sort of home you could talk about easily to the girls at St. Mary's. They might pity you or, worse still, look down on your mother. When Mrs. Boothe got dressed in her prettiest clothes, and drove out to Garden City with Mrs. Cobb to visit their daughters, Clare was very proud of her indeed. Mrs. Boothe would quite literally rather have died than have her daughter's friends know how she lived. So would Clare. She kept her mouth tight shut, and, when the other girls were exchanging confidences, Clare buried her nose in a book.

So, in the Class Book, they named her the "most conceited." That was a first for Clare: her first unfavorable press. It hurt her terribly.

Another first was Clare's first published poem, which appeared in the school *Annual* in 1916. As the precursor of millions of printed words, it deserves republication.

Westminster Abbey at Night

'Tis midnight, the clock has struck the hour,
Mournful it rings from Westminster tower.
And as it was beckoning to me,
With fiendish laughter and dev'lish glee,
Ghosts came pointing and laughing and sneering,
Wailing, sighing, and moaning and jeering.
There are brave lives wrought with countless good,
Men who firm by their country have stood.

There are kings whose rule,
Was hard—yes, cruel,

Fair ladies whose lives were filled with pain,
Heroes who were by traitors slain;
Martyrs, ladies, traitors, kings and all,
Come gliding to me from that dread hall.
But as I watch, they fade away
And gladly I see the light of day!

Clare's second year at Garden City was worse than the first, because Buff caught some sort of bronchial infection. When her weight got down to eighty pounds and she looked as sad as a canned string bean, her alarmed parents whipped her off to Florida.

Alone once again, Clare concentrated more than ever on her studies and all the outside reading she could get her hands on. That period generated the tremendous inner drive which to this day has never diminished. She was forced by pride and hurt to excel, and the habit of ambition became too strong for even happiness to break. Incidentally, it infuriates her when people speak of her ambition as though it were a shameful thing. "Of course you want to do the best you can," she says. "If that's ambition, let them make the most of it!"

The immediate result at St. Mary's was that she made the honor role, one of two girls in her class.

Clare was naturally an extrovert like her mother. Circumstances turned her inward. It took another, happier school to turn her right-side-out again.

By the autumn of 1917 Mrs. Boothe was distinctly better off. It may be presumed that the startling upward flight of the stock market had something to do with this fortunate circumstance. In any event, she sent her daughter to the Castle School at Tarrytown, New York. The next two years were the happiest of Clare's whole life.

The Castle had always been a happy house. This biographer knew it well, for it originally belonged to his grandfather, Alfrederic Hatch. There that patriarch raised his eleven children in a sort of riotous harmony—nobody minded if they roller-skated over the marble floors, and when they married they usually brought their wives home to live in the Castle. Eighteen sat down for dinner on nights when there were no guests, which was seldom.

When Miss Cassidy Mason founded her famous school there, it was just as happy. The headmistress was a big, handsome woman with curly white hair worn in a pompadour, and fine gray eyes. Her views were as broad as her person. She was an ardent feminist who inspired her girls with ambition to go out into the world and do things, which was not the way young ladies were usually "finished" in fashionable schools.

Among other progressive ideas, Miss Mason was an aviation enthusiast. Her 1919 prophecy according to Clare's diary was: "Within no great number of years we will . . . have great big passenger liners flying across the ocean" . . . *Wireless across the sea: Hello, Miss Mason, come spend this weekend with me in Switzerland, you'll be here in a few hours.* "According to her," adds skeptical Clare.

Under such guidance the Castle was a wonderfully stimulating little world. Add the romantic atmosphere of great stone, battlemented towers overlooking a fifty-mile sweep of the Hudson, vast rooms with groined and buttressed ceilings, and an authentic secret stairway running up through the fat column in the center of the huge circular drawing room—Clare's first short story was based on that—and you have a place for youthful dreams.

Not that Miss Mason carried her progressive principles very far in the management of her pupils. The school was pretty strict by modern standards. The rising bell bonged out at 6:40 A.M. From that time on scarcely a minute of the day was unaccounted for until "9:30 Lights out. Perfect quiet required." The girls were allowed no beaux at school. Only occasionally did they go down the steep hill to Tarrytown walking two by two in a crocodile with a teacher at both ends. They were required to wear uniforms by day and simple white dresses in the evening, which they kidded in a song:

> "Sweet little white dresses
> Shy little white dresses. . . .
> We're safe in Miss Mason's arms
> Far from all boyish charms
> Sweet little Castle maids."

On the other hand they had occasional proms, when boys *were* admitted. They played hockey, coasted down the icy hill in winter, and gave plays frequently. Miss Mason saw to it that the senior class took advantage of being so near New York by going frequently to the opera and theaters.

From the moment Clare arrived at the Castle with a group of girls in the big carryall drawn by two fat horses—the hill was pretty steep for automobiles—she seems to have completely metamorphosized. For one thing, she had nothing now to hide. Her mother lived in a pretty white frame house in Greenwich, Connecticut, and no longer worried about the cost of postage. Because she could let herself go at last, Clare's wit and beauty made her immediately popular with the Castle girls, who came from all over the United States. That first year, when she was a new girl in the sophomore class, she did not make any special mark, but in her second and final year she was regarded by many of her classmates, in retrospect at least, as "The Princess of the Castle."

In the summer of 1918 Clare made what seemed to her a major decision. Miss Mason had said that she was so far ahead of her class, particularly in French, that she should skip ahead to the senior class. Clare's ambition jumped at that, though her former classmates wrote her almost hysterical letters about "deserting the Class of 1920."

Despite her happiness, Clare had not slacked off. Dorothy Burns Holloran, her best friend at the Castle and still close to her, says, "She was always interested in reading and learning about art or French and English history—driving herself through some inner compulsion to find out the why of everything. When the rest of us were reading Elinor Glyn, she would be deep in Racine. While she brushed her long, shining hair she'd read Gibbon; and while she soaked in the tub she'd have Plato propped on the taps in front of her. But," adds Dorothy, "she was no goody-goody. If anybody annoyed her, she had a tongue like a black snake whip."

So Clare came back a senior at fifteen and soon, as is her way, became an intensely loyal member of the Class of 1919. The class motto, she notes, was *Veritas Omnia Vincet;* and her personal one *Je vis en espoire.*

Clare became a leading contributor of stories, articles, and decorative drawings, as well as business manager of the school paper, *The Drawbridge,* and editor of *The Annual.* In her new personality she even took up sports. She played field hockey in a remarkable uniform consisting of baggy bloomers, long purple and gold stockings (these were the class colors), a bandeau to match, and a purple jersey with *1919* emblazoned on it in gold. Her superb coordination made her a fine player. She was also the best swimmer in the school, having had plenty of practice in the sound off Greenwich.

Those were the years of World War I, and though the Castle was isolated from its direct effects, Miss Mason saw to it that it was not insulated from the impact of America's struggle. Red Cross work went on at the school, and that year the Castle won second place in the Westchester War Savings Stamp Drive. Clare followed the reports of American troops in action with intense concentration, not only because of her fervent patriotism and the intellectual excitement of seeing history being made, but because of a vital personal interest.

Her brother David had enlisted in the Marines at the age of sixteen. He had grown into a powerful young man, as swarthy as his sister was fair, with black hair and dark brown eyes—the girls thought he looked like Richard Barthelmess. So when he lied about his age, the Marines believed him.

That war ended before David got into it, though nearly a quarter of a century later he lied to the Marines about his age again, and at thirty-nine became a fighter pilot, flying more than fifty missions in the Pacific.

In her diary Clare vividly describes how the news of an armistice (the false one) came to the Castle:

"Thursday at 10 o'clock the news reached us that Germany had surrendered. The Castle went wild. We rang our Castle bell though it could scarcely be heard amid the boom of the West Point guns and the Tarrytown siren. We climbed the Castle tower and attempted to hoist the Flag, singing meanwhile 'Taps,' 'Star-Spangled Banner,' 'Marseillaise,' and 'God Save the King,' until we wept and our voices cracked. That night, amid great excitement we managed to procure four autos. In New York, Mother met us. We had a glorious ride in through the crowds. New York was mad, delirious, insane with joy. The crowds surged around the cars so that we were forced to go very slowly. Newspapers were littering up the streets ankle deep. We left Mother at her hotel and then stopped for some sodas and sandwiches and arrived home at 12 o'clock very worn out and tired.

"Mother bought Middie, Mary, and me some flags. Mine I shall keep forever.

"*November 11th*. The day the Armistice was really signed."

Peace also brought disillusionment:

"*December 1st*. Lloyd Miller, who I firmly believed to be dead and buried in the fields of Flanders came to see me at the Hotel. The puppy love which I confess I had nursed at the thought of his heroism died out completely. He is a lieutenant in the Aviation Corps, stationed at Mineola, L. I."

With the coming of peace, Miss Mason added to the seniors' schedule of operas and plays. That winter Clare heard Scotti, Geraldine Farrar, Martinelli, and others at the Metropolitan, and saw virtually all the best plays on Broadway. Some of her comments are enlightening:

"Went to *Three Faces East*. Didn't like it." "*Dear Brutus*. Good but wishy-washy. . . ."

Topflight lecturers came to the Castle. Clare again incisively separated sheep from goats:

"*January* 26. Miss A, Red Cross worker gave a foolish and insincere talk.

"*February 9*. John Kendrick Bangs gave a vivid lecture called 'The Lights and Shades of War.'

Her judgment of people was sharp and ruthless. She could even recognize her own limitations quite as clearly:

"*May 27th*. Miss Mason's Birthday. Big Deal. Mrs. Richards read my palm. She advised me to take up public speaking, journalism, or art. However, she said I'd have none of these unless I developed my stick-to-itiveness and will power (!). She also gave me some very kind motherly advice about my egotism, lack of sympathy, or 'coldness.' I promised myself to try to improve. I am to have a very serious *affaire de coeur*."

For all her clarity of mind and her almost overwhelming literary sophistication, Clare was still more child than woman. Parts of her diary are touchingly innocent. For instance there was one page on which you were supposed to list:

MEN I HAVE MET

1. Mr. Barnum—Rather medium-sized, good dancer.
2. Mr. Madden—Emmie's cousin. Tall blond, good dancer and very attractive.
3. Mr. Clowney—Clowney's brother. Large and wears glasses. A great kidder.
4. Mr. Blackman—Hotel proprietor.
5. Ensign Van Cleek—Seen for barely a second in Hotel Biltmore. Red headed, peppy, and small.

A girl is really scraping the bottom of the barrel when she has to dig up a hotel proprietor and an ensign seen for a second.

Another page lists:

MY FAVORITE CLOTHES

1. Turquoise blue coat; huge collar and cuffs of brown-flecked squirrel.
2. Gold embroidered terra cotta silk with panniers and tassels, swathed sleeves.
3. White rajah silk.
4. Gray.
5. Dark blue.
6. Green, gray.
Prom Dress. Yellow georgette draped with yellow silk and trimmed with blue georgette and ostrich feathers. Carried blue feather fan—yellow shoes and stockings. [Her mother had made it for her and she loved it.]

As Clare's last year at the Castle drew to its close in the riotous burgeoning of spring, her days were happier and more glorious, shadowed only by that rapidly approaching Graduation Day, to her like looking over a cliff into infinity. She could not think beyond it, nor did she want to.

"*April 10*, my Birthday. The Happiest Day of my life. Went to dinner with Mother at the Pickwick Arms."

Clare got some wonderful presents, and she listed over fifty, among them:

1. This book *[memory book]* from Mother.
2. Aviation insignia collar device from Lt. Price. . . .
6. Half a dozen white kid gloves from Mother. . . .
8. Diary with lock and key. Brother. . . .
43. The most exquisite silk underwear for graduation I have ever seen or read of. White duck silk trimmed with wonderful real cream lace and cream satin ribbons. Made and joined entirely by hand by dear Mrs. McBath—from Mother.

As graduation approached, Clare worked extremely hard. Her senior essay, which earned her the highest honors the Castle could give, was an examination into the causes of World War I. Despite the violent emotions of the time it is impartial, almost juridical. It is written in a clear, simple but exact style—in French.

The graduation exercises lasted for almost a week—a marathon of ceremonies, parties, excitement, and emotion. It began with Senior Day, when eighteen girls escorted by Miss Mason went to New York for "A merry luncheon at Schraffts, the matinee of *39 East,* dinner at the Biltmore, and *A Little Journey.*" This was followed by Founders Day with appropriate ceremonies, and Saturday when all classes presented Episodes from History. The seniors presented one from Anthony and Cleopatra, and the freshmen Columbia's Gift of Rare Women to the World: Pocahontas, Priscilla, Martha Washington, Julia Ward Howe, Susan B. Anthony, and on down to Clara Barton. One wonders if other freshmen might not add a Castle girl to the list.

From that they went on to military drill, chariot races, horseback riding, and Finnish exercises.

So it continued with baccalaureate sermons, teas, dinners, speeches, a tree-planting ceremony, and Miss Mason's address in which she gave advice that at least one of her pupils lived by: "Cultivate sleepless energy. Keep in your hearts the spirit of adventure, and be of spiritual strength!"

The class prophecy about Clare was not too far off: *Famous author and illustrator*—"There's Ann Clare Boothe. Have you seen her last book? I'm quite crazy about it and the illustrations are so clever. My dear, she is prettier than ever, and did you hear that she dedicated the book to the Castle? Yes, really!"

So they came to the final day and the end of all the ceremonies and speeches; the end, too, of uncomplicated happiness. Clare wore "a white georgette, straight lines flowing from the shoulders and my beautiful underwear." She looked incredibly lovely with her high coloring and her blue eyes brilliant with excitement. Her thick gold hair was braided in a coronet on her proud head.

Last of all, the seniors trooped through the great window of Miss Mason's office carrying their big bouquets of yellow roses and purple sweet peas. They lined up by the gray stone battlements, and sang the Castle song with tears streaming from their youthful eyes and the people in the courtyard below wept with them.

Clare's memory book ends with a characteristic combination of sentiment and acid:

"The program was just as on the next page—such a happy, longed-for day. Mother, Mrs. Adler, and Mrs. Linsey came out. Also Milton and Mrs. B., who gave me a pain, and I threw a rose to 'K.' Armytage, Rosalie, Peggie, Florence, and Laura. Wept copiously at the very last minute. The slip of paper is from my diploma and certificate. The ribbon's the same. It isn't possible that I will never be a Castle girl again. . . ."

CHAPTER FIVE

THE BRIDE OR THE NUN

O<small>NE OF THE FIRST THINGS CLARE DID WHEN SHE FINISHED</small> school was to have herself an adventure as prescribed by Miss Mason; though it is doubtful if that lady would have approved. She ran away from home and got a job with Dennison's in New York under the *nom de guerre* of Jacqueline Tanner. They put her to work making little paper nut cups for the Christmas trade. She made the best paper nut cups Dennison's ever had, she says immodestly.

It was not, however, the sort of thing that could hold her interest long. As soon as the fine feeling of independence wore off, she got horribly bored with folding colored paper all day long for eighteen dollars a week, and going back alone to a cheap boardinghouse at night. If she could only think of some face-saving way of getting home again! Then, conveniently, she got herself an attack of acute appendicitis and rushed back to Greenwich for an operation.

At this point the beneficial incidence of appendicitis on Clare's fortunes was quite spectacular. Hardly had she recovered than her mother suffered a similar attack. Mrs. Boothe was operated on by Dr. Albert E. Austin of Greenwich. He was a quiet man with graying hair and a restful bedside manner which he took with him everywhere. He fell madly in love with his beautiful patient. They were quietly married the following year.

That finally ended financial anxiety. Though Dr. Austin was not rich, he had a very substantial practice in Greenwich. The Austins lived in a white frame house with a lawn that ran down to the water on Sound Beach, Connecticut. Clare was happy there, though she did not stagnate. That was the period of her Olympic tryout, and her brief, inglorious association with Clare Tree Major. She also studied typing and shorthand in Bridgeport. She read as ferociously as ever, the French philosophers now: Montesquieu, Diderot, Voltaire, and Rousseau.

She also kept up with the Castle girls—as far as she is able she still does. There was a visit to Dot Burns in Chicago. According to her, Clare had slimmed down and, in her favorite blue coat with the squirrel collar, was so radiantly beautiful that men stopped on the street to stare at her. The boys her age fell madly in love, and she tormented them as young beauty always does. To one young man whom she met at a dance in Chicago, she pretended she was French and could speak no English. When he bemusedly came to call the next day, she kept up the gag, carrying it off in spite of Dorothy's incipient hysteria.

Then Dot Burns and Mildred Price came to visit her in Sound Beach, and there was a Castle reunion with the whole class on June 1. That may have been Clare's final schoolgirl fling. In the summer of 1922 she sailed for Europe with her mother and stepfather to a rendezvous with her choice of destinies.

Clare's second trip to Europe was very different from her previous one: it was first class all the way. Dr. Austin combined business with pleasure, attending medical congresses in Belgium, Germany, and Austria, and studying European hospitals and new operative techniques. Clare did not waste a precious second of her time; she saw all the lovely things there were to see.

In spite of her mental overload of eighteenth-century philosophers and their fulminations against the Church of Rome, she loved the perpendicular beauty of the great Catholic cathedrals. They stirred deep but enigmatic emotions in her, though she resolutely resisted their religious significance. Their spiritual quality, she told herself, was due simply to the glory of design or their "magnificent emptiness," and had nothing to do with the dubious doctrines preached from their splendid altars. "It seemed such a pity," she has written, "that you couldn't have cathedrals without Catholics."

Clare was intensely interested in the theater and went to plays wherever she could. The Austins remained in Berlin for quite a while, and Clare delighted in the new plays presented by Max Reinhardt at the Shauspiel House, which represented Berlin's intellectual resurgence from the despair of defeat. She focused the concentrated beam of her intelligence on studying German, and quickly learned to speak it quite well.

In the autumn they all sailed home on a crack Cunarder. In the quick, easy intimacy of shipboard, Clare met a god and goddess from the machine—quite different machines. The first to notice the young girl, striding along the promenade deck like a dismounted Valkyrie, was Mrs. O. H. P. Belmont of Newport, New York, and the continent of Europe. This remarkably dynamic lady had switched careers in midstream. As Mrs. William K. Vanderbilt she had attained the very apex of society, earning the envy of all Four Hundred of them by browbeating her daughter into marrying the Duke of Marlborough. Then, finding life on that windless peak utterly boring, she divorced Vanderbilt, married Oliver H. P. Belmont, and became a militant suffragette. When the male politicians unconditionally surrendered by approving the Nineteenth Amendment which gave the vote to women, Mrs. Belmont was left without a cause. But she quickly invented another one, organizing the Women's National Party, designed to gain control of the United States government by voting American women *en bloc*.

Miss Mason's conditioning in feminism made Clare's mind mesh with Mrs. Belmont's. She thought the older woman intensely stimulating—which she was. Mrs. Belmont saw in Clare a magnificent tool for her present purpose. Indeed she was so impressed by the triple threat of Clare's beauty, brains, and adventurous spirit that she remarked to her plump young assistant, Elsa Maxwell, "If that girl gets only one third of the advantages she deserves, you will be very proud to know her in twenty-five years."

Which entitles Mrs. Belmont to a respectable ranking among the minor prophets.

Clare's other shipboard acquaintance was even more exciting: an authentic great one of the theater world, forty-five-year-old Max Reinhardt. He, too, fell for her beauty, her knowledge of the

European theater, and her piquantly accented German. *It was for this,* Clare thought, *that I studied so hard.*

They spent most of the few shipboard evenings together, while Reinhardt talked of his plans for a spectacular religious play to be called *The Miracle.* On the last night he said to her, "I am going to America to find a young woman to play the part of The Nun. But I could turn back, for I have already found her."

In the hurried good-byes on the windy dock Clare quite forgot to give Reinhardt her address. She had been vegetating on Sound Beach for a week when she was called to the telephone. It was Dr. Rudolph Kommer, Reinhardt's agent. He was in a terrible temper. "For a week I have been wasting time looking all over New York for a girl named Clare Boothe, who was idiotic enough to disappear without leaving an address," he snarled.

"Well, here I am," Clare said a little faintly. "Does Mr. Reinhardt want to see me?"

"Do you think I act the amateur detective for fun?" Kommer snorted. "Max has been hounding me all week. Get in here tomorrow!"

The next day Clare met the producer in New York. "So you really meant it," she said.

"I always mean what I say," Reinhardt replied. "I'm much too busy for flattery. Do you want the part?"

"Of course I want it," Clare said, remembering Clare Tree Major. "But am I up to it? What do I have to do?"

Reinhardt twinkled at her. "You just run up and down in the cathedral and say nothing. Absolutely nothing!"

It was all set. Reinhardt was going back to Austria for the summer, but would return for the production in the fall. Meanwhile a wonderful world opened up for Clare. Dr. Kommer took her around to meet leading producers, among them David Belasco, whom she had not seen since her ten-year-old stint in *A Good Little Devil.* Reinhardt invited her to glamorous dinners with such stars as Jane Cowl, the Barrymores, Otis Skinner, and Martinelli of the Met. Clare was immensely stimulated by these people, and wonderfully at ease. She was much too realistic not to know that she was as beautiful as the best of them, much too impressed not to act with proper modesty, and far too intelligent to sit around mumchance. So she made a small niche for herself in their magical circle. Simultaneously, she was entering another glamorous world where the glitter was more golden.

Mrs. Belmont had not forgotten her young Valkyrie. Almost simultaneously with Kommer's call, she telephoned to offer Clare a position as secretary at the headquarters of the Women's Party. Clare took that job too.

Working with Mrs. Belmont entailed a great deal more than taking shorthand, which Clare could not do very well anyway. The idea was to exploit the girl's beauty in the good cause of getting publicity for the Party. At one point Clare found herself sailing around the skies over Rochester, New York, in a rickety biplane, bombing an unappreciative electorate with sheaves of feminist literature. It was great fun.

Her job also led her into the attenuated atmosphere where her mentor moved among almost legendary figures that had been to Mrs. Astor's celebrated ball some thirty years before. The remains of the Four Hundred also seemed to like Clare. Though they were certainly not as interesting as actors and writers, the girl got a thrill out of the pomp and panoply of their existence. In the Castle one might sometimes pretend that the great stairway was lined with flunkeys holding flaming flambeaux to light one's upward progress. The footmen in knee-breeches and braided uniforms who swung back the massive bronze doors of the Fifth Avenue mansions of Mrs. Belmont's friends were real enough, but it still seemed like romantic make-believe to Clare.

It was a lovely day in spring that the very blue-blooded Mr. and Mrs. James Stewart Cushman, who had taken a great fancy to Clare, asked her to go with them to the Fifth Avenue Presbyterian Church to hear Dr. Harry Emerson Fosdick. Clare was certainly not an ardent churchgoer, but she did not want to hurt the Cushmans' feelings, and she liked Fosdick's vigorous, intelligent sermons, in which he reconciled science and Christianity. So she accepted.

The Cushmans were shown to their pew. Just as the service was starting, a very handsome older man, dressed in a cutaway and carrying a glistening high silk hat, nodded to the Cushmans and sat down next to Clare. All through the service she felt his eyes on her profile, and occasionally she met his glance and smiled at him. When church was over, the Cushmans introduced Mr. George Brokaw.

They all moved out into the sunshine of Fifth Avenue and stood talking for a few moments while the long limousines rolled up to the curb and the traffic snarled on the Avenue. Mr. Brokaw saw them to their car and stood bareheaded as they drove away.

By this time Clare was a good enough student of the Social Register to know that George Tuttle Brokaw was the richest bachelor in society—some people said he had fifty million dollars; the lowest estimate was thirty. She also knew that he had never married and that this was not because debutantes and their mamas had not been trying for twenty years. She was pretty sure that he was interested, indeed he had been quivering like a bird dog. But, mixing her metaphors, she concluded that he was too wary a bird to light on a strange bush.

Mr. Brokaw called up the next day. In his punctilious, old-fashioned way he asked not for Clare but for her mother. Introducing himself, he inquired if she would have any objections if he invited her daughter to dine and go to the theater with him. Mrs. Austin had none. Clare was amused and very excited.

The courtship of George Brokaw was conducted in the rhythm of a minuet. He took Clare to dinner and the theater and respectfully left her at her hotel, while his chauffeur stood holding the door of his car. He invited her to tea with Mrs. Brokaw, Sr., in the enormous stone chateau on Fifth Avenue, where mother and son lived alone with a dozen servants. Oddly enough, old Mrs. Brokaw took a great fancy to Clare. She made her sit in the strong light of the window, looked at her intensely, and then turned abruptly to her son.

"George," she said, "this is a good girl. And she is intelligent. It is high time you got married." Almost eighty, the old lady did not think she would last much longer. Perhaps, she thought to herself, this girl might stop his drinking . . .

And, Mr. Brokaw had stopped drinking the day he met Clare. She did not know about that. All she knew was that he was as charming as only an older man who has lived all over the world can be. It is true that he did not exactly scintillate; but the stories of important people and the places he had seen and his knowledge of high life temporarily gave the same effect. Clare was beglamored by him. She began to wonder what it would be like to be Mrs. George Tuttle Brokaw.

She soon found out. In the smiling presence of his mother Mr. Brokaw proposed in the courtly way in which he conducted his whole life. Clare hesitated and was lost. A modestly chaste kiss sealed the bargain, and a ten-carat diamond, which his mother told him to "go out and buy at once," made it official.

Mrs. Austin was ecstatic when she heard the news. Indeed, the only one of Clare's friends who did not offer hearty congratulations was Rudolph Kommer. From Reinhardt's Castle Leopoldskin came a series of "angry, almost insulting" letters from the good doctor. The least of what he said was an astounded squawk: "It is incredible that you should pass up this great and golden opportunity to play a principal role in the production of *The Miracle,* to get married.

Many years later, when Clare visited Max Reinhardt at Leopoldskin, the old gentleman spoke the final word: "That was a fell mistake," he said.

Sometimes it seems incredible that she made it. But it was actually perfectly natural. No use putting it down merely to materialism; there was far more to it than that. Of course, Brokaw's wealth and the stately way he lived was part of it. But Clare was too spirited, too sure of herself to be avaricious—after all, she did have The Nun waiting for her if she chose. The fact is that at twenty Clare was curiously innocent. Her intellectual sophistication was still separated from her real self as it had been at the Castle. The things that happened in books left her own life untouched. Indeed, it is doubtful if she had ever been thoroughly kissed. Love and romance and glamour were all mixed up in her mind. Though she almost certainly was not really in love, glamour and romance fooled her into thinking so. Though her fiancé was twice her age, he seemed in many ways twice the man any of her callow young beaux were. His less attractive traits were not apparent, for he, at least, was truly and romantically in love. At his most charming,

George Brokaw, even at forty-three, could be a reasonable facsimile of a prince on a white charger.

However, Clare did have a bad attack of bridal jitters on her wedding eve. She burst upon her mother sobbing, "I can't go through with it! I don't want to live in that dark house. I don't really want to be a society matron. I'll have to be that. I know it!"

Mrs. Austin was naturally frantic. All the momentum generated by a big wedding rolled down on her: the public announcements, the hundreds of guests, rooms full of presents, the caterers, the music, the church. Stopping it would be like trying to roll back a tidal wave.

"You can't back out now!" she cried. "You can't give it *all* up!"

For answer Clare rushed upstairs and locked herself in her room crying hysterically.

Just when she was feeling worst there was a commotion at the window. David Boothe was outside clinging to the drainpipe he had climbed. "You don't have to marry him, Sis!"

Clare stuck her tear-puffed face out of the window. "Why don't I?"

"I've still got some money I saved in the Marines. We can run away together."

It was infinitely touching. Clare never forgot her brother's gesture and later forgave him many things because of it. But even as she wept afresh, she could not picture herself and David fleeing ignominiously from a splendid destiny. It would not have been like her.

In the bright sunshine of the next day, August 10, 1923, it all seemed pretty silly. Clare, radiant in bridal white, wearing the necklace of diamonds and emeralds George had given her, was married by the Reverend George Thompson, Rector of Christ Church. There was a huge reception at the Pickwick Arms, where once was spent *The Happiest day of my life. Had dinner with Mother.* Everything went off almost perfectly. Many of the Four Hundred were there, as well as hundreds of the Austins' friends. Only George's brothers, Howard and Irving Brokaw, and their wives would not come. They gave as their excuse that they were "in mourning for President Harding." Throughout Clare's marriage they were as unpleasant as Cinderella's wicked stepsisters. After all, each had three daughters, who were expected to be the heirs of Bachelor George.

The bride and groom went off to Europe in a sumptuous royal suite, George was enormously proud of his beautiful bride, and he made their honeymoon as magnificent as anyone possibly could. For the first time Clare knew the infinite luxuries of great wealth— not only the big things like the royal suites and the great automobiles, and the constant, almost embarrassing, attentions of anxious servants, but the subtle little things like fresh flowers always in the rooms, the scent of expensive soap, and your own fine linen sheets replacing the almost equally good ones of the big hotels. The subtlest thing of all, and the hardest to get used to, was never having to wonder what anything cost.

It was a tremendous experience. And George was very attentive and kind. He only got drunk once or twice. However, nobody knew it because he never showed it. The only way Clare discovered it was that he could not remember anything that had happened the week before.

CHAPTER SIX

FROM NEWPORT TO VANITY FAIR

THE HOUSE THAT CLARE CAME HOME TO WAS A COPY OF A FRENCH Renaissance chateau with bastions and towers and pointed pinnacles. It looked a little like one of Maxfield Parrish's enchanted castles, but instead of being on a cloudy peak it was right on the corner of Fifth Avenue and Seventy-ninth Street. Inside, it was massively gloomy—Parrish's castles probably were, too. The great square hall was paneled in yellow marble with a huge fireplace and mantelpiece carved by workmen especially brought here from Italy. The high ceiling was intricately patterned with gold leaf, and the twisted columns supporting the arch of the grand stairway had golden capitals. At the rear were stained-glass windows of plump, allegorical ladies representing: *Abundantia, Hospitalitas, Concordia, Recreatia*—in time the irony became pretty painful.

To the left of the hall were twin drawing rooms divided by a wide archway. Each was lighted by a magnificent crystal chandelier and excessively furnished in the French gilt and ormolu style. On the right an oval library led to the long dining room paneled in dark oak. Brokaw showed his wife a secret button that caused one of the panels to spring out, disclosing a massive six-foot safe where she could keep her jewels.

Life there was like a stately dream peopled with animated dolls that walked and talked and said nothing. Clare never had to do anything for herself; indeed, she could not without hurting some servant's feelings. No matter how late she and George came home, there was always a footman in livery waiting merely to swing open the heavy front door. Imperceptibly the dream turned into one of those nightmares in which your limbs are too heavy to obey the will and you try to run and cannot.

The next spring they went to live in George Brokaw's pretty country house at Port Washington, Long Island, and they lived there quietly, for Clare was expecting a baby. George was drinking more, but he was still very kind and thoughtful. He wrote a letter to Dorothy Burns in Chicago, telling her that Clare seemed despondent and lonely. "Please come to stay with us as long as you can, and cheer her up."

Dorothy came, and her jolly, sensible companionship did cheer Clare up. Dorothy was a devout Catholic, but they were careful never to talk about religion. The visit ended abruptly at the end of July, when Dorothy's father died suddenly.

Clare's baby was born in August, 1924, a little dark-haired girl. She was christened Ann Clare Brokaw.

Though Clare loved her, a baby did not occupy the place in her elaborate life that it would in a more modest home. This was not peculiar to the Brokaws, but to almost everyone who lived as they did. There were, there had to be, trained nurses who were jealous of their charges and only grudgingly admitted a mother's right to play with her baby. Later a governess would take the place of the nurse, but the situation would be the same. In the houses of the very rich, parents and children met almost as courteous strangers and seldom got to know each other really well until the children were almost grown—if even then. Later Clare blamed herself bitterly for not having been closer to her child, but it was not her fault; it was a pattern of existence which she was too inexperienced to break.

The fact that Clare's marriage lasted for six years is proof that she really tried. Not that anyone is going to pretend that there were not enormous compensations for its difficulties. The Twenties were the September Song of the great tycoons, their flaming sunset, when, aided by modern science, their luxurious living made the Caesars in their unsprung, iron-tired chariots and their drafty palace on the Palatine Hill look like monks in a cave by comparison.

From New York to Palm Beach to Newport, to the Riviera, Clare traveled in such comfort as the world had never seen. Nor was it all materialistic. She moved amid great beauty, visiting in classic houses artfully placed among rolling lawns and lakes, or on cliffs looking over Narragansett Bay. There were graceful yachts sailing over the changeable silk of tropical waters; and mountain lodges among the Adirondack pines. All the arts were commanded to enhance the pleasure of life; glowing masterpieces hanging, not in a museum row, but as they should, alone on the walls of gracious rooms; the splendor of great music performed by the finest artists of the time. Even the tools of living, the table silver and cobweb cloths, the rugs Clare walked on, and the sheets she slept in, were exquisite pieces of craftsmanship.

But it was all no good because of the purposeless pattern of their existence and the vapidity of their friends.

George did his dull best to please her. He went along with her love of the theater, backing a stock company in Newport, where they put on some excellent plays. Clare joined the Amateur Comedy Club and played the lead in their production of *Tweedles* by Booth Tarkington and Harry Leon Wilson. What with the less exacting demands of a friendly audience and the professional polish she had acquired so many years before, she made a smash hit. And also, an almost invariable penalty of wealth and beauty, she roused considerable jealousy among the female Comediennes.

A picture of the first night: the Brokaw limousine drawing up to the theater, and Clare, breath-taking in a crystal and silver gown by Lanvin, sweeping into the theater followed by George and a footman with their arms piled high with boxes of orchids and gardenias for the ladies and gentlemen of the cast. Clare intended a gracious gesture; it was unenthusiastically received as being too much the Lady Bountiful.

As the years of the marriage went on, Clare became more and more bored and miserable, and George drank harder and harder. The time came when he would wake up in the morning only a little drunk and promptly rectify the deficiency. Even then he never showed it, for he drank, as he did everything, like a gentleman. But he remained in an alcoholic daze. So they moved through the great houses of Newport and New York, Clare, her lovely eyes shadowy, withdrawn, with George following her in an owlish stupor. The curious affection that existed between old Mrs. Brokaw and her daughter-in-law somehow kept the marriage going. Then, one spring, she died. And Clare felt that the time had come when she could not stand it any longer. She felt physically suffocated; her brain, of which she was so proud, was being stultified. She tried to write plays which nobody wanted to read. She had a library of books in her dressing room and read and read—"How odd of her," some of the women said, when she told them she preferred reading to playing bridge.

Clare did not take divorce lightly. Dorothy Burns, who saw her just before she left for Reno, records that she was unhappy. "She had honestly expected to make her marriage last."

It was even hard, in a way, to leave George. Though later there was a tremendous legal hassle over the custody of Ann, with George Gordon Battle representing Brokaw and brilliant Arthur Garfield Hays in Clare's corner, while William M. Chadbourne, beaming benevolently on everybody, acted as unofficial referee, the actual divorce was amiable. Finally Brokaw offered Clare an alimony tax-free of seventy-five thousand dollars a year, so long as she did not marry, or four hundred and twenty-five thousand dollars. Clare chose the latter. With the agreement signed, Clare set out on the rough road to Reno.

Of all the cities in the world, Reno is the most dismal. They should call it the City of Desperate Women, for not even the three-time losers take divorce as lightly as they pretend; and to a sensitive young woman it is a harrowing experience. Certainly Reno injected a streak of bitterness into Clare that turned her wit to vitriol and fired her personality with a hard glaze that did not entirely disappear until she joined the Catholic Church. She distilled the essence of it into the famous Reno scene in her play *The Women* in which Sylvia, the cat, who is a little tipsy, is talking to the aging, often-married Countess:

Sylvia: "I gave him my youth."

Countess (dreamily): "Hélas, what can a woman do with her youth but give it to a man?"

Sylvia: "Hélas, she can't preserve it in alcohol."

When Clare came back she rented an apartment at the Hotel

Stanhope on Fifth Avenue. She had pictured freedom as release from boredom; instead she was utterly miserable. The crash in Wall Street that fall deepened her sense of futility. Four of her good friends committed suicide in the next few months. Though she regarded herself as a cynical woman of the world, she could not quite harden herself to think of people who preferred death to life as mere neurotics. Finally she became so despondent that she sought the help of a psychoanalyst.

Even at its gloomiest, Clare's mind was much too acute to fall for the Freudian hashish that her particular quack dished out to his patients. Right in the middle of a treatment, "I realized that this man's technique was nonsense, and walked out. Then I realized: *What I need is a job.*"

The next thing was to assess her capabilities. The only thing Clare thought that she could do was to write. But she knew that that alone was not enough; she felt she needed the discipline of having to go to work at fixed hours, and a boss to keep her on the tracks. The answer was obviously to work on a magazine. Characteristically, Clare went to the top.

Condé Nast was the only man she knew in the magazine field, so she called on him at his penthouse on Park Avenue. Nast listened to her with his eyes twinkling amusedly behind his rimless pince-nez, and gave her a long anti-sales talk about all the women who wanted jobs on *Vogue*. When Clare persisted, he gave her a courteous runaround. "You go to see Edna Chase at *Vogue*," he said, "I'm off to Europe in a couple of days."

The very next morning Clare called on Edna Woolman Chase, the remarkable lady who, with Nast's backing had raised *Vogue* from a fifth-rate dressmaker's delight to a commanding position in the world of fashion. Mrs. Chase was equally courteous . . . and elusive. Clare was determined. She called again. This time Mrs. Chase announced that she, too, was going to Europe. "When I come back, perhaps. . . ."

The fact is that no one believed that a woman as pretty and well off as Clare would be worth a Mexican nickel in business. Indeed, her great friend Margaret Case of *Vogue* says, "Clare's beauty was actually a handicap to her literary career. Because of it nobody would take her seriously. But she showed them!"

Condé Nast and Edna Chase reckoned not on Clare's stubbornness. She left the editor's presence and wandered down a long corridor peering into offices. Finally she came to one in which, "a dear little old lady was sitting all alone." It was the caption writers' office. Clare walked in and pointed at an empty desk. "Whose desk is that?" she asked.

The dear little old lady answered, "No one's, at present."

"Then it's mine."

"What are you going to do?"

"Write captions," Clare said briskly.

The dear little old lady seemed pleased. She handed over a group of photographs, saying, "Well, here are some to write."

They were captions for pictures of what the well-dressed baby will wear.

Clare worked in that office every day, and nobody knew she was there until the girl came around with the pay envelopes. "I'm afraid I don't have one for you," she said to Clare.

"That's quite all right," Clare answered hastily. "Think nothing of it!"

The second week when the paygirl came around, Clare was fairly caught. She was sent to one of the editors, luckily a man. He questioned her keenly and a little crossly, but she knew she had made an impression. Then he asked the people who had worked with her how she was doing. It seemed she was doing fine. Donald Freeman, managing editor of *Vanity Fair*, also pleaded her cause with Miss Margaret Case who was in charge while Mrs. Chase was abroad. "She's young and beautiful and very smart," he said.

"Oh no!" said Maggie.

"Oh yes!" he countered and gave Miss Case some of Clare's work.

It *was* good, so they decided to risk giving her a job—at twenty-one dollars a week.

Clare worked on *Vogue* for five months, but she was already aspiring to *Vanity Fair*. This was the magazine that Nast had founded in 1914 under the brilliant editorship of Frank Crowninshield and later Donald Freeman. It was interested in everything that was interesting: politics, business, all the arts, sports, and people—especially people. It also published some excellent off-beat fiction. The tone was witty, cynical, and intelligent; and the people who wrote for it were a diamond-minded lot: George Jean Nathan, Paul Gallico, Walter Lippmann, George Sokolsky, Frank Sullivan, Robert Sherwood, and a dozen more, while the great photographer Edward Steichen made its picture pages fine art of another kind. It was just Clare's dish of tea.

As soon as she got to know Crowninshield fairly well, she went to work on him. Crowny finally said, "If you want a job, you must submit a hundred ideas for *Vanity Fair.*"

He was joking, but Clare took it straight—and produced them over a weekend. She got the job.

Then it was back to writing captions, but this time more interesting ones, for *Vanity Fair's* "Hall of Fame." One of her first assignments was young Mr. Luce of Time, Inc.

Clare took her job seriously. Through his secretary she made several appointments to interview Mr. Luce. Each time he broke them. Finally he sent word that he was much to busy for such nonsense. Failing to meet the great young man personally, Clare went to his friends. They did not have much to give her in the way of color or anecdote. All of them emphasized how hard he worked.

Then Clare sat down to write her caption:

"We nominate for The Hall of Fame:

"Henry Luce. Originator of the news magazine idea; because at the age of thirty-two he is the successful editor and publisher of 'Time' and 'Fortune' magazines; because he was born in China; because he was a humble newspaper reporter on the Chicago Daily News; and lastly because he claims that he has no other interest outside of his work, and that his work fills his waking hours."

Clare says that as she stabbed the last period in with her pencil she said to herself, "What a dull fellow that must be!"

CHAPTER SEVEN

CLARE'S FIRST PINNACLE

IN THE SUMMER OF 1930 CLARE RENTED A COTTAGE AT EASTHAMP-
ton, where Ann could enjoy the fine sea air and a whole beachful
of sand to play on all week, and she could spend the weekends. At
the Maidstone Club she literally ran into Buff Cobb, and they
hugged each other in dripping bathing suits. All their old affection
for each other blazed up and never cooled again.

That fall Clare rented an apartment at 444 East Fifty-second
Street and did it up in modern style, as different as possible from
a French chateau. Rosamund Pinchot, who had made a tremendous
hit as The Nun whom Clare had forsaken for matrimony, had one
on the same floor. Despite the odds against it the two young beau-
ties became great friends. They both loved to entertain interesting
people and sometimes joined forces, opening both apartments for
especially gala occasions. Through their portals poured the most
glittering intellects in the world, from Noel Coward to Herr
Brüning the last Chancellor of the German Republic. Incidentally,
Clare became very fond of the wise old German who tried so hard
to save his country from Nazism.

Other close friends who came, then and later, to her brilliant
parties were George Jean Nathan, Condé Nast, Frank Crowninshield, Elsa Maxwell, Ferenc Molnar, Harrison Smith of *The
Saturday Review,* Buckminster Fuller, inventor of the Dymaxion
car and the house that hung on a pole, Dorothy Hale, Père Lorenze
of *Time,* Donald Freeman of *Vanity Fair,* and Bernard Baruch. As
one friend describes it, "Around Clare there were painters painting

pictures, authors writing, musicians playing, actors acting, and everybody talking about the arts, economics and politics."

This was the sort of thing Clare had longed for, as different as possible from discussions of the servant problem or the high cost of keeping a yacht. But still she was not happy. She describes herself at this time as a sort of intellectual weathercock, whirling to the wind of each new *ism*. The general direction of her thinking was from left to far left. She read Karl Marx and his disciples, and, as the Great Depression deepened and the apple sellers set up stalls on windy corners, she became, "very inclined to believe that Marx had found the perfect blueprint for a happy society." But she never went so far as to recommend the immediate overthrow of the American Constitution.

She must have been a pretty picture of inconsistency with her blue eyes outflashing her splendid jewels as she delivered philippics against the international bankers and panegyrics to the classless society. There was, however, one point on which everybody—that is, all right-thinking liberals—agreed: Christianity was a flop. "The opiate of the people" had given the human race a bad hang-over.

Such a lot of fine free-thinking should have been exciting, if not inspiring. Instead, Clare still felt futile. Though she would never have admitted it then, she needed some larger answer to life than was to be had in Socialist dialectics.

The thing Clare enjoyed most was her job on *Vanity Fair*. The high spot of the week was the office luncheons to which the rather small staff all came, and usually one or two distinguished guests, such as André Maurois or Julian Huxley. The food was delicious, sent up from the Savarin Restaurant downstairs in the Graybar Building. Clare, conscious of once having been buxom, never ordered anything but salad. However, old *Vanity Fairers* say that by the time she got through tasting everybody else's dishes, she had made a good square meal.

Of course, Condé Nast was usually there and Frank Crowninshield—"Crowny was a wonderful wit—he could write with his feet." Everybody would catch the spirit of gaiety and the long table was kept in gales of laughter.

Clare did a lot of talking and everybody listened to her slow, soft voice, because what she said was very worthwhile hearing. Many of the articles that appeared in the magazine under various by-lines were in effect written right there at the table, beaten out in witty badinage.

Clare suggested several of the features that became famous tidbits of *Vanity Fair*. "Married in Name Only," (for instance, Helen and J. P. Morgan). "We Nominate for Oblivion," and "Improbable Interviews." "The Improbable Interview" she wrote between Mussolini and Huey Long cost the magazine the account of the Italian Line: about fifty thousand dollars a year.

When Clare first went to work she thought she ought to dress like a businesswoman. She had two mannishly tailored suits, one brown, one gray; but she remained a swan in a mouse's clothing. Helen Brown, author of *Latins Are Lousy Lovers* whom Clare brought to *Vanity Fair*, describes her at that time as a dazzling golden blonde. "Even after the latest night she always came to work on time, looking fresh and beautiful."

Incidentally, Clare never used any beauty preparation to stay dazzling; to this day she washes her face with Physicians and Surgeons soap.

While Helen Brown may be partial, her description of Clare should, after all, be reliable since she, too, is a very attractive woman. "When Clare came into a room full of people," she says, "she had a sort of radiance like a strong light inside her that made all the other women look washed out."

Apparently the light went on and off, for when Clare was bored, she could not hide the dismal fact. Dorothy Thompson says, "One thing about her that irritated people was her low threshhold of boredom. She would go absolutely white from it."

Clare's inner flame glowed more steadily for men than women, but this seems to have been less coquetry than because men usually had more interesting things to say. In this connection Helen Brown tells of introducing Clare to young Irwin Shaw, author of *Bury the Dead*. Beforehand, Shaw was sure he would dislike her. She began talking to him very simply and earnestly, looking up at him, asking his opinion, but illuminating the discussion with penetrating comments. Shaw's prejudice visibly collapsed. Indeed, Helen says, "He went all to pieces."

When he finally got out in the cold night air, he shook his head as though to clear it. "I did not believe she was so beautiful," he said.

"And so feminine," Helen prompted.

Shaw gave her a quizzical look. "She's about as feminine as a meat ax," he said. "But wonderful!"

That direct quality of Clare's mind is probably the reason why so many people, who don't know her, dislike her. For there is no question but that she arouses an almost pathological antipathy, especially among women. It is often said that this is just plain jealousy of anyone so beautiful, rich, and successful; but such venom, which is shared by some men—who don't know her—requires a better explanation. It probably lies in her terrible candor and the ruthless way she has of stripping away the shams and illusions with which less gifted mortals cover their inadequacies. Her penetrating intelligence could always discern a phony, and she had no mercy on them.

However, the important thing to note is that the people who hated her then—and now—are almost all people who never knew her well. The women who worked closely with her on *Vogue* and *Vanity Fair* adored her. One of these was Margaret Case, who became her lifelong friend and confidante. Another was Jean Ballot, who shared her office at *Vanity Fair*; and the third was Helen Brown, now Mrs. Jack Lawrenson, who says, "She was always fair to people who worked for her. If she brought up one of my ideas at a conference and it met with favor, she would always say to Condé and Crowny, 'This is Miss Brown's idea.' It is rather rare for one's boss to do that.

"Another thing," Helen adds, "I was in a motor accident, and suffered a bad cut over my eyebrow. The moment Clare heard about it, she called me up and insisted that I go to her doctor. 'It won't cost you anything,' she said. 'He owes me a lot of favors.'

"Without that expert care I would have had a disfiguring scar," Helen says. "I know Clare paid for it. That is just the sort of thing she does all the time for her friends."

Less surprising than the evident devotion of her women friends on *Vanity Fair* is the fact that most of the men fell in love with Clare, in greater or lesser degree. Writers John O'Hara and Paul Gallico and even Condé Nast himself, were among those who might be called smitten. Bill Hale and Donald Freeman, the brilliant, ugly, kind managing editor, were romantically in love. Clare loved them all and was in love with no one.

It is interesting to leaf through the back issues of *Vanity Fair* and watch the growing maturity of the articles signed Clare Boothe Brokaw. The early ones are sharply satirical, very funny nonsense. A collection of fictional sketches of this period formed the basis of her first book, *Stuffed Shirts,* published by Horace Liveright in 1931. It is a venomous lampoon of New York society into which she poured all the gall her unhappy marriage had engendered. By it she supposedly burned her social bridges behind her, but her later successes rapidly repaired them.

Gradually the subjects of her *Vanity Fair* articles became more serious and the treatment more philosophical until she was writing of politics and economics with surprising wisdom that was enlivened by a thunderbolt flash of phrase. More important, the human understanding deepened issue by issue.

Paul Gallico and Donald Freeman, both superb craftsmen, taught her a great deal about technique, while Steichen was teaching her photography. Nobody was ever able to teach her to spell— Clare writes phonetically.

Incidentally, not all of Clare's work in *Vanity Fair* was signed by her. Sometimes she had two or more pieces in a single issue under different names. The first one the magazine printed was under a literary alias. When she was just starting out, she says, she was dying to have a piece in the magazine but dared not submit it under her own name. So she signed it Julian Jerome and slipped it into Freeman's basket. He read and bought it without knowing the author. The price was one hundred dollars, which was pretty good considering that Paul Gallico got only fifty dollars for a short sketch. [And the entire editorial cost of the issue, including pictures and color plates, was $9866.05.]

Another thing on which the old *Vanity Fair* crowd are agreed is that Clare had not the faintest tinge of snobbery or racial prejudice. Nor would she satirize things that were important. One time at an editorial conference Condé Nast proposed a satirical cover on "The Forgotten Man." Clare looked her boss coldly in the eye and said,

"I don't see anything even remotely funny about people being hungry."

The silence was so thick you were like to drown in it. Then somebody changed the subject. Nast was glad to forget "The Forgotten Man."

Clare's preoccupation with the distress and misery engendered by the depression had a good deal to do with changing the character of *Vanity Fair*. It seemed to her that those dark days of toppling banks, unemployment, privation, and social unrest were no time for the gay frivolity that had suited the tempo of the Golden Twenties. She was influential in bringing Henry Pringle and John Franklin Carter, Jr., to the magazine as part-time editorial advisers. Carter, who was to become a mainstay of Franklin Roosevelt's New Deal and one of about twenty people who claim to have contributed that phrase to the Roosevelt Brain Trust, wrote for the magazine as Jay Franklin.

Carter's article in *Vanity Fair* called, "Wanted a New Party," sparked the founding of the short-lived New National party, which was financially backed by such fashionable but socially conscious ladies as Mesdames Harrison Williams and James Forrestal; and spearheaded by Clare herself.

It was about this time that a meeting occurred which was pure good fortune. She went to dinner at the Colony Restaurant with Bill Chadbourne, and among the people at a large table she saw the classically rugged head, and the sagacious eyes behind much-cartooned pince-nez of sixty-year-old Bernard M. Baruch. Clare had met him at large functions, but had never really talked to him. Baruch waved jovially to Chadbourne and called a greeting.

"Do you know him that well?" asked Clare.

"Yes," the lawyer answered. "Do you want to meet him?"

"I want to talk to him," Clare said.

Bill accomplished the introduction with his usual flowery turn of phrase that made Clare sound like a combination of Ilium's Helen, Lesbos' Sappho, and Mrs. Amelia Bloomer of New York. Clare blushed a little, which did her appearance no harm; and Baruch noted her beauty and wondered if she could possibly have the brains Bill implied. In retrospect he says, "She was so lovely to look at. I remember the little, wispy, golden-brown curls on her forehead and her classic figure."

After that they met quite often at the glittering buffet supper parties Condé Nast used to give at his Park Avenue apartment, which usually started after the theater and continued amid good music, dancing, and wonderful talk until the sun jumped out of the East River. It was at one of these that she said to him, "Mr. Baruch, you're not very nice to me."

"I thought I was being nice," he answered, twinkling. "What do you want me to do?"

"Will you help me to understand the economic problems we're facing?" she asked unexpectedly.

As Baruch puts it: "It certainly didn't hurt your eyes to look at her, so I was willing to help her."

Their first long talks completely eliminated Baruch's doubts as to the quality of her mind. He says, "In her thinking two and two always equal four; her logical approach and clear thinking never change. In fact, there is nothing feminine about her but her looks. She is very *soignée*, but under the dress by Jacques Fath is a matter-of-fact, thoughtful person. And when courage was given out, she was sitting on the front bench."

As he got to know her better, Baruch decided that Clare's beauty was much more than physical perfection: "When she comes into a room she attracts everybody's attention by the glow that emanates from her," he says. "Her extraordinary spirit shines out of her eyes; she glows with the spiritual beauty of her character. She reacts automatically against injustice—against anything that is wrong."

The elder statesman of democracy delighted in imparting his wisdom to Clare. One of the first questions she asked him was, "How can you tell if a thing is so or not?"

"Ask yourself these questions," Baruch replied. "Is it possible? Is it probable? Is it, then, true? Finally, can it take place at this time and place, allowing for the human equation?"

On another occasion Clare asked him his opinion on the then-vexed question of German reparations. After listening to him thoughtfully, she wrote an article on the subject and handed it in to Nast, telling him it was by the unorthodox British economist

John Maynard Keynes. Nast read it and said it was great stuff and was prepared to print it, but Clare had to break down and confess her authorship. The article was never published.

But Baruch was dead against the New National party, in which Clare tried to interest him. "Third parties don't work in America," he told her, "and a good thing that is. You must work through your own party."

To advance her education in politics, Baruch took Clare to her first national convention, the Democratic one of 1932 in Chicago, which nominated Franklin D. Roosevelt. Others in his party were the Morton Schwartzes, Mrs. Condé Nast, General Hugh (Iron Pants) Johnson, Admiral Cary Grayson, and Mrs. Woodrow Wilson. Under such an aegis Clare saw the inside workings of a great convention; the politicians like James H. Farley trying to persuade Baruch to throw his great influence to Roosevelt; others arguing for John Garner of Texas or Al Smith. To them all Baruch was cordial and noncommittal. "I don't believe in being for anybody until after someone is nominated, then I'll work like mad to get him elected."

Clare also heard the inside story of the deals and counterdeals and watched the exciting counts of the votes and the frantic scrambles to corral wavering delegates between ballots, until, in the early hours of the morning Jim Curley, Boss of Boston, got on the telephone to William Randolph Hearst at San Simeon to swing California to Roosevelt, while Sam Rayburn of Texas persuaded Jack Garner to put that state in Roosevelt's column in exchange for the Vice-Presidency.

Then came the fourth ballot with Chicago wardheelers desperately crowding down among the delegates to cause confusion and head off the stampede for Roosevelt; the count of states, and McAdoo of California shouting, "California. Forty-six votes for Franklin D. Roosevelt." And the wild crash of cheering as the delegates realized that the deadlock was broken and Roosevelt would be nominated.

Clare had tried to do some lobbying herself for the New National party, but she got nowhere, as Baruch had predicted. As soon as she reached home she dissolved her party by firing its only employee, a secretary.

Both at the convention and afterward Baruch introduced Clare to many of the leaders of America. General Johnson became her close friend and later, at Baruch's suggestion, appointed her on the committee to write the Theatre and Motion Picture Code for Roosevelt's NRA. Though Clare hated the exfoliating bureaucracy and Socialistic implications of NRA's attempt to put all American business under a statist form of federal control, she served faithfully on the committee and thereby met many moguls of the theater, among them Max Gordon, who later produced *The Women*.

Other people whom she met through Baruch were Al Smith, Owen D. Young, the great journalists Mark Sullivan and Arthur Krock, as well as virtually all the head men of the Democratic party. During the election of 1932 she worked hard for Roosevelt as a minor member of his famous Brain Trust.

The most exciting introduction of all happened a few years later. Clare, who was in England for the Hearst Syndicate, was dining with Baruch at the Savoy, when Winston Churchill came in. The great Englishmen headed straight for his old friend and was introduced to Clare. It looked as though the introduction had not taken, for Churchill merely acknowledged Clare's presence and plunged into conversation with Baruch.

However, two days later when Baruch was staying with Churchill at Chartwell, the latter asked, "Who was that awfully pretty girl you introduced me to in London?"

Baruch told him something about Clare and Churchill said, "Let's get her down here."

Turning to his son, he commanded, "Randolph, go call her up. Get her to come down."

Clare came for the rest of the week end. Baruch says that she asked Churchill some very acute, embarrassing questions about the war debts. "Questions that I would not have dared to ask." But Churchill did not mind.

During those few years Clare was often asked on the house parties Baruch gave at his superb, secluded place in South Carolina, Hobcaw Barony. There, among many others, she met John Golden, who said to his host, "That girl will write a great play if she ever gets down to it."

At Hobcaw, Baruch taught Clare to shoot. He says that she went at it with the same "concentration and determination with which she does everything else. In a short time she became a first-class shot."

Baruch adds that the only other person he taught to shoot who put the same single-minded purpose into learning was Senator Taft.

Time has not withered but strengthened the friendship that began so casually in the Colony Restaurant. Clare's devotion to "Bernie" is equaled only by his affection for her. Lately he told her the story of how one time the aged French statesman Georges Clemenceau refused a favor to Mrs. Charles Dana Gibson. Mrs. Gibson said, "I don't believe you love me."

"Madame, I love you with all the fervor of my eighty-five years," Clemenceau replied. "Someday you will die and go to heaven. Just after you pass the gate you will see a little anteroom on the left. I will be waiting for you there."

Quite evidently Baruch, who is eighty-five, meant that he, also, would be waiting there for Clare.

By the autumn of 1932 Clare had become a mainstay of the magazine, both as writer and editor. Her promotion to managing editor came about through a tragedy that shook her deeply. On October 2, Donald Freeman, motoring out to Connecticut, lost control of his car, which crashed into a bridge abutment, killing him instantly.

His death was not only a great loss to the magazine but a personal blow to everybody on it, most of all, perhaps, to Clare. Her loyalty to him was transferred to his sister, Gladys Freeman, who is one of the many women who can always call on her in any emergency. When Clare was married to Harry Luce, she commissioned Gladys, who had become an interior decorator, to design the furnishings for their house in Greenwich, their apartment in the Waldorf Towers, and, later, their present beautiful house in Ridgefield, Connecticut.

Condé Nast and Frank Crowninshield felt that Clare was the editor best fitted to fill the gaping hole in *Vanity Fair*'s ranks. That she justified their confidence is evidenced by the fact that the quality of the magazine did not suffer but if anything improved.

Buckminster Fuller says, "Nast, Crowninshield, and Clare were a brilliant triumvirate when they ruled *Vanity Fair*—a great team."

As managing editor Clare steered the magazine even more toward political and economic interests. However, her most significant contribution was stillborn. With an almost eerie prescience she said to Nast one day, "I've been thinking it would be a good idea to start a picture magazine. In fact, I've even got a title for it: *Life*."

"There is a magazine called *Life*," he objected.

"Of course there is," said Clare. "I've found out you could buy it for twenty thousand dollars. The name is worth all of that."

"Write me a memorandum about it," Nast suggested. "We'll go into it further."

Clare wrote a twelve-page memorandum. Condé buried it in the files and thereby missed no ordinary boat but a regular luxury liner. However, that memorandum later came in very handy.

All her life, until she joined the Catholic Church, Clare was driven by her fiercely restless inner self. She has written that "some vast uneasiness, restlesness, discontent suffused the very interstices of my being." Even in the happy Castle days she pushed herself beyond need or reason, and later, in Greenwich, she was at times so beset that she would drive her car at night over twisting back-country roads at tremendous speed, escaping something—perhaps herself—or seeking something she knew not what. Not fortune or success: she won them and went on. Not sex or any carnal thing. Love, perhaps, or possibly faith.

So when she reached the attainable summit of Condé Nast Publications she was content to remain there only briefly. To her a pinnacle was never a place to remain but rather a vantage point to scan the horizon for new worlds to conquer.

In 1934 she resigned her ten-thousand-dollar-a-year job as managing editor and started a newspaper column for Paul Block's newspapers and the Hearst Syndicate. Then she gave up her apartment and took off for Europe to look over "This World of Ours" as her column was called. Her clear-eyed view of the disintegrating European scene was too strong for an American public that was used to the pabulum of pacifist optimism; while her sense of America's obligation to provide some sort of leadership to arrest the cancerous growth of totalitarianism ran head on into Hearst's isolationist idiocy.

So he fired her, and with Block's not-unwilling assent, she came home. There was a play in her mind fairly shouting to see footlights. Its title was *Abide with Me*.

CHAPTER EIGHT

"THAT DULL FELLOW"

THE THAYER HOBSONS WERE GIVING A DINNER PARTY. IT WAS A
rather special dinner because they had secured a rather special
guest. Henry Luce was anything but a party boy—that *"work, work"*
caption of Clare's was quite true. Because he was so hard to get,
everybody wanted him. As the extra woman who could be more
suitable than Clare Brokaw, lately back from Europe with all sorts
of inside information that would be sure to interest the father of
Time? It was a natural, thought the Hobsons.

They did not put Mrs. Brokaw next to Mr. Luce at dinner, but
when the men came back to join the ladies, Hobson maneuvered
him onto a sofa next to Clare and left nature to take its course.

Despite her snap judgment as to Luce's lack of color, Clare
was excited. An aura of mystery and power is almost irresistible to
a woman. Besides, Harry Luce was bold-nosed handsome, as a man
should be, and his gray-blue eyes were ever so slightly slanted, as
though they had been shaped by the environment of his youthful
years in China. In addition, he had a reputation for being imper-
meable. Confidently, Clare decided to give him the works.

She was doing very well, she thought, talking extremely intelligently about the rise of Nazism, when Mr. Luce pulled out his
watch. "My bedtime," he said. "Nice to have met you. Good-bye."
And left her with her mouth open in mid-sentence.

The next time Clare saw him was at somebody's crowded cocktail
party. And again she unlimbered her heaviest mental artillery, this
time choosing her subject cannily. Knowing the rumor that *Life*

was germinating in the Luce mind, she said, "Mr. Luce, you must start a picture magazine."

Harry's eyebrows came down and his lips quirked up. "How would you cover the death of the Mikado?" he asked.

"By taking pictures," said Clare, dead-pan.

It was quite lively while it lasted. But Clare says, "Just in the middle of things he hauled out his watch—and left!"

He left her seething. She swore that, "If I ever see that guy again I'll fix him!"

When next Clare encountered an editor from *Time*, she let off steam: "Without doubt the editor of your magazine has the worst manners of any man alive. He just picks your brains and leaves you flat."

The editor no doubt wondered how many men Clare had done the same thing to. Clearly Greek meeting Greek, this one.

Elsa Maxwell's party for Cole Porter on December 6, 1934, was intended to be a really tremendous affair, with all the glitter and splash that had made her name a synonym for hostess. But she hardly expected it to influence the history of an era. Accidentally she gave destiny a shove by suggesting to Condé Nast, who was giving a small dinner—for fifty—before the ball: "Why not ask Harry Luce to your party?"

"That will never do," Nast objected. "Clare Brokaw is coming and she dislikes him intensely. They met at some dinner and had a cat-and-dog time."

When Elsa sets her sights on somebody, nothing stops her. "Go ahead and ask him anyhow," she urged. "I want to snaffle him for my party."

Luce accepted his fellow publisher's invitation, but he and Clare kept apart at the dinner. To Elsa's delighted surprise Harry went on to her party at the Starlight Roof of the Waldorf. The place was so jammed with celebrities that it would seem that one more or less hardly mattered; but rejoicing over the strayed lamb is not confined to heaven.

At about midnight Clare was sitting with her escort of the hour at a table for two. He got up to leave her for a moment, and passes nameless out of history. "I was sitting alone at the table," Clare says, "when I saw Harry coming across the room with two glasses of champagne. *There is that dreadful man,* I thought. I decided to treat him the way he had treated me—by leaving him in the middle of a sentence. But first I had to get him to sit down at the table, so I stopped him and asked sweetly, 'Are you bringing that champagne for me, Mr. Luce?'

" 'Humph, I suppose so,' said Harry."

Clare's luck was a lady that night. At precisely the right moment all the lights in the room went out for the show.

"Won't you sit down?" Clare said in the darkness.

There was nothing else Harry could do.

Once she had him trapped, Clare found that "I really did not feel like fighting that night."

So they sat and talked. Spotlights blazed on some of the greatest talent of London, Broadway, and Hollywood. Cole Porter played and Merman sang, "I Get a Kick Out of You," at the top of her lungs. Famous comedians exchanged badinage that would have brought the police at a public performance. Hoofers hoofed; tenors tremuloed; the orchestra tore itself to tatters; and Elsa cracked the whip like the ringmaster she was of one of the greatest shows on earth. But Clare and Harry talked . . .

It must have been nearly three o'clock when Harry said abruptly, "Will you walk to the lobby with me? I have something important to tell you."

Clare thought it odd and wondered if he was going to offer her a job on *Time.* She was going to have the fun of turning it down flat. When they reached the lobby, she asked lightly, "What is this shattering news?"

Harry Luce did not smile. His eyes were deadly serious and, strangely for him, he fumbled for words. "It isn't easy to say it," he muttered. "I've just made an important discovery. I hope you will think it's important too. I've discovered that you are the one woman in my life."

Clare gasped and could do no more than mutter something feeble. Then she watched incredulously as Harry hauled out his watch once more. "I've got to get back to the party," he said, "Where do you live?"

"At the Sherry-Netherlands."

"Fine," said Harry. "I'll call on you Wednesday afternoon at five-thirty, and we'll discuss this further."

Henry Robinson Luce is the son of American Presbyterian missionaries to China. He loves that land and likes to talk about his life there.

"I was born in Shantung Province on the big promontory of China where Confucius came from," he will tell you. "Father, Dr. Henry Winters Luce, was associated with higher education in China. In 1897, when he arrived, there was nothing to speak of in the way of higher education in all China. During his time he saw and played a great part in the development of high schools, colleges, even universities, in Shantung—Christian University and Yen Ching, where Leighton Stewart was president when the Japs came. Father was assistant to the president during his last ten years in China.

"The place I remember best in China is Wei Hsien, a city of one hundred and fifty thousand—Hsien means county seat. It was almost in the middle of the province. The first union college was founded there, a union of several missionary societies, both American and British—the first time the British would agree to cooperate. The compound was therefore much larger than normal missionary compounds. It had about thirty families, English and American, and was a mile and a half from the city, 'way out on a plain. You could see the hills in the distance, but it was almost like the Western prairies except for the graves; thousands of large dirt mounds about six feet high all over the place. There were villages every mile or so; you could see six or seven villages from the compound. The roads were just ruts in the plain, worn down through the centuries until they were perhaps fifteen feet below the level of the fields. Big-wheeled carts were the only vehicles, with donkeys and human beings as motive power. You cannot say it was primitive, because it was so ancient a civilization, but it was very preindustrial.

"There I saw the whole life of China. We were, of course, out on the campus, but still I saw the flow of life—the bridal processions winding among the graves, market day with the country people pouring in before dawn and wandering back at twilight, some of them staggering—quite high.

"About once a week we went into the city, where I saw the crowded, jostling alleys of that shopkeeping town. I came to know the Chinese with their strange tenderness—sentimentality—and their paradoxical cruelty. There was no famine in our area; the villagers got along all right. There were beggars, of course, some real, some fake. And there was always the police, whom the Chinese felt were to be avoided at all costs.

"Culturally, I was brought up an American. My mother made a special effort on my education, reading the classics aloud to me— the origin of my love of reading aloud. Therefore, I knew little of Chinese art or literature, although people think me an authority. Of course I've learned a lot, but that came later.

"I went to an English-American boarding school. It was run in the manner of a British public school, fagging, caning, and such, like *Tom Brown's Schooldays*—a provincial Rugby on the coast of China, with none of the swank and all the severity.

"The school was organized by the China-England Mission. They were people who did not care about progress but were just out to save the Chinese from hellfire. There were millions of rules— we boys were always in trouble. The worst rule, and most strictly enforced, was that we have no communication with the Chinese. The teachers did it to save themselves trouble. As a result, I never spoke Chinese when there, and I do not speak it as I would like— just kitchen Chinese."

That was the environment in which Harry Luce was raised with his two sisters and a younger brother. They were a closely knit family and still are, with a strong belief in themselves and each other. Clare says, "The Luces take for granted that anything done in the family will be done superbly well. You don't get praise, but if something is badly done you get ticked off. However, if you get into trouble they are there with all the help in the world."

That family solidarity is a natural result of living in a compound in that far-off foreign land. So is their unshakable belief in their Presbyterian faith. "You must remember that the foundation of our lives, our reason for being, was this missionary thing. There was that strong religious motivation."

Harry Luce came to America in 1912, when he was fourteen years old, to attend Hotchkiss School in Lakeville, Connecticut. He was a thin, shy, serious boy with a foreign air about him, but more ardently American than most of his schoolmates, who had never had to think about being Americans. The fashionable preparatory school was certainly a pleasant change from that ersatz Rugby on the China coast, and the lovely wooded hills with their snug houses and slender white church steeples far prettier than the vast, flat, dusty plains of Shantung. But sometimes Harry was homesick for the land of his birth, even for the dirt and smell of it. China was in his blood, and all his life he has felt an intense interest in it and in the problems of Sino-American relations. "It is fascinating to see the same kind of clashes coming up through the years as we had then, now on the great stage."

Harry went through Hotchkiss with ease and on to graduate from Yale in 1920 with a Phi Beta Kappa key. In between he trained as a second lieutenant in the field artillery during World War I, though he did not get overseas. Then he studied for a term or two at Oxford University, after which he worked as a reporter on the Chicago *Daily News* and the Baltimore *News*.

In 1923, at the age of twenty-five, Luce joined with Briton Hadden to found *Time*, the first news magazine. Hadden died in 1929, and by 1930 Luce was master of *Time* and had founded *Fortune*, which became a sort of oracle of American industry as *Time* had become almost required reading for literate Americans.

Thus at thirty-six, when he met Clare, Harry Luce was one of the most powerful publishers in the world, though his greatest success still lay before him. No wonder his life had been "work, work, work." For to achieve such a resounding success so early takes more than a brilliant mind or even genius; it requires unremitting, relentless energy and a total self-immolation in the enterprise, a sort of consecration.

In 1923, the same year he founded *Time*, Harry Luce married Lila Ross Hotz. They had two sons, Henry Luce III and Peter Paul Luce. But in those first frantic years of *Time* Harry was so deeply involved that he had neither energy nor emotion to spare. They drifted apart imperceptibly and by the Thirties Mrs. Luce, who disliked New York gatherings and the clash of ideas, lived mostly in their country house at Rumson, New Jersey, while her husband stayed in New York, watching over his magazines and attending as a bachelor such parties as he thought necessary to keep up the contacts vital to his work as a publisher.

Harry's dedication to his magazines was a facet of that "strong religious motivation." He believed in them utterly and at times fairly staggered under the awful weight of his responsibility. Those who agree with him and those who don't, who like his publications or detest them, almost all admit that he is completely, sometimes ruthlessly, sincere in his determination to make them a great force for the good of America, and after that, of people everywhere—as he sees the good. He was exclusively absorbed in them—until he met Clare.

Not the least amazing thing in their extraordinary careers is that two such sophisticated, egocentric, and *spoiled* people as Clare Brokaw and Harry Luce fell so unpremeditatedly, so romantically, so *vernally* in love. Not that Clare succumbed immediately. She tried to escape—from Harry or herself. She rushed off to Havana to give him time to cool off. When she got back Harry resumed his relentless, oddly brusque, touchingly brusque, wooing. In the end she fell in love with all her heart.

Harry had known he was in love that night at Elsa Maxwell's party. As he said good night to his hostess, she teasingly asked, "What are you doing here so late? I thought you hated parties."

Harry, smiling bemusedly, answered, "But this was a very special party."

Mrs. Allen Grover saw them after Clare came back from Havana at Buff Cobb's apartment. "I had heard nothing about anything," she says, "but I knew at once. If ever people had stars in their eyes, those two did." And to Bill Chadbourne, at a formal dinner at her Sherry-Netherlands apartment, Clare, seeking approval like any young girl, asked fondly, "What do you think of that young man?"

Naturally the way of it was not smooth. Harry Luce was married, and his strong religious convictions and family feeling made divorce particularly distasteful to him. But, as one of his friends put it, "It was one of those things that had to be."

In order to be out of the way and not influence him Clare invited

Buff Cobb to go to Europe with her in the spring of 1935. Though she knew it was out of season and would be hotter than a tin roof in Death Valley, Clare wanted to see Africa. Buff was game.

They arrived in Biskra by motor in mid-June. Algiers and Tunis had seemed fantastically torrid, but Biskra in the desert behind the mountains was unbelievable. The white buildings shimmered in the heat haze, and the desert wind seemed to blow out of a dragon's mouth. All the big hotels were shut, so they stayed at a third-rate commercial hotel that even the hardiest traveling salesman avoided at that season.

Clare was not slowed down at all. This was Africa and she did not propose to miss a single experience. First on the agenda was a camel ride.

Buff Cobb says, "It was rather ridiculous. On one side was the desert, and on the other a streetcar line and suburban villas. We were jerking around on top of those great, dirty beasts while a villainous guide, with one eye and no teeth, walked beside us."

From their high perch they could see over the garden walls. There was one particularly fine house, with colorful blinds and an exquisitely cool garden. Clare asked the guide who lived there.

"Madame Sheradeen," he answered.

"He must mean Claire Sheridan," she exclaimed. "Bernie Baruch told me to look her up. Hey! Stop this beast! I want to call on her."

The guide sneered unbecomingly. "She is a very famous lady," he said. "She would not receive people like you."

For once Clare was put properly in her place. She and Buff got a bad case of the giggles thinking that a guide had passed final judgment on their social position. Later they got a car and went back to call on Mrs. Sheridan, who, wearing her famous snowy Arabian burnoose, was delighted to see them.

That night Clare had to see the Oulid-Nails dance, so they left the car at the twenty-foot-high doors of the Kasbah and, following their one-eyed mentor, walked through narrow alleys, jostled by scurrying Arabs, to a small, smoky café. There was not another European or another woman present, just row after row of white-robed swarthy men, black-bearded, dark eyes staring. As the native girls danced sinuously, the pitch of excitement tightened until Buff found it almost unbearable. Clare sat with her silvery, snow-princess look, as unaffected as though Noel and Gertrude were demonstrating a waltz in her own drawing room.

Even the sultry night, smelling of rotting fruit, acrid African sweat, and sewage was a relief after that den. Buff thought grate-fully of the waiting car and looked toward their small hotel like home. Then the guide pointed up a shoulder-wide alley with garbage-littered stairs. "The most famous of the Oulid-Nails lives up there," he said. "Would you like to call on her?"

"Do you think she would receive the likes of us?" Clare asked caustically.

"Do you like to go?"

"Let's not push our luck," Buff urged.

"How many Americans have been bumped off in Biskra?" Clare asked. "Yes," she said to the guide.

They climbed the slippery steps in pitch blackness, until they came to a tiny plaster house. It had a single room in which a small native girl was sitting cross-legged on a cushion. The only other piece of furniture was a Vuiton trunk she had acquired when she danced at the Paris Exposition. The smell in the room was really horrendous. Even Clare felt a little faint. She saw a balcony on the other side and, saying courteously that she would like to see the view, moved toward it. She stepped out of the window onto the stomach of a fat, dirty Arab.

The man rolled out from under and began drumming furiously. The guide started to giggle.

"What's he drumming for?" Clare demanded haughtily.

The guide whooped and hollered and rolled on the floor, gasping out, "He announce arrival of two new girls—one blonde."

Traveling by limousine seemed pretty tame to Clare. "You should either travel on a red carpet or third-class so you meet people," she told Buff.

She wanted to dismiss the car and take one of the rickety native buses back, but Buff rebelled at that.

Coming back from Tunis on the coastal road, it was still very hot. The tawny land was as empty as the day after the flood; the sea looked wonderfully cool. The two American women looked at each other and nodded. Ordering the chauffeur to stay in the car behind a sand dune, they scrambled down to the edge of the sea. They undressed under lately acquired burnooses and splashed through long shallows to deep, wonderful water.

As they were swimming gaily around, they heard a shrill whistle. A young goatherd and his flock appeared on the skyline. Almost immediately, what seemed like hundreds of Arabs came leaping down the dunes with their white robes floating behind them. Clare hugged herself like September Morn and said, "I can't get out of the water. I'll have to stay here the rest of my life."

Buff took a realistic view. "You'll never see any of these people at the Colony Restaurant," she said. "Come on!"

They ran for the beach and dressed under their burnooses. The chauffeur was very angry—he had lost face.

From Africa they went to Cap d'Antibes, where they took a "funny little house that clung to the side of a cliff." An acid English maid named Mabel came with it. The sitting room was especially dainty, with a wonderful view of blue water patterned by the bright-colored lateen sails of the fishing boats, and edged with foam lace and red rocks. When Buff commented on the pretty room, Mabel gave a very British sniff and said, "It looks like a love nest to me. There's a couch in every corner."

Just around the other side of their cliff Somerset Maugham lived in splendid confusion. Clare's acrid wit and Buff's homespun humor were the great man's dish. He took them to his bosom and showed them the life of a Riviera Riley from Mentone to San Rafael.

Clare came home in September to superintend the production of *Abide with Me*. Her play was backed by Malcolm Pearson and Donald Baruch in association with Al Woods. The splendid cast included Cecilia Loftus, Earl Larimore, and Maria Ouspenskaya. Clare hurled herself into the business of rewriting and rehearsal with nonpareil dynamism. She also found time to prepare for her marriage to Harry Luce.

Abide with Me was set to open at the Ritz Theatre on November 21, 1935. It had everything in its favor, and all the signs and portents were auspicious. But there is nothing in the world quite as

tricky as the theater. The greatest experts in the world can't seem
to tell whether a play is any good or not until it hits Broadway.
Abide with Me did not make the grade.

That dismal denouement did not appear the first night. If anyone
had dropped a bomb in the Ritz Theatre that evening, it would have
decimated the intelligentsia of these United States. Most of them
were Clare's friends, and if her enemies are pitiless, her friends are
loyal above and beyond the call of duty. As the final curtain fell
they applauded and stamped like La Scala greeting Toscanini.
Above the crash and thunder of hands and feet came the sweet
lowing sound of "Author! Author!"

Radiantly happy, Clare joined hands with Cissy Loftus and Earl
Larimore to acknowledge their tribute expressed in a final burst
of approval.

After that came the deluge. Clare read the morning papers with
incredulous eyes and a sick lump in her stomach. The critics simply
tore her play to tatters. "Too horrible to be real . . . too hysterical,
too literary . . ." said Lockridge of the *Sun*. Brooks Atkinson of
the *Times* said, *"Abide with Me* is merely a gratuitous horror play
about an abnormal family jar"; while Howard Barnes in the *Herald
Tribune* observed, "Miss Brokaw's first step in the theater is stumbling. . . . The unhappy predicament of her heroine married to a
sadistic drunkard is authentic enough for any drama [but] she has
not let these protagonists reveal themselves in significant action.
Having sat and chatted for most of two acts, they are suddenly
galvanized into frenetic and rather ridiculous action. Where a
neophyte might be pardoned for a good many slips in dramatic
structure, it is not so easy to forgive sheer bad writing. . . ."

Nor did the critics stop at criticism of the play. With bared fangs
they bayed at Clare for taking the curtain call, which she had
naïvely supposed to be a tribute to her play instead of an expression
of loyalty. That unjustified attack hurt her far more than the harsh
criticism of her play, which she considered legitimate. Indeed, the
scars still sometimes show, and she is very tender toward a fellow
sufferer.

Ilka Chase tells of a time years later when her play, *In Bed We
Cry*, got rough treatment. "The reviews were excruciating to me,"
she says. "I felt as though I were standing in garbage. Clare tele-

phoned me first thing. 'I know just how you feel,' she said. 'It happens to me all the time.'

"It was an awfully kind thing for her to do," says Ilka. "I really did not know her that well."

Clare's dreadful day did not end with the evening papers. There was one more tribulation still to go. Down in his office on Rockefeller Plaza the drama critic of *Time* was sweating blood. The floor was three feet deep in crumpled yellow paper. Finally he rode desperately to the sacred thirty-third floor.

"Mr. Luce," he said. "What shall we do about *Abide with Me?*"

"We'd better ask Mrs. Brokaw," said Harry gravely.

So they adjourned uptown. Harry stated the problem and added gently, "I'm afraid it really isn't a very good play, darling."

"I'll write you a review," Clare said.

She sat down at her desk, and her pencil tore across the paper. When Harry read it, he grinned. "This won't do either," he said. "No play is *that* bad!"

They worked out a compromise, and Clare's aftermath of Waterloo was finally over. Unlike Napoleon, she had just begun to fight.

The following day, November 23, 1935, Mrs. Clare Boothe Brokaw was married to Mr. Henry Robinson Luce.

CHAPTER NINE

A TRILOGY OF TRIUMPHS

THE LUCE'S HONEYMOON WAS STORMY—NOT FIGURATIVELY BUT quite literally. It took place on a small yacht off Cuba, and the ocean failed to cooperate. The crew consisted of Harry's chauffeur, Alonzo, who had boasted of his prowess both at sea and in the galley.

Harry and Clare were good sailors, but as their small craft swooped over the waves, Alonzo began to fade. "You won't be wanting much dinner tonight, sir," he said hopefully to Harry. "Just some nice sandwiches and a cup of coffee, maybe?"

Harry's eyes glinted with deviltry as he thought of the tall tales Alonzo had told of his seafaring days. "You signed on as an able seaman and cook," he said. "Now go ahead and cook."

Three courses the skidding Alonzo served that night, and Harry gravely ate them all. "It was a terrible dinner," he said, "but I called that fellow's bluff."

Of course there were other kinds of storms as well. Two such individualists as Harry and Clare Luce could hardly adjust to each other without rough edges grating. But their agreements far outweighed their differences. Quite early Harry began his custom of reading aloud to Clare, while she did the exquisite needlepoint which she had recently taken up to ease her nervous tension. He read the great classics and contemporary literature; he read the papers and political speeches. And he read Clare's plays aloud to her. She says that "Harry reads rather slowly. I knew that if my dialogue stood up with such timing it was good."

Even their arguments were usually impersonal. They had some

ding-dong fights about foreign policy, politics, personalities, and religion. On the last-mentioned subject Clare's skepticism challenged her husband's rockbound faith until one day he said to her, "You know, Clare, if you ever join a church, you will go all the way and become a Catholic."

They still sometimes get heated to the point of shouting over politics. But Clare never let them come between her and Harry. It was quite the opposite. Because it is no fun to argue with someone who agrees with you, their very different points of view built up the intellectual excitement of being together. They were each enormously proud of the other's brilliant mind; and though their methods might clash, their fundamental aims were identical.

Then, too, their separate careers and interests kept custom from wearing interest thin. Because they were so often apart or else lost from each other in crowds of people with whom they inevitably passed much of their free time, spending an evening alone together has always been an excitement and a delight.

However, though their separations preserved the freshness of their appreciation of each other, it prevented them from ever having a real home. Their first residences were a big apartment they rented at River House on East Fifty-second Street and a house hired for the summer at Stamford, Connecticut. Then they bought a huge Georgian mansion in Greenwich made of red brick with marble trim and high classic columns. This they simply called "The House." So sporadically did they inhabit it that Allen Grover, vice-president of Time, Inc., recalls one time when the butler there addressed him as "Mr. Luce."

In 1938 they took a splendid apartment on the forty-first floor of the Waldorf Towers, where they lived for almost twelve years. But despite the touches of beauty that Clare brought to it, the place was still a hotel. Mepkin, their plantation in South Carolina, was the nearest they have come to a home; but when tragedy overshadowed its happy memories, they gave it up.

This peculiar penalty of their wide interests and intense activity still dogs them. Harry Luce says, "We have had no time to make a real home. We started at Mepkin. Then the war came, and later it seemed better to give that up. So we are still transients in our own houses."

However, though they have never been able to settle down for long, each place in which they have lived was made beautiful by Clare's taste and imagination. Architectural limitations never stopped her. If a room needed to be larger and a wall was in the way, she would simply have it moved. The matter of how to do it without bringing down the house was a detail for her architects to worry about.

Clare always worked through decorators, but the houses, even her hotel apartments, bore the stamp of her personality. Sometimes they were classic in conception, sometimes modernistic or, as in the case of "The House" a peculiarly harmonious combination of these supposed opposites. Whatever they were, a person had only to enter them to know that Clare lived there.

The only place the Luces built from scratch was well-loved Mepkin. They first saw it on a trip through the South in the spring of 1936—seven thousand acres of jasmine-starred woods, rough fields for upland shooting, and reedy swamps where the wild ducks rafted along the Cooper River. They bought it immediately and started to build a home.

Tradition suggested stately columns and shady galleries with smiling servitors galloping about with trays full of mint juleps. Clare outraged the neighbors by building a very beautiful house as modern as a country place on Mars. As in everything she does, her reason was logical, if not sentimental. "I know they criticize me," she said at the time. "I'm accustomed to criticism, though I never can understand why they always criticize me personally and not the thing I do. Whether it's plays or houses, people always jump on me.

"Why should I build an old mansion on the Cooper River? I have no roots there. This is none of my tradition, and it would be false to ape the old ways."

So the main house had picture windows and air-conditioning. Its low, geometric outline did not clash with the formal gardens and moss-hung cypress trees; rather it merged comfortably with its setting. The five small guest cottages that surrounded it were almost always full when the Luces were there. Often they were full of children, the Luce boys and their schoolmates and Ann and her friends.

It became the Luces' custom to leave for Mepkin with the children on the day after Christmas, and spend the rest of the vacation there. There were horses to ride and shooting for quail or from the dove blinds. Clare became a crack shot and taught Ann and the boys and any of the women guests she could entice out. "Shooting is one sport that women are really better qualified for than men," she told them. "And you can do it well until you're eighty."

They went down at Easter, too, when the woods were sweet with jasmine, when spring flowers blazed in the splendid formal garden and the Cooper River outgrew its banks, flooding the lowlands with sky-blue mirrors in which cranes and herons waded, while the ducks pointed their vees to the North. Mepkin was the place in all the world that Ann loved best.

Mother and daughter grew much closer together during those next years. Ann was developing into a person in her own right. She was a very pretty girl. Clare has written of "the gay, pure face of my daughter with glowing red-brown hair." Her lithe grace matched Clare's own perfect coordination. More important, her mind had a clear, penetrating quality that made her a congenial companion for her mother.

When Ann was about fourteen, they made a delightful voyage to Hawaii together. Harry and his sister Mrs. Severinghouse were with them for a while. They took a cottage outside of Honolulu. Its one big living room had a high ceiling with arched rafters, and cool modern furniture. Clare and her daughter rode the mile-long rollers on surfboards piloted by Captain Louis Hale, whom everybody called "Sally." Clare says, "I usually fell off." But Ann became as surefooted as a Hawaiian beach boy.

In the evening there were often big feasts called *luaus* with a whole roasted pig as the *pièce de résistance,* supplemented by pineapples and octopus. After dinner the Hawaiians would bring their steel guitars and sing the soft, sweet songs of the Islands or "The Cockeyed Major of Molokai" and "Little Grass Shack."

In every respect that trip was successful for mother and daughter.

Mrs. Isabel Hill came to work for Clare Luce on April 1, 1936. It was April Fool's Day for her, because she was told there was really very little for her to do and perhaps she could help Mr. Luce a bit

too. Clare went off to White Sulphur Springs the following week
end and came back with a stack of pencil-covered yellow paper a
foot high—the manuscript of *The Women*.

There have been various stories and many profound doubts as to
the writing of *The Women*. The play was actually written in three
days. "That was the first draft," Clare says, "but it was the one
Max Gordon bought. Of course I spent two months rewriting it
when we went into production."

From the day Clare got back from her week end, Mrs. Hill hardly
had a quiet moment for the next twelve years. First *The Women*
must be typed, revised, and retyped. Then Clare sent it off to Brock
Pemberton. It came back home to roost. Next she mailed it to John
Golden, and that gentle-minded producer dropped it as though it
had burned his fingers.

Clare thought it was good, and wanted Max Gordon to read it,
but he was disinterested. She happened to mention this to Bernard
Baruch, who promptly called his old friend Max. "I want you to
read a play by Clare Boothe," he said.

"Why should I?" Gordon asked. "Who is she anyway?"

"Don't you remember the pretty girl who worked on the Theatre
Code with you?"

"No."

"Well," said Baruch, "she is—very pretty. Call her up and ask
for the play."

"That would give her too much advantage," objected Gordon.

"Go ahead and do it for me," said Bernie Baruch.

About ten minutes later Clare called him again: "Bernie, the
most wonderful thing happened. Max Gordon called up and he
wants to read my play."

"Did he now!" said Baruch. "That's fine."

There was a long pause. Then Clare's voice, laughing: "Bernie!
You scoundrel!"

Of course Gordon bought the play. For the next six months Clare
threw herself into the work of production. She had particularly
definite ideas about casting and did much of it herself in consulta-
tion with Gordon. For example, Ilka Chase seemed suitable for the
part of that supersophisticated female werewolf, Sylvia Fowler. Not

knowing her well, Clare invited Ilka to lunch at the Waldorf to sound her out. Ilka describes her that day as looking very pretty and neat in a tweed suit with black and white stripes and a cuffed skirt. "She wears pretty clothes rather than chic ones."

Clare opened the conversation by saying, "Harry has never forgotten the one time he met you. That political argument you had made him perfectly furious." Then she added, "I rather envy you; I've never been able to make him mad."

Said Ilka sweetly, "You will, dear."

It was obvious that Ilka was perfect for the part. Clare took her right around to Max Gordon's office and signed her up.

That was the beginning of friendship. Ilka says, "Up to *The Women,* I thought I did not like Clare, but during rehearsals I learned to admire her. She worked so hard—real, honest work. Somehow no matter how hard she worked or how hot and tired the rest of us might be, she always managed to look fresh and dainty—impeccable.

"I remember one evening when she stopped by a late rehearsal. She was on her way to a party, wearing a superb evening dress, sables, and terrific jewels. Max asked her for some changes in one scene. Then and there she scribbled some very amusing lines."

It is often said that Clare did not really write *The Women.* This is complete nonsense—it has her signature on almost every line. But she did have some expert advice. George Kaufman helped to doctor it, but when asked if he had not written it, he said, "If I'd written it, why should I sign it Clare Boothe?"

Another man who taught Clare a good deal about stagecraft was Alex King. King was an original character out of a book nobody will ever write because he was too improbable. Once he wrote a play of his own, but he hated the idea of all the fuss and exasperations of producing it. So he simply hired a theater and invited the critics and the great of the intellectual world. They all came. It was probably one of the most brilliant audiences a first-and-only night ever had. Alex wore a new yellow necktie and his old blue suit.

He opened the proceedings by sitting on a piano and telling some riotous anecdotes. Then he began to read. Buckminster Fuller says, "Though there were no actors and no scenery, that play is still more vivid in our memories than most of those we have seen played in the full panoply of the theater. In fact it is hard to realize that we did not see it acted."

Next day the critics gave it rave notices. Of course, Alex was delighted. "I'm famous," he said, "and it only cost me six hundred dollars."

The Women opened at the Ethel Barrymore Theatre on the night after Christmas, 1936. Word had got around that it was something special and the audience was, if possible, more spectacular than that which had seen *Abide with Me*. This time they got something worthy of their glitter. Not that the critics exactly acclaimed it. The play, it seems, was too acrid for the more squeamish. Brooks Atkinson of the *Times* had his hatchet all resharpened. "Not the ladies but The Women are the brew in Clare Boothe's kettle of venom," he reported, . . . "Miss Boothe's alley cats scratch and spit with considerable virtuosity. . . . [There are] two or three poignant scenes, but *The Women* is mainly a multi-scened portrait of the modern New York wife on the loose, spraying poison over the immediate landscape. . . . Miss Boothe has compiled a workable play out of the withering malice of New York's most unregenerate worldlings. This reviewer did not like it."

But New York's unregenerate worldlings did. And so did people everywhere from Singapore to Oslo and way stations in between. Not even Clare knows how many countries it has played in, but the certain total is at least twenty-five, not counting the movie and television. Inevitably it made astronomical amounts of money for all concerned.

Now that the dust storm kicked up by controversy has settled sufficiently to allow a cool, clear look, the play is accepted as a classic of the theater. It is probably the most ruthless, brilliant, scathing satire that struck Broadway in all the years between the wars. Certainly there were theatrical tricks in it as well as sound stagecraft. Betty Lawford, as Crystal in her bubble bath, alone was enough bait for wolves. Indeed the whole play in which men provide the basic motivation and yet are never seen, while forty-four women make up the cast, is a remarkable *tour de force*. The amazing technical dexterity which enables you to know these gentlemen intimately, yet never miss their corporeal presence is as fascinating a piece of theatrical legerdemain as a great virtuoso performing improbably difficult musical feats, or that family riding their bicycle on the high wire in the circus.

But such components are mere bright trimmings. The fact remains that the play has a universal bitter verity that strikes home wherever women—or men—live in civilized and even semicivilized conditions.

Clare did not wait around New York to savor her triumph. Mepkin was ready for the first time, and the whole Luce family went down for New Year's. On that first visit it was not quite as modern as it looked, for Harry telegraphed Isobel Hill, "We found snakes in our bathtub—real snakes."

London awaited *The Women* with avid expectation. Clare and Harry went over to see it open there and make a smash hit that echoed throughout the Empire.

If Clare had a hero at this time, it was George Bernard Shaw; she used to keep a picture of him on her dressing table. With *The Women* making theatrical history, she felt able to cope with him, though perhaps she was overoptimistic.

So the Luces made the pilgrimage to the vine-covered Tudor rectory at Ayot St. Lawrence. Shaw, dressed in his outdated rough tweed suit with plus fours, received them amicably. Clare's opening gambit was an uncharacteristic schoolgirl gush: "Oh Mr. Shaw, if it weren't for you, I wouldn't be here."

Shaw's eyes twinkled under his Mephistophelean eyebrows. "Let's see," he said. "What was your sweet mother's name?"

Harry's *coup de grâce* was delivered in a note Clare received from Shaw some time later which concluded "Kindest regards to you and Mr. Boothe."

One would have thought that with *The Women* piling up profits in every known currency, producers would have been breathing down Clare's neck while she wrote her next play. The fact is, she scared them. She took a month to write *Kiss the Boys Good-by*, the story of Cindy Lou, a saccharin-cyanide Southern belle, and a movie producer who is looking for an actress to play a part a good deal like Scarlet O'Hara in *Gone with the Wind*. Its farcical comedy has serious overtones sharply critical of Southern reactionaries. Among the nervous impresarios who decided it was too hot to handle were Max Gordon who advised Clare, "File this in your wastebasket," and Gilbert Miller. Brock Pemberton, who had doubtless been kicking himself around Longacre Square, decided to risk it.

He got his just reward. *Kiss the Boys* was another smash hit, though it did not have the stature of *The Women*. During rehearsals Clare was as indefatigable as ever. In fact, she watched a preview the night before the Broadway opening and then rewrote most of the third act in time for an early-morning rehearsal.

As usual Clare owed little of her success to the critics, and there were some roars of wounded pride from people who imagined themselves caricatured in the play. Heywood Broun was monumentally upset by what he took to be a likeness to a left-wing columnist, and wrote of Clare's attempt "to degrade the human race." Later they kissed and made up, and Broun wrote a eulogistic foreword for one of Clare's published plays.

Clare wrote the third of her trilogy of hits in just ten days in 1939. *Margin for Error* was a first-class mystery melodrama, with a bemonocled Nazi villain, who in defeat becomes a pathetic figure because his ruthless government allows its servants "no margin for error." Clare's hatred of Nazism cracking through the dialogue gave the play the force of moral indignation in addition to its exciting drama.

Characteristically, Clare tried it out in Washington under the very nose of the German Embassy. Their gnashing teeth were sweet music to her ears.

Margin for Error opened in New York at the Plymouth Theatre on November 3, 1939, to the usual critical disclaim. The timing was superb. Two months before, Hitler had sent his *panzers* crashing across the Polish border. The scream of his Stukas diving down to make a charnel house of Warsaw filled Americans with fear and fury. People flocked in droves to see a Nazi get his comeuppance at the Plymouth.

While his wife had been scaling her second pinnacle of fame and fortune, Harry Luce had not been simply sitting still. In November, 1936, the first issue of *Life* appeared. When Harry told his

Right: Ann Snyder Boothe.
Clare's mother was more beautiful than she.

Below: The Boothe family at White Plains. Clare's grandparents right. Billy Boothe leaning against column center.

At thirteen Clare was already an authentic beauty.

Clare and her brother David. "She was fat and sassy and full of fun."

A child actress at ten. Clare with Ernest Truex (*right*) in *The Dummy*. She fell in love with the star. (*Courtesy of Culver Service*)

Returning from Europe in 1922, Clare met Mrs. O. H. P. Belmont and Max Reinhardt, who gave her a choice of destinies. (*Photo from European*)

She married New York's most eligible bachelor, George Tuttle Brokaw. Mr. and Mrs. Brokaw attending the races at Belmont Park. (*Photo from European*)

Clare and grown-up Ann by their swimming pool in Greenwich. (*Photo by Max Peter Haas*)

After her divorce Clare took a house at Easthampton so her daughter, Ann Clare Brokaw, could enjoy the beach. (*Photo from European*)

Left: Clare pulled a bone
the first time she me
Wendell Willkie; but the
became great friends.

Below: It was quite a fea
to startle Elsa Maxwel
and H. G. Wells. *(Photo
by Max Peter Haas)*

Right: Bernard Baruch once told Clare that when she got to heaven she would find him waiting, "just to the left of the gate." *(Photo from European)*

Below: Campaigning for Congress, Clare "listened as well as glistened outside the factory gates."

Left: "It was inevitable that Clare should get along fine with Third Army's prickly commander, General George S Patton, Jr." *(International News Photo)*

Below: Clare first met the man she helped to become President on a congressional tour of the front lines in 1944.

Above: "I'm in love with the whole Fifth Army!" Clare broadcasting to the troops in Italy. Christmas, 1944. *Below:* Clare spared herself nothing. She went to newly captured Buchenwald when wagonloads of dead bodies still stood before the crematorium. (*International News Photos*)

In 1946 Clare was received into the Catholic Church. In 1949 she had a private audience with Pope Pius XII. (*Associated Press Photo*)

Clare's last picture with her beloved Ann, who died a few days later, January 11, 1944. (*Los Angeles Times Photo*)

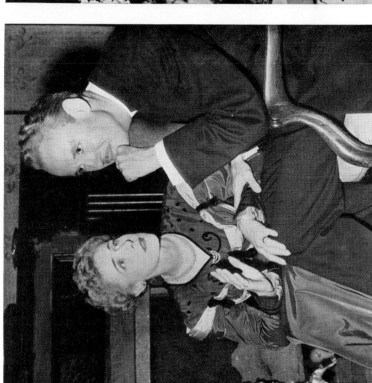

The critics had a Roman holiday with Clare as the Christian when she appeared in summer stock as Candida with Paul McGrath in 1945. (*Associated Press Photo*)

Though she fought with President Roosevelt, Clare said of his wife, "No woman has ever so comforted the distressed, or so distressed the comfortable."

Above: Chief Justice Vinson administered the ambassadorial oath to Clare on March 5, 1953. *(Photo from European) Below:* Ambassador Clare Boothe Luce with her boss, Secretary of State, John Foster Dulles. *(International News Photo)*

Above: Veteran diplomat Robert Murphy arrives in Italy to help solve the Trieste problem. *Below:* At a *Te Deum* in Rome. Mr. and Mrs. Henry Luce, Italian Minister of War Attilio Piccione. Far right, the Prime Minister and Mrs. Mario Scelba. (*International News Photos*)

"Well done!" Harry Luce is immensely proud of his beautiful wife.

General Mark Clark and Ambassador Luce at Nettuno Cemetery to pay homage to the dead of their beloved Fifth Army. (*International News Photo*)

Front row, left to right: Lord Cherwell, Sir Winston Churchill, Ambassador Clare Boothe Luce, Mrs. Emmett Cassady. *Back row, left to right:* Anthony F. Moir, Colonel (now Brig. Gen.) Emmett Cassady, air attaché in Rome Embassy; Emmett Hughes, staff writer for *Life*; Henry R. Luce, John Colville. *(Life photo by Carl Mydans)*

A good team. The Ambassador and Mr. Luce.

wife that he had bought the old *Life* for sixty-five thousand dollars for its name, she looked a little smug and said, "You paid forty-five thousand too much. Condé Nast could have had it for twenty thousand in 1933."

That forty-five thousand turned out to be peanuts as *Life* caught on like a flash fire and its circulation zoomed past *Time*. When a little later Luce was sued for a huge sum of money by some characters who alleged that he had stolen the idea for a picture-news magazine from them, Clare rushed to her husband's rescue waving her old memorandum to Condé Nast to prove that it was an idea that anybody might conceive; and won the suit.

New Year's Day, 1939, found the Luces all at Mepkin again. It was a gay party of young people, with a few of the Luces' older friends. But underneath surface serenity and laughter, Clare and Harry were conscious of the dreadful unease of the times. That was the winter after Munich, where democracy's abject surrender to totalitarian power had bought not "peace for our time," as British Prime Minister Chamberlain had hoped, but a few months of armed truce. The Luces were too well informed and too acutely conscious of European undercurrents to take comfort in a soothing phrase. They both felt that 1939 would be a cataclysmic year.

Personal tragedy struck Clare before the public catastrophe that she foresaw. A telephone call from Florida told her that her beloved mother had been instantly killed in an automobile accident. Her grief was mitigated by the need to comfort Ann, who had loved her pretty grandmother dearly. When the grim cycle was repeated in another January, there would be no possibility of comfort.

CHAPTER TEN

THE SPRING OF DISASTER

It took hitler just three weeks in september, 1939, to destroy the Polish Army and enslave the Polish nation. After that came the strange period of inactivity that was called the "phony war." It was as terrifying as the sunshiny lull in the eye of a hurricane.

The phony war was tremendously confusing to Americans who are always impatient for action. And Americans were already terribly confused. Our disillusionment after World War I, the conviction that we had been taken for an idealistic buggy ride, had convinced the vast majority of us that we must never again be inveigled into a European war. This belief was embodied in the law of the land, the Neutrality Act, which in effect forbade Americans to travel in war zones or trade with belligerents, though it was modified to permit selling war materials to the Allies on a cash-and-carry basis.

On the other hand, the incredible brutality of Nazi methods and the terrible demonstration of Nazi military power made Americans uneasy in their minds and consciences. It was inconceivable that Hitler could conquer France and England; but if he did, what would it be like living across a narrowing ocean from the massed might of Europe in the hands of a megalomaniac? And what of our ideals of freedom and democracy? It was a good deal more comforting to think that the war really was phony and that nobody actually intended to fight.

Clare Luce says that she was one of the people who were most confused. Her finely informed, analytical mind rejected the phony theory. The idealism that had once made her tolerant of communism—since the Russian-German pact of August, 1939, she had hated communism with a consuming passion—that idealism, together with her realistic appraisal of America's position if England should fall, inclined her to the unpopular belief that America should concern herself in the fight against tyranny. But there remained the doubts and dangers of European involvement and her intense hatred of war.

By February, 1940, Clare was in such a swelter of doubt in the vortex of contradictory rumor and conflicting opinion that, being extremely American, she had to resolve her confusion by action. She decided to go to Europe to see for herself and find out what she really thought. *Europe in the Spring,* the book she wrote about her trip, is dedicated to "H.R.L. who understood why I wanted to go."

Harry Luce not only understood Clare's psychic necessity to find out; he aided and abetted her. Since the State Department would not issue passports for travel abroad without good reason, Harry commissioned Clare as a correspondent for *Life.* But he wanted her to have a woman companion. Clare turned to her old friend, Margaret Case of *Vogue,* who was able to get a passport to report the Paris collections—the great French *couturiers* actually showed their collections as usual in the spring of 1940.

The two inquiring reporters landed in Naples on March 3, 1940, a beautiful spring morning. They took the insanely fast electric train to Rome and put up at the Excelsior Hotel in an ornate suite just vacated by Under Secretary of State Sumner Welles, who was also touring Europe "in a cloud of obfuscation" to try to find out what was going on.

Though Italy was still technically at peace, Mussolini was frantically preparing to implement his alliance with Hitler. Rome was jammed with Fascist officers wearing stunning uniforms and gold-hilted dress swords, and with very expensive-looking women. They were all very confident and foolishly happy—indeed, the city had a frenetic gaiety.

Clare had allowed herself five days in Rome. Surprisingly, it was her first visit since childhood to the father of cities, and she felt a compulsion to sight-see as well as to investigate the Italian mind. So she says she "circled all the wonders of the seven cypress-and-pine-crowned hills like a miniature whirlwind."

The main purpose of her trip was served by going to endless luncheons, cocktail parties, and dinners, and listening with her extremely acute ears for talk of war and politics. But she would not have been herself if she had not also called up newspapermen, stuck her lovely nose into dingy shops and small cafés, and questioned waiters, maids, and even people sitting on benches in the sun.

She had a very hard time making the Romans talk politics with her. They always changed the subject abruptly or, if she pressed them, said, "I'm afraid an American wouldn't understand the Fascist angle on that." It was her first experience with people who lived in fear.

One day at a luncheon Clare said to the princely Italian beside her, "Oh, all right, we won't discuss the war any more. Let's talk about love. There isn't a Fascist angle on that, is there?"

The prince sighed and said, "Ah, *si*, the Fascist angle on love is making more babies."

Clare went to a state dinner that Ambassador and Mrs. William Philips gave at the American Embassy. But nobody talked politics there either. To make it easier not to, Ambassador Philips showed his guests the movie of *Drums Along the Mohawk*. The Italians seemed to enjoy it greatly—perhaps they imagined that in Ethiopia they were pioneering too.

Clare's best chance to find out something was at a dinner Donna Caetani gave for Count Ciano, who was Foreign Minister of Italy and married to Mussolini's daughter, Edda. Since *Time* had recently published a remarkably unenthusiastic profile of Ciano, his hostess asked him if he minded meeting Clare.

"Is she pretty?" Ciano asked.

"Very pretty."

"Then put her next to me."

Clare had been told that Ciano was very pro-American. The first thing she saw when she came into the smoke-filled private room at the Excelsior, where the dinner was given, was Countess Edda Ciano, looking as emaciated as a *Vogue* silhouette, with her red-gold hair, green cat's eyes, and a cigarette in a long holder at an acute angle in her sullen mouth. *Nothing doing there,* she thought and ignored the Countess to concentrate on her blond, handsome husband, who talked slightly dated American slang.

True to the Roman custom, Ciano preferred discussing art to politics. They talked about the new excavations of old Roman ruins and then about the modern Fascist buildings. Clare slipped a snare into the talk: "Wouldn't it be a pity," she said, "if Italy got into this war and all those fine new buildings Mussolini has built became *prematurely* ruins. It wouldn't be nice if the archaeologists had to excavate them in 2042."

Ciano laughed. "Don't worry about modern ruins," he replied. "They have no future. The kind of ruins you get after a modern war wouldn't be worth excavating."

The talk at dinner was in Italian and Clare did not understand a word of it. Afterward, while the others played cards, Ciano took her into a side room, and they talked for two hours. But not a word would he say of politics. Instead, he talked about a play he had written long ago called *The Golden Land.*

"You don't know what those critics did to me," he said wanly. "You've never had a failure."

"Oh, yes I have," said Clare, and told him about *Abide with Me.*

"My God, you *do* know," beamed Ciano.

They reached a complete accord—but only about their views on dramatic critics.

The only satisfying happening of Clare's stay in Rome was her audience with Pope Pius XII. It was arranged very hurriedly, and there was not time to buy the required costume of a high-necked black dress, black stockings, and a black veil. But Donna Caetani sent her maid over with a lovely lace mantilla and some black chiffon, which the girl fixed on a round-necked black dress Clare owned. So she went to the Vatican as she had gone to her confirmation, held together by pins.

"Where are your great jewels, *Signora?*" the maid asked, when Clare was ready.

"I have none with me," Clare said. "Why do you ask?"

"Always the ladies wear their great jewels when they go to see the Holy Father."

Clare found that idea oddly shocking to her puritan upbringing and concluded that Catholics were different.

There were about forty people waiting in the velvet-hung reception room of the Pope's private apartment: a few Italian men wearing white ties and tails at eleven o'clock in the morning, many ladies in black with "great jewels," and a contingent of nuns. Clare was surprised to find that she was trembling as she stood waiting. In a few moments the door at the end of the room opened and the Holy Father came in. Clare knelt with the others in a circle around the walls of the room.

At first the Pope's back was toward her. She could only see that he was very tall and thin and a little stooped. He wore a white skullcap on his dark hair and a red sash around his waist. There were little red slippers on his narrow feet. As he moved around the circle of kneeling people, she watched their faces break into "such happy and purified smiles."

Then she saw his face, the kind, intelligent eyes magnified by his rimless spectacles, and his expression of benevolence. She started to smile even before he reached her. When he did, he asked in his pure English, "Are you the American lady?" And she answered that she was.

"I loved your country when I was there," he said.

Then he smiled at her and made the sign of the cross. "God bless America," he said.

That was Clare's first audience with Pope Pius XII. She wrote at the time: "I am not a Catholic; I am not even very religious; but like all human beings who are not utterly lost to Grace, I am humble and respectful and awed and ashamed before very good men who do God's work greatly. . . ." She added that as she left the Vatican "I felt, for some exceedingly strange reason, so much better in my heart. . . ."

In the limousine going back to the Excelsior she prayed silently for a miracle to save the world.

As Clare left for Paris on the Rome Express, the King of Italy's gaudy special train pulled in, bringing Nazi Foreign Minister von Ribbontrop to confer with "pro-American" Count Ciano.

Morale in Paris was high. It was especially high at the Ritz, where Clare and Margaret Case had rooms on the garden. There were flowers in all the vases and cards from many friends: Henri Bernstein, Sir Charles and Lady Mendl, Madame Dupay . . . A pneumatic drill rattled the windows as they built a new air-raid shelter in the garden.

"Doesn't that make you a little nervous?" Maggie Case asked.

Clare answered cockily, "Bombs never make hits on the people who stay at the Claridge or Ritz."

"Why, that's poetry."

"No, political philosophy," said Clare. "Widely popularized by a man called Karl Marx."

Clare had no trouble finding people in Paris who would talk politics—they would talk of nothing else. Even when they talked about the war, she found they were really talking French politics. Virtually nobody agreed with anybody else, either about strategy or French internal policy or even what to do about Germany after they had won the war. However, they were all agreed on three things: That the Maginot Line was impregnable; that France would win the war; and that this time *Il faut en finir*: it must be finished.

Because of Harry's magazines and her own wide connections, Clare was able to talk with virtually all the men who were responsible for the government of France; and with their womenfolk. She went to one dinner that American Ambassador William Bullitt gave at the embassy, where it was perfectly safe to address any man as *Monsieur le President,* because nearly all of them either had been or hoped to be premiers of France.

There was banker Bonnet, round and smiling Mandel, and worried old Herriot, Blum, the left-wing Socialist, peering through his spectacles, and Pierre Laval, that hard-faced realist wearing a stiff, round collar and a white tie like the one in which some eons later he was executed as a traitor to France. Bill Bullitt called them all by their first names. He was immensely popular in Paris because

everyone thought he was a true friend of France—which he was—
and would bring overwhelming American help if anything awful
happened—which he could not.

As always, Clare talked to as many different kinds of people as
possible. The workers and shopgirls, and white-collar clerks, the
officers and *poilus* on leave, were perhaps less confused than the
politicians, because they, at least, had a clear conception of their
war aims, which were just to defend the beloved soil of France.
They, too, all agreed that this time, "It must be finished."

Early in April cautious, do-nothing Deladier's government fell,
as Clare had predicted in a cable to *Life,* and Paul Reynaud was
confirmed as premier by one vote in the Chamber of Deputies. He
was little and wiry and full of fire. Everybody said, "Now we'll get
on with the war." French morale rose higher than ever. Everybody
continued to eat the wonderful French food and listen to Maurice
Chevalier sing patriotic songs at the Casino de Paris, and nobody
worried very much. Clare did not worry either. Writing after the
debacle, she said, "Now let me be honest. In early April I had also
believed . . . that the requisite for victory was largely 'sticking it'
. . . I never doubted the Allies . . ." She never doubted until she
went to see the Maginot Line, that tremendous impregnable forest
of fortifications that France had built at a cost of billions of francs
all along the German border, but *not along the border of Belgium.*

As a good reporter, Clare was dying to see the Maginot. She was
the *marraine,* the godmother, of one of its stupendous forts, Mont
des Welsches, which meant that she sent the troops their cigarettes
and candy and a flag with their motto embroidered in gold: *Ils ne
passeront pas.*

Back in March she had applied for permission to visit her fort.
The French military authorities took a very dim view of American
women in the war zone. Clare was quite willing to accept their
decision, but her influential friends—and even a lot of people she
did not know—thought it was a shame that she could not visit her
embattled godchild. Entirely without urging they turned the heat
on the army. Before the affair was settled, at least thirty people
were pulling wires. Finally the Commander-in-Chief, General
Maurice Gustave Gamelin, himself denied her permission.

On April 4 Clare went to see M. André de Laboulaye of the Ministry of Information and said, "Please, Monsieur, tell all these charming people, who are working on my behalf, to lay off. The 'no' of a generalissimo of France is 'no' to me. I don't want to do anything incompatible with the military policies of France. In fact I am going to Norway and Sweden next week."

"That is an excellent solution, Madame," said M. de Laboulaye. "It is most generous and charming of you."

"Then it is settled?" Clare asked.

"*Absolument!*" said M. de Laboulaye.

The next morning Clare received a note from Captain Charles Emmanuel Brousse of the Bureau d'Information saying that he was assigned to conduct her to the Maginot Line. It appears that General Gamelin was so overcome by her unprecedented consideration for his worries that he decided she was the sort of person who *should* see the Maginot. "Perhaps she will understand it," he said. Unfortunately she did.

Very early on the morning of April 6 Clare, accompanied by Captain Brousse, started off in a snappy little staff car for the front. By late afternoon they were driving through Lorraine. The gentle sunshine of that lovely spring day touched the delicate greens of the rich farmland. It also glinted on the sharp metal fangs of the tank traps and the muzzles of ten thousand cannon hidden in hayricks and fake cottages and the sweet-smelling woods.

Clare spent the night at the small, chilly Hotel Royal in Metz. Even there she encountered a friend, young Count René de Chambrun. He was a great-great-grandson of Lafayette, and his American mother was Nicholas Longworth's sister, and his wife was the daughter of Pierre Laval.

Young de Chambrun expatiated on his magnificent Maginot. It was to him the ultimate expression of France's determination to defend herself. That his country desired no conquest was proved, he said, by the fact that millions of dollars' worth of guns were embedded in five hundred million dollars' worth of concrete. That phrase sent the first chill of doubt through Clare's mind. Nazi guns were mounted on tanks that could go forty miles an hour. She said, "Oh, René, are you sure the Germans will come this way?"

Count de Chambrun thought so. "Even though last time they

came through Belgium. But we are extending the line there, too."

"Why didn't you do it before?"

"Because it cost too much, and besides, the Belgians might have thought us aggressive."

"Even with guns anchored in concrete?" asked Clare.

The next morning Clare went to see Mont des Welsches. She likened it to a battleship sunk in the earth, only vastly bigger and more powerful than any battleship that man could build, with its turrets in which the guns swung and its bombproof magazines; its control rooms and barracks sixty feet underground and its immense stores of ammunition, food, clothes, oil, and supplies of every sort.

The commandant took her all through it. He was very proud of his fort—and hers. Once again she asked the question that was bothering her: "What if the Germans don't come this way?" The commandant was happily sure they would, because they would not want to take on three million Dutch and Belgian soldiers in addition to the great armies of France.

As Clare came out of the fort and stood blinking in the sunshine, a small, pale *poilu* was shoved toward her by his fellows. Awkwardly he handed her a bunch of red roses. *"Madame est très courageuse."*

Clare thanked him amid applause from the soldiers. Then to the commandant she said, "Do you keep roses in the fort as well?"

The officer laughed proudly. "That boy walked all the way to Metz at dawn to get them for you," he said.

Clare began to cry, partly because of strain and excitement and partly because the French were such gallant, charming people— but mostly because of a logical, sickening sense that guns anchored in concrete were no good against guns that traveled at forty miles an hour.

On April 9 Clare had luncheon with the general commanding the 7th Division in a rectory in the French village of Kemplich, and a superb lunch it was. In that small room, incongruously decorated with religious pictures, the general and his staff ate heaps of wonderful *hors d'oeuvres,* oysters fresh from the sea, and *poulet de Bresse aux Champignons,* washed down with white wine or red.

"No matter what happens to France," Captain Brousse said, "her officers will always dine like kings."

Right in the middle of lunch the radio operator burst in and handed the general a dispatch announcing that the Nazis had occupied Denmark and were invading Norway. The general read it aloud, and for a moment they all sat silent, solemn and bewildered. Then the general shrugged and said, "Oh, well, this is England's affair; they have the navy."

When Clare got back to Paris she found that the news had given French morale another shot in the arm. Now there would be action at last! As the British landed at Narvik and Trondheim in Norway to close with the enemy, everybody agreed with British Prime Minister Neville Chamberlain's jocose remark that Hitler "has missed the bus." They were all very happy that the Nazis had made the mistake of opening up a real front. Clare was happy, too, until she talked to Colonel Horace Fuller, Military Attaché of the American Embassy.

In *Europe in the Spring* Clare says that the most intelligent, best-informed and clearest-sighted people she talked to in Europe were in the American embassies. Colonel Fuller sadly told her a few facts of life. "Hitler missed the bus all right, but he caught a transport plane," said Fuller.

The attaché explained the frightful odds the British Navy was facing in the death-trap fjords of Norway while Hitler's air power held the sky. He then went on to predict that the Nazis would soon launch a great offensive through the Lowlands of Holland and Belgium. He pointed out that the Germans had vastly superior strength to that of World War I, concentrated on *one* front instead of two; and that this time France stood almost alone. There were only ten British divisions in the Allied Army and no Americans. In addition, the German Air Force would control the sky.

"You don't really believe the Nazis are going to win, do you?" Clare asked, feeling heartsick.

"Yes," said Colonel Fuller grimly, "unless some miracle happens."

That was when Clare cabled her husband begging him to join her because "The curtain is going up." Harry caught the fast

Italian liner *Rex* on what proved to be her last voyage. He joined his wife in Paris, and together they crossed the Channel to England to search for reassurance. Colonel Fuller had said, "The British will keep on fighting. That's the best hope."

London, too, was gay that spring. All the windowboxes were dramatic with bright flowers, while cuckoos called and nightingales sang above the air-raid shelters in the parks, and people danced to the fine orchestras at Claridge's and the Savoy.

Clare and her husband talked to many of the men who were guiding the destiny of England. Most of the Conservative British were violently anti-American because we had not "come in." Clare got into some pretty hot arguments, while Harry took it all more philosophically. Clare admired the candor of American Ambassador Joseph P. Kennedy, who loved the English yet made himself unpopular by daring to tell them the truth: that America could not, and would not, "come in" unless the U.S. itself was attacked by the Axis.

Then the Norwegian campaign began to fail. As the battered British fleet pulled out of hard-won Trondheim fjord, Harry Luce says "The talk in the great houses was 'Chamberlain can't go on.'" A favorite candidate to replace him was septuagenarian Lloyd George, who had presided over victory in World War I.

On Sunday, May 5, the Luces were having tea at an ancient, gray-walled house with lawns that flowed down to the Thames, when J. L. Garven, the "Gladstonian-looking" editor of the London *Observer*, used for the first time that despairful phrase "too little and too late."

The following week end was the long Whitsuntide holiday. Trondheim and Narvik notwithstanding, there would be nobody left in London to talk to. Rather than rusticate the precious days away in some country house, Clare decided to take what she felt might be a last look at Holland and Belgium. She and Harry flew to The Hague on May 7, 1940.

American Minister to the Netherlands George Gordon greeted them with anxious inhospitality. "You have come at a bad time," he said. "There's a nice, big, juicy crisis brewing."

Sitting next to Holland's Permanent Secretary-general for Foreign Affairs, Herr Snouck Hurgronje, at dinner that night, Clare learned more about the crisis. German troops were massing on the Dutch border, Herr Hurgronje told her. He had the information from the same sources that had predicted the invasion of Norway five days before it happened.

"Aren't you uneasy?" Clare asked.

Herr Hurgronje went on happily eating planked beefsteak. "We've had three crises since the war began. This may also pass," he said philosophically. "It's just another agony to fear what cannot be prevented."

That was typical of the Dutch attitude toward invasion. Baroness Van Tuyll, a great lady of Queen Wilhelmina's court, expressed an even stranger view. "If they come there will be death and destruction, and people like me will lose everything," she said. "That part will be unpleasant."

"What could be pleasant?" Clare asked.

"It is interesting to be allowed to see in your lifetime a new world trying to be born. For good or evil the old, old dream of every wise European may become a reality: the unification of Europe. *Pan Europa!*"

At the embassy in Brussels, Ambassador Cudahy had good news for them. "The scare is over!" he said.

They had arrived late and talked on until one o'clock. Then they went, very tired, to bed and slept heavily.

Harry was roused at five by someone shaking his shoulder. He saw a little maid with a white face and charcoal-black eyes, who gasped, *"Les Allemands reviennent!"*

Harry put on his robe and shambled sleepily over to Clare. He stood looking at her for a moment, then he touched her bare shoulder. "Wake up, Clare," he said softly. "The curtain has gone up."

Clare was wide awake all at once. With excitement and pain in her eyes, she asked, "It's begun then?"

"Yes, the Germans are coming again."

Husband and wife moved together to the open window and looked out across the quiet square. It was a beautiful summer dawn. Early sunshine slanted over the gabled rooftops to light trees and flowers and the diamond-paned windows of the houses with red gold. The air was very sweet. Despite the disturbing news they stood there letting serenity flow around them.

Harry says he had just rested his chin in his hand when WHAM!— he was knocked back across the room as the first bomb of the blitz fell across the square. Flames and boiling black smoke stained the sky, blotting out tranquillity, while the antiaircraft guns crashed noisily into action.

The Luces dressed and hurried downstairs, to find the Ambassador, his guests, and his staff milling about in confusion. Everybody talked and nobody said anything. After a while they stopped talking and just looked at each other uncertainly. As Harry says, "Just what are you supposed to do when a war starts at five o'clock in the morning?"

Clare had the answer: "Let's go make some coffee and scrambled eggs!"

After a good American breakfast the Luces went for a walk. They turned into the Rue Belliard. The German Embassy was in the middle of the block, and at the corner was a house blown inside out. "The right block but the wrong house," Clare said bitterly.

They walked on to La Place Charles Rogier which seemed pretty peaceful still, with men in khaki sitting around the entrance to the station, smoking and waiting for the trains to take them to the front.

When the Luces got back to the embassy, the Ambassador said, "I've got a car you can have. You'd better leave at once for Paris."

Clare glanced at her husband; neither of them rattle easily. Harry said, "But you are giving a dinner for us tonight."

"Dinner or not, you'd better go. If you stay, I take no responsibility."

"We'll stay," said Harry.

The dinner was held. Everyone wore evening clothes and tried not to notice when the great crystal chandelier trembled as the antiaircraft guns fired or a bomb dropped on the airport.

The next day Harry wangled a car from the American Express Company and went to pick up Clare at the Hotel Metropole. He was startled when she came out with three young British pilots in sky-blue uniforms lugging huge duffel bags. It seems they had been interned in neutral Belgium, but since it was not neutral any more, they were free. Clare had offered them a lift to Paris.

Fortunately, Mrs. Hugh Gibson, wife of the former Ambassador, was driving her own car back to France, so they set off in convoy on the road to Ghent. Soon they caught up with the crowds of refugees going nowhere, stumbling blindly away from fear.

Near the border of France a long column of camouflaged trucks filled with British soldiers thundered past, going very fast, also Brenn gun carriers with their tractor treads shooting sparks of speed, and flocks of shrieking motorcycles. People stood in the village streets throwing flowers at them. Still further back came marching troops, the Scots Guards and the Queen's own Westminsters, singing "Tipperary" as they marched. In a few hours the Luces passed almost the entire mobile reserve of the Allied armies marching into the trap from which most of them barely escaped with their lives at Dunkirk.

They slept that night at Lille. Half the British Imperial Staff was there, headed by Lord Gort. They had already been to the front and had come back to plan.

The next morning the Luces started very early and reached Paris in time for lunch. The dining room of the Ritz was crowded as usual, and the high-pitched clatter of voices sounded as it always did. It was all the same as usual until about halfway through lunch, when Harry says a very interesting and terrible thing happened. Quite suddenly a wave of panic swept that rich and crowded room. The voices began to scream instead of cackle. People got up and milled, and sat down and sobbed. The veneer of civilization on those carefully groomed faces cracked and naked terror peered out of their eyes. The Luces, sitting quietly together, looked on with both pity and disgust. As Harry observed, "The frightened rich were not a pretty sight."

The rest of that spring of disaster is history. The Nazi *Panzers,* led by General Erwin Rommel, crashed through at twice-fatal Sedan, where the Maginot was not yet built, and encircled the Allied armies in Belgium. As catastrophe piled on defeat, Harry Luce hurried home to take charge of his great magazines and try to tell the American people the truth of what was happening, and to advise them as best he could on what to do.

Clare, remaining in Paris for a little while, saw that now it was really at war, with all the young men gone to join the Army and the trains loaded with refugees, dumping their pitiful cargoes of broken men and women and frightened children on the station platforms to be taken care of somehow by the wonderfully kind people of Paris, aroused at last.

But as the news got worse, all the people were asking, "Who has betrayed us?" And they said to Clare, "Go home and tell the Americans what has really happened. Tell them we need them. How we need them!"

So that seemed to be the thing to do. On the last day of May she went to Le Bourget to take a plane to England. She found the British were at war, too, now, with Chamberlain out at last, and Winston Churchill as Prime Minister, epitomizing all the virtues of Britain. England rejoiced as most of her men, by the grace of British courage and improvisation, came miraculously back from Dunkirk. But all the guns and tanks were lost.

On June 8 Clare flew to Oporto in Portugal and hired a car, for a wild, reckless drive of three hundred and fifty miles over wagon-track roads to Lisbon, the last part in the dark with no headlights.

The Hotel Avis was jammed, as were all the other hotels, because Lisbon was celebrating eight hundred years of Portuguese independence with a fiesta. So she telephoned the American Minister, Herbert Pell, whom she had known long ago in Newport, and, of course, the Pells asked her to stay with them. Bertie Pell was a great, big reassuring man, who gave her a copy of yesterday's New York *Times*. It was very comforting.

The next day news came that Mussolini had declared war on France. That day also Clare's clipper came in from Horta in the Azores, bringing Noel Coward, Madeleine Carroll, and Simon Elwes, who were all going back to England to do what they could, anything they could, to help.

Around midnight Clare joined them in a little café, where they drank red Portuguese wine while she told them what France and England were really like. And they told her about America and how smug and complacent people were, and how everybody said, "We've got plenty of time to prepare."

"Speaking of Hollywood," Coward said, "they're all turning to the South American market, 'until the war in Europe blows over.' "

"Blows over what," said Clare between her teeth, "the Atlantic?"

There in that very foreign place she suddenly realized how very much England, in spite of the stupidities and irritations of Englishmen, meant to her and to all Americans. In *Europe in the Spring* she wrote:

"The English not only feel the same things about Justice and Liberty we do, but say them in the language I love and know . . . I knew that if England were going to die, a large part of American me would die with her. Because (I thought) we are the children of Mother England . . . When your mother goes, you know at last that you are no longer somebody's child; you are an adult. This is a bitter frightening moment for a man, or a colony or even 'an independent nation.' And they never know how bitter it is until it really comes to pass."

So as Clare got up to leave she said to her English friends who were going back to do anything they could for England, "Good-by and God bless you all, from John O'Groats to Lands End."

And Noel Coward answered, "Don't worry so much about England; we'll muddle through. You'd better start worrying about America."

The next morning Clare boarded the clipper, which took off from the broad Tagus River and, passing low over the pastel houses of Lisbon and the Castle of Cintra on its mountaintop, left the last cape of Europe behind and headed home.

Clare holed up in "The House" in Greenwich to tell people in *Europe in the Spring* what she had seen. The book she wrote was a best seller, and it deserved to be, for it was a good book for Americans to read.

To begin with, it was superb reporting. Reading it even now, with the knowledge of all the incredible things that happened in these fifteen years, it stands up. The judgment of people and probabilities are good and true, and nowhere can one say this is absurdly prejudiced or that is superficially conceived. But the book is far more than good reporting. It is inspired and informed by the fact that Clare cared so very much about the things she wrote of. Her passionate love of freedom and justice, her compassion for the people who in their bungling way were trying to defend them, her terror lest her country should not know the danger and rise to meet the challenge, and her determination, which has shaped her whole life's purpose ever since—that America should never find herself militarily and spiritually bankrupt as France had been—give it the significance of a great social document. Though, its purpose served, it is for the time forgotten, the truths she wrote there are eternally valid. In it Clare reached intellectual and emotional maturity.

CHAPTER ELEVEN

"LADIES, PLEASE!"

THE SECOND WORST *faux pas* CLARE EVER MADE HAPPENED A FEW
days after she returned from Europe in June, 1940. You cannot
say that she has a one-track mind, for the lines of her interest are
multiple; but when her train of thought gets started in one direction,
it is practically impossible to switch it. Now she was so wrapped up,
so emotionally involved, in the war and the blitz, that she hardly
thought or heard of what was going on in America—how could she
when France had just surrendered to Hitler? So she literally buried
herself in "The House" to work with burning-glass concentration
on her book.

One afternoon her husband called her from his office. "I have
accepted an invitation for us to dine with Russell and Marcia Davenport this evening," he said. "The Wendell Willkies will be there.
Is that all right with you?"

It was not exactly all right. Clare only wanted to work and work,
but if Harry wanted to go, she would drop everything. So she said,
"Sure! It sounds like fun."

On the way to a party the Luces usually briefed each other about
the people they were going to meet; but this particular evening
there was so much else to talk about that they did not. Of course,
Clare knew the Davenports well and she remembered vaguely that
Mr. Willkie was president of a great utility company, the Common-
wealth and Southern. She also knew that the Republican party soon
would meet in a convention to nominate a candidate for the

Presidency, and that nobody knew who would be nominated. She was in fact "aware of everything except the central point."

The Luces were greeted rather excitedly by the Davenports, Russell craggy and homespun, Marcia dark-eyed and brittle. The Willkies soon came in. Clare noticed that Mr. Willkie looked rumpled but full of tremendous vitality. Edith Willkie was as delicate and neat as though she were made of Staffordshire china.

The talk at dinner was all on politics and Clare found her mind drifting off to her book. Toward the end of the meal Davenport said, "There is no question about it, we need a businessman with vision to head the Republican party."

With a twinkle in his deep blue eyes Wendell Willkie remarked, "That makes Henry Luce the logical candidate."

Clare thought he meant it and she was seething. There had been rumors about Harry aspiring to the Presidency, which was completely untrue. Indeed, it was probably constitutionally impossible because he had been born in China. Clare wondered if Mr. Willkie could really be that silly, or if he were trying "to butter up Harry."

After dinner they sat in a circle in the drawing room, still talking about a liberal businessman for President. Finally Clare boiled over. In her soft, slow voice, the words dropping with deadly clarity, she said, "Mr. Willkie, if you think an American businessman can be nominated, you may be right; but no businessman can be elected in 1940—*ouch!*"

Harry had ungallantly kicked her in the shin.

Very soon after, Harry rather abruptly pulled the watch trick. As soon as they were in the car he said, "Why in blazes did you say that to Mr. Willkie?"

"The man's a fool to think that you'd be President."

"He doesn't want me to be President," Harry grinned. "*He* wants to be President."

Less than three weeks later Wendell Willkie was nominated as the Republican candidate for President of the United States.

It was about this time that Harry Luce conceived an idea that had enormous historical results. England was being starved to death, both economically and literally, by wolf packs of Nazi submarines. Her navy was stretched beyond the breaking point—

she just did not have enough ships to guard the seaways. Meanwhile, we had a large fleet of obsolescent destroyers built for World War I, rusting their lives away in anchored rows. Why not give them to England? Harry thought.

Through an emissary, he conveyed the idea to President Roosevelt, who promptly invited the Luces to dinner at the White House.

It was a gay and intimate meal, with only Harry Hopkins and the President's friend and secretary, Missy Le Hand, present. Roosevelt in his wheelchair mixed the strong old-fashioneds and insisted on a second round. After that even the somber state dining room could not dampen the conversation. When they returned to the second floor, Clare was left in the family sitting room with Hopkins and Missy Le Hand, while Harry went to the Oval Study with the President.

Hours went past while Clare made conversation, lively at first and then sagging with stifled yawns. It was half-past two in the morning when Harry Luce finished pleading his cause with the President. Later he told Clare the upshot of their discussion. The President liked the idea—he was willing to do almost anything to save England—but he maintained that it was politically impossible in the present temper of the American people. Luce argued that the people would realize the urgent necessity of the move.

Finally the President said, "If you will take on the job of changing public opinion, I'll do it!"

"All right," Harry answered. "I'll go right through with it to the end."

At the agreed-on time, *Life* ran pages of pictures of the old destroyers and strongly urged the plan of giving them to England, with *Time* in hearty support. Other papers joined the crusade, and it was lifted right out of the realm of politics, becoming, in effect, the first nonpartisan piece of American foreign policy. There is little question that the fifty over-age destroyers which President Roosevelt gave in exchange for American bases on British possessions in the Western Hemisphere were a vital factor in saving England from destruction.

Despite this alliance with Roosevelt on the destroyers, Harry Luce backed Willkie for President with all the power of his magazines. Clare, for the time being, remained aloof. She had not interested herself in politics since the fair false dawn of the New Deal, and, besides, there was the book to finish. When it was on the press, she threw herself enthusiastically into the movement for Union Now; a nonpartisan group that advocated immediate union with beleaguered Britain to save Anglo-American civilization.

Then something happened that sent Clare into action. Despite his support of the Destroyer Deal, President Roosevelt publicly called Harry Luce an isolationist. Those were fighting words to Clare, who says, "When somebody attacks Harry unjustly, I get pretty mad."

That was the beginning of a feud that lasted while Roosevelt lived.

It was inevitable that Clare and Roosevelt would clash, and not just because Harry Luce opposed him, for she was rarely swayed by her husband's political views; and her attitude toward the President became far more rigorous than his. In part her rage against Roosevelt was induced by disappointment after her high hopes in 1933. She had welcomed many of his reforms, but as one after another of the idealists whom she had known and worked with, such as John Carter, Raymond Moley, and General Johnson, were heaved off the ship of state and their ideals corrupted for party advantage, disillusionment set in.

Three other things turned her against the President. One was his failings as an administrator: the waste and inefficiency of the ever-expanding government operations, while bureaus and bureaucrats multiplied like rabbits. Second, was Roosevelt's devious way of conducting affairs. Clare was always a straight-from-the-shoulder type—possibly too much so as Margaret Case Harriman recognized when in a profile for *The New Yorker* she called Clare "The Candor Kid." In any event, Roosevelt's inclination to political double-talk infuriated Clare.

The final and most important element of friction was that Clare felt that the President did not recognize the danger of communism. As she saw it, Roosevelt was influenced by his left-wing advisers to take a deludedly tolerant attitude toward the extremely realistic masters of the Kremlin, who, for her money, were just as dangerous as Fascists.

To her logical brain, the President's thinking seemed to emanate from a nebulous haze of irrational idealism. She could not bring herself to trust the judgment of a man who reached his conclusions in such a haphazard fashion.

The ill will between Clare and Roosevelt gradually changed from political opposition to intense personal animosity. This was due partly to Clare's pointed gibes at the President, and partly to his vindictive attitude toward her.

And yet, Clare says, "I never saw him on his way to address the Congress, walking stiffly with infinite difficulty down the aisle of the House, without feeling compassion and admiration for his courage, his imagination, and his impregnable gaiety."

Clare got into the campaign of 1940 when columnist Dorothy Thompson, who had opposed Roosevelt vituperatively for years, suddenly switched and announced that she was for Roosevelt because he was better qualified "to see this thing through than Willkie."

Clare challenged her in a speech she delivered on October 15, 1940. After noting that Miss Thompson had fired a gun at the Nazis from Clare's own godchild fort in the Maginot and must therefore disapprove of them, she said: "In the last five years Miss Thompson has attacked the President with an almost physical violence. Now she says the range and precision of his military, naval, and political knowledge inspires every person with whom he talks. If the President knew what the power of the German military machine was, why are we Americans unarmed today? . . .

"Eight years ago Miss Thompson had an interview with Adolf Hitler, and afterward she wrote that he would never come to power. Her judgment of the qualities it takes in a man to lead a nation, fight a war, or win a peace are surely open to question."

Clare also described Miss Thompson as wild-eyed and babbling, the victim of acute fear.

To say that Dorothy Thompson took umbrage at this questioning of her judgment is understating it. With her yellow hair flying and her blue eyes blazing, she launched a violent personal counter attack: "Miss Boothe is the body by Fisher in this campaign. She is the Brenda Frazier of the Great Crusade. She has torn herself away from the Stork Club [Clare was there once] to serve her country. [She is] the Power's model . . . the Snob Copy of the campaign. . . ."

Clare could be pretty umbrageous herself, and she took a few more cracks at Dorothy whom she called "The Molly Pitcher of the Maginot Line." She also invited Dorothy to debate with her at Town Hall, which Miss Thompson refused to do. Clare now admits that this showed great good judgment on Dorothy's part, for the newspapers were whooping it up for a "Cat Fight," as they called it, and all sorts of wisecracks were being made such as, "Ladies, please! Remember there are gentleman present."

With England in the first desperate stage of the Battle of Britain and America torn by divided counsels, Clare felt it was no time for personalities.

Buckminster Fuller says, "Few people saw the powers at play before the war as Clare did. Wherever she went—and she went everywhere—there were intimate gatherings at which people talked freely, a tearing away of surfaces. She would tell me of trends that turned out to be very accurate."

Armed with her special knowledge, Clare went on to make many speeches for Willkie. Her theme was: "America, wake up before it is too late!" And her standard was courage: "The will to reform and defend this country can only be steeled in the fires of our courage and our faith in the future of our historic way of life." She said at the *Herald Tribune* Forum:

"How many of us this year cast our votes, not in faith, but in fear, a fundamental devastating fear, breeding a Pandora's box of fears. . . . Fear that we won't get into the war in time. Fear that we will get in too soon. Fear that we will get in at all. Class fears, racial fears—all these fears admitted to the councils of government or behind the curtains of a polling booth—these are treason's other name."

And she said, "A soldier with a gun in his hand is only half prepared. A soldier with a gun in his hand, and faith and courage in his heart, is fully prepared. . . ."

According to Joe Martin, who was Willkie's campaign chairman, Clare originated the idea for the final great rally, when people from all over the country were brought in on a nation-wide radio hookup for the first time in political history.

Despite her ardent partisanship, Clare never fooled herself. Her doubts as to the outcome of Willkie's campaign are shown by a telegram she sent to Raymond Clapper just before election saying in part, "Whatever the outcome, you and I will know that we were right."

Yet, like the good American she was, a few weeks after Roosevelt had won, she told a meeting of the British War Relief Society, that the country must support the President because under his leadership, "the United States has done all that can be done to aid Britain under the present neutrality law, and must now face the fact that whatever further is done will be at the known peril of entering the war."

Though her candidate and her party had lost, Clare had gained invaluable experience. Even the fray with Dorothy Thompson had its advantage. "At that time," Clare says, "I learned a lesson I have never forgotten. I learned that if two women have a political dispute, everybody calls it a cat fight or hair-pulling brawl. If two men say just as harsh things to each other, no one would think of calling it a dog fight.

"When I saw the glee with which the press wrote about our argument, I decided that I would never again make a derogatory remark or engage in controversy with any women in public life— or private. I never have."

"When Helen Gahagan Douglas was elected to Congress the papers tried to start something. 'Brunette Actress and Blonde Glamour Girl Due to Tangle.'

"As soon as Mrs. Douglas reached Washington, I telephoned her and asked for a private appointment. When I saw her I explained why. She agreed with me, and we made a compact and shook on it.

"We agreed that we would never appear against each other or address remarks to each other. We had dozens of offers to debate, and we refused them all. Nevertheless, if she spoke in the House and I spoke eight hours later, or even the next day, the papers would headline it, "Luce and Douglas Clash.""

Incidentally, when Mrs. Douglas made her maiden speech before the House, President Roosevelt was so eager to hear her that he had the radio turned on during his cocktail hour and shushed all his guests. After listening for about five minutes the President said wearily, "Turn off the radio. She can't hold a candle to Clare."

As for Dorothy Thompson, she and Clare remained good friends. As Dorothy says, "I like Clare because she does not carry political animosities to her friendships."

CHAPTER TWELVE

THE HEROIC BACK YARD

IN THE SPRING OF 1941, HARRY LUCE DECIDED TO GO TO CHINA TO
see how things were there. To his mind, which had been oriented to
the Far East since childhood, it seemed that this might be as important to America as the dire happenings in Europe. Certainly,
with the Japanese holding all the richest and most progressive part
of that great country, and the Chinese armies entrenched on that
last great barrier, the Yellow River, the situation was just as desperate. Clare went with him to Chiang Kai-shek's beleaguered
capital, Chungking.

When they landed from the clipper in Hong Kong, Clare excitedly felt that she was now in China. Harry told her that this
was no more China than Bermuda was America.

From Hong Kong they took off at 3 A.M. in a commercial DC-2
for the five-hour flight, most of it over Japanese-held territory, to
Chungking. Once the lights of the British city were left behind,
there was no sign of life in all that darkened land.

They were over Szechwan Province, still held by China's last
armies, by the time the sun came up. Under the vibrating wings of
their old plane Clare saw the Chinese countryside—abrupt, small
mountains rising like anthills from the plains, each terraced
nearly to the top with tender green rice paddies in all sorts of shapes,
from conventional squares and rectangles to delicious little new-
moon slivers. Scattered all over the verdant plain were small villages
the color of earth. As they flew farther west the mountains became higher and the plains more spacious. Presently Clare saw

two great rivers looping down out of the hills; where they joined stood the city of Chungking.

Their plane landed in the middle of the river bed—a drought had shrunk it. They were met by some Chinese officials and Teddy White of *Time,* looking very British in a white sun helmet, shorts, and an open-collar white shirt with a black tie knotted sailor-fashion. He had brought sedan chairs in which they were carried up the city cliff and then went in an automobile to the home of Dr. H. H. Kung, head of the civil government of China. Dr. Kung, looking surprisingly young, with a round, smiling face and horn-rimmed glasses, welcomed them jovially and provided a hearty breakfast, American style.

Clare's first real look at Chungking came at lunchtime at the Kialing Hotel overlooking the city. It seemed very drab, a higgledy-piggledy conglomeration of mud-gray houses, and piles of mud-gray rubble left by Japanese bombs. Harry, too, was disappointed.

"Chungking was at the end of the moon to me when I was a boy," he says. "It took longer to get there from Shantung, where I lived, than it did to San Francisco on a slow boat. In fact, travel was so difficult that some of the English boys at my school who came from there never saw their parents for years. So Clare got her first look at China, at what was, in effect, its Wild West. I regretted that it was not the China I knew but the back yard—and a bombed-out back yard at that."

But it was a heroic back yard. Japanese bombers from Hankow, two hours' flight away, came over nearly every day—it had become a pattern of life which the inhabitants took in their stride. The second day Clare was there, the warning sirens went off at 10:30 A.M. Since that meant two hours' grace, she and Harry drove through the heavy traffic of oxcarts, automobiles, buses, and hundreds of rickshaws, past columns of air-raid wardens marching to their posts and people leisurely closing up their shops, to the American Embassy on the slope of a hill outside of town.

Ambassador Nelson Johnson greeted them and took them out on the terrace overlooking the river and the city. The sun was hot in a cloudless sky. People, like lines of ants, were moving down the cliffs to the safe caves tunneled into them. The first Japanese raid in 1939 had killed five thousand Chinese. Now the inhabitants

had become so disciplined in taking cover that a similar raid cost
no more than a hundred casualties.

Quite soon the last straggler disappeared into the hillside, and
the city looked as lifeless as a lunar landscape. Just around a bend
in the river a little American gunboat, like a small old-fashioned
yacht, nuzzled against the bank. The air was motionless and op-
pressive.

The Ambassador and his staff compared watches as the zero
hour approached, and cocked their heads, searching the sky. Suddenly Johnson said, "There they come!"

Clare could see and hear nothing until heavy explosions shook
the earth and a mile-long wall of smoke billowed up from behind
the city hill. Following the Ambassador's finger pointing upward,
Clare saw many tiny flecks of silver in the brilliant sky. The air
attaché counted forty-two planes coming their way.

A series of teeth-loosening explosions came from immediately
below them as the Japs dumped a mixed load of high explosives
and incendiaries on the shacks and junks at the river's edge. Clare
could see the phosphorous bombs burning red-gold in the sunshine.
Then it was all over, and the stillness was like a pall as the smoke
thinned and drifted away.

The following day Clare sat out a raid in the tunnel-like, underground shelter of Dr. Kung's Bank of China. This time the bombs
were closer and the noise was terrific as the earthen walls seemed to
rock like a ship. After the raid she learned that a five-hundred-
pounder had landed directly on top of the shelter. Luckily it was
a dud.

Clare found that morale was high in Chungking, but it was very
different from the phony morale in Paris just a year ago, for these
Chinese people knew the worst and were facing it unafraid. They,
too, had their theaters, as many as were open on Broadway that
spring. On a rainy night—it was better so because rain meant no
bombs—Clare went to Chungking's Broadway with a Chinese
friend named Mr. Kwong. He explained before they started: "Re-
gardless of all dark shadows over Chungking, many residents are
always looking forward to Drama which makes their lives full of
fascination and thrill. This is why theater is such fashionable
recreation among masses."

In rickshaws, with the aprons pulled up to their chins and awnings down to their eyebrows to keep out the driving rain, Clare and Mr. Kwong started out for what he called "Taking samples of all kinds of theater in Chungking." When the street turned into a narrow ladder-like flight of stone steps they changed to palanquins carried by sweating, rain-soaked coolies, who carried them upward through the stench of rotting vegetables, dead dogs, and human ordure that was like a gas generated by warm rain water.

That night they saw part of a modern patriotic movie and an excellent play written by a young Chinese author who had studied theater at Harvard. Finally they looked in on a classic Chinese drama in a brightly-lit theater crowded with happy Chinese, moving constantly, shouting at friends, reading papers, eating nuts, and spanking babies, while actors in grotesque masks and magnificently embroidered costumes went through a ritualistic performance in a pattern set a thousand years ago, to the music of clashing cymbals and wailing flutes.

"In China old drama is dying," observed Mr. Kwong. "It does not help fight Holy Resistance War."

Clare met Generalissimo and Madame Chiang in what was perhaps their finest hour, when it seemed that they were the symbol of China's will to stay free. The meeting took place in the large, shadowy drawing room of the Chiangs' house. Madame Chiang, the delicate embodiment of Chinese beauty, with a mind that almost matched Clare's, received them first and gave them tea, talking very fast in American-English. Presently the Generalissimo, in a plain uniform, slipped into the room. Clare stood up with the others, while Madame Chiang presented them. To each the ruler of China said, "How!" which was the extent of his English. Then he said, "How . . . How," and motioned them to sit down, taking the place next to Harry Luce.

From then on the men did most of the talking, with Madame Chiang acting as interpreter. Even through so difficult a medium it was clear that the Generalissimo had an acute mind and intense determination.

The Luces came away convinced that the Chiangs were magnificent people. And so they were, then. For, however much things may have deteriorated later, when America came into the war and the Chinese, sure of victory, relaxed a bit, at that time, holding the remnants of China together by their inspiring courage, the Chiangs were a dedicated pair.

The little single-engined Beechcraft fluttered over the twelve-thousand-foot Tsinling Mountains like a gnat. The air was thin up there and very rough. Clouds engulfed it and cleared in time to see a towering peak right ahead. It was enough to make any man nervous, but Clare sat reading, apparently relaxed. Perhaps she really was, for physical danger seems to mean absolutely nothing to her.

The plane taking the Luces to the Yellow River Front, stopped for the night at Chengtu, and then flew on to a makeshift landing field at Sian among the golden wheat fields of Shensi Province. At the headquarters of the Northern Front in the courtyard of a temple, they met the Generalissimo's son, Lieutenant Chiang Wei-kuo, a strong-nosed young officer with a mat of thick black hair and a big smiling mouth.

After dinner with the governor of Shensi, they took a train for two-hundred-mile ride to the end of steel, that is to the front. At three in the morning they got off the train and into an automobile that had been sent along on a flatcar for their special use. Two hours later, in the sunrise, they came to a small hill of loess—the most ancient dust in the world. Their car was hidden under an earth-colored tarpaulin.

Mongolian ponies were waiting and, following General Chow of the 167th Division, they rode toward the front. Clare lent her camera to a Chinese officer who took a picture of them starting out. With a white Stetson hat shading his stern visage and his rumpled gray business suit, Harry looked a little like an itinerant missionary; Clare looked like a college girl in a big straw hat, a pleated white blouse, and a black skirt hiked up by the saddle. Just after it was taken Clare's horse ran away. She lost her camera but hung on to the horse.

In the six miles to the front the Luces rode through three large villages, crowded with people. The food shops were piled with the produce of that rich land. At the gates of a ruined town on the edge of a swirling yellow torrent, General Chow dismounted and led them on foot along the wrecked railroad embankment, past machine-gun nests and big gun emplacements, to the wall of the city facing the Japanese across the river. There they had tea with the colonel of a front-line regiment, with fresh flowers on the table from the garden he had planted in the lee of the wall.

After tea they mounted the wall and, as Harry says, "The general rather wanted us to keep our heads down."

They were looking over the great bend of the Yellow River. The enemy lines were about two thousand yards away. Clare could see their gun emplacements on the cliffs across the river and spotted a Japanese sentry. Through her field glasses she could see the red-ball flag of Nippon.

Then they rode back through the ruined city.

Clare's trip to China made an indelible impression on her mind and swung it from its hitherto exclusive preoccupation with Europe. As always, she talked with everybody she could find who spoke English, from Madame Chiang and all the top government officials to engineers and students and houseboys. In this unfamiliar environment her mind did not exercise its usual clear critical quality. She could write quite affectionately of an "unshaven, shy little general . . . who once had a price of eighty thousand dollars on his head and then helped to save the Generalissimo's life." His name was Chou En-lai.

For the most part she relied on her husband's interpretation of the things she saw. Harry Luce's deep affection for the land of his birth gave him a wonderfully warm and wise understanding of the Chinese, though it may have made him unduly optimistic. He woke in Clare a passionate interest in China that has never dimmed, and she shared his uncritical enthusiasm.

In an article for *Life* called "Wings Over China," she wrote: "East is East and West is West, but when you look down on fighting China from an airplane you see . . . the two great halves of the world are being joined. . . . There are no hemispheres in an air world. When all the world takes to wings, we'll see that. Perhaps then we'll get the Great Peace, the World Peace—the Peace of Ameurasia."

CHAPTER THIRTEEN

GATEWAY TO THE CHINA SEAS

CLARE CAME HOME EARLY IN JUNE, 1941, TO ONE OF THE HAP-
piest summers she ever spent. First she hurried to Foxcraft School
in Middleburg, Virginia, to see Ann graduated *cum laude.*

Her daughter had really worked for the scholastic honors she
won. In fact at one time she drove herself so hard—even as Clare
drove herself—that the mother of one of her schoolmates warned
Clare that her daughter was making a nervous wreck of herself
trying to live up to the standard set by her mother.

Clare dropped everything and rushed down to Foxcraft to see
Ann. With the characteristic candor that marked their relation-
ship, she told her daughter exactly what had been said. Ann answered furiously, "If I want to make a nervous wreck of myself
trying to be like you, I'll do it no matter what anybody says!"

Clare recognized her own indomitable independence and with
loving wisdom decided not to interfere.

When they got back to "The House," Ann found that a brand-
new convertible was her graduation present. She promptly named
it "Aloysius." Dorothy Burns' sister, Ruth, who had come to be
Clare's secretary in Greenwich—Isabel Hill mostly stayed at the
office in New York—taught Ann to drive it.

Ruth Burns—they all called her Burney—became completely devoted to Ann. Everyone who knew the girl loved her, for in addition
to her fine brain she had a wonderful simple sweetness.

Harry Luce adored Ann, and he was her ideal of what a man

should be. She called him Dad; and any pronouncement he might make became the law to her.

Clare spent long hours with her daughter. They played tennis and rode and swam. Ann's young friends swarmed all over the place, and Henry III and Peter Paul Luce, who were growing up, too, stayed with them most of the time.

All the children were brought up to be careful of money. Ann had no idea that when she was twenty-one she would inherit her share of George Brokaw's millions. One day Ruth Burns heard her tearing up the stairs shouting, "Burney! Burney! Did you know I was an heiress?"

"What makes you think that?" she asked.

"It's right here in Cholly Knickerbocker's column. I'm listed along with a Vanderbilt and a couple of Rockefellers!"

"Well, if you're such an heiress," said Burney, wet-blanketwise, "how about paying me the sixty-five cents you owe me?"

Ann had a reasonable allowance from which she was supposed to buy her own clothes. Clare advised her to get simple basic dresses and change their appearance by using different accessories. The economic disciplining only concerned material things. Ruth Burns says that in anything that Clare thought would develop her daughter mentally, "the sky was the limit." Every time Clare went to New York she picked out a group of records for Ann's collection. The girl loved music and, in fact, knew more about it than her mother.

Sometimes Ann went to church with Ruth Burns, who was a devout Catholic. On their return from one such occasion, Clare asked, "Are you trying to make my daughter a Catholic, Burney?"

"No, she wanted to come with me."

"I don't care," Clare said. "I envy people who can believe. If she were a *good* Catholic, that would be fine."

It was assumed that Ann was going to college at either Smith or Bryn Mawr, but she had been doing a lot of independent thinking on the subject. One day at luncheon she asked Burney, "Why did you, a Middle-westerner, come East to college?"

"Because I wanted to learn about other parts of the country," Ruth Burns answered.

"Then it might be good if I went West to school?"

"I think it would, Ann. You would learn many things you would not around here."

"Any ideas where I should go?"

"Leland-Stanford is a very fine university," Burney said at random.

Ann dashed away from the table and upstairs to the room where Clare was working and eating a sandwich.

"Mummie, what do you think Burney thinks I should do? Go West to California to college. Leland-Stanford!"

Clare looked coolly at her secretary, who had followed Ann upstairs. "Couldn't you think of any place farther off?" she asked.

But when Burney explained her reasons, Clare caught fire.

"Of course you're right," she said. "Do you think we can get her in? I could call Mr. Hoover."

It was not necessary to telephone Mr. Hoover. Ann's scholastic record made her a welcome student anywhere. So it was settled.

The next question was whether Ann should be allowed to take Aloysius. She begged. Clare stood firm. There was quite an argument which Ruth Burns joined. "I think Ann should take her car," she said.

"You'd give her the moon," Clare retorted. "You spoil her. What makes you say that?"

"Because she's a fine driver and very careful. I'd rather she drove herself than ride around, as she's sure to do, with wild, young Californians."

Clare pondered that and came to a decision. "You win, Burney," she said. "Ann can take her car. But if anything happens, it's on your soul, not mine."

All summer Clare was working very hard. She would not have been happy had she not been. She wrote the articles for *Life* and *Vogue* about her Chinese trip, and a play that was not finished for ten years. Often she worked until one or two in the morning. Then she and Burney would raid the icebox.

Since she was considered an authority on the war and European affairs, the *Times* and *Herald Tribune* literary magazines sent her many books to review. Among them was Anne Lindbergh's *Wave of the Future,* which seemed to take a sympathetic view of Nazism.

Clare was working on it late at night when she buzzed Burney. "What was that dreadful conundrum your father told me when I was a schoolgirl, about apples and worms?"

"What's worse than finding a worm in an apple? The answer is half a worm."

"That's what I'm going to say about this book," Clare announced. "It's so beautifully written that you take a big bite before you find the worm."

As always, "The House" was a center for writers, politicians, foreign statesman, journalists, and refugees. Anyone who could contribute interesting thoughts was welcome. They poured in that summer and the talk at the Luces' table was of an extraordinarily thoughtful character.

Among their more intimate friends who came again and again, were Buff Cobb, Clifton Webb, Somerset Maugham, Gladys Freeman, Sir William Wiseman, the Willkies, Vincent Sheean, the writer, John Gunther, Marcia and Russell Davenport, the Whitelaw Reids, Ambassador Cudahy, Maggie Case, C. D. Jackson and other *Time* editors, Henry's sister and brother-in-law, the "Tex" Moores, and most especially and most welcome, Bernard Baruch.

Harry Luce's father and mother often came to stay at "The House." Dr. Luce loved to get up at dawn and watch the sun break in splendor over the Sound. If anyone asked him why he made such an effort, he would gently quote a favorite saying: "He who does not know the dawn, does not know the day."

There were always domestic crises in "The House." Once the houseman drove the car through a plate-glass window in the dining room just as luncheon was served. On another occasion Ely Culbertson arrived complete with ulcers, while his frantic secretary telephoned the menu he had to have. As a result everyone else was served while Culbertson sat gloomily looking at an empty plate. Finally he asked Clare, "Are you mad at me or something?"

However, he was duly grateful when the nonulcerous food finally arrived.

Then there was the kitten that Clare and Harry rescued on a back road one rainy night. Clare loved cats and became so attached to this one that it had the run of the whole house. After some

months it repaid her hospitality by having kittens of its own on a
five-hundred-dollar yellow brocade bedspread in the best guest
room. The bedspread was ruined but, as Clare said, "The kittens
were awfully cunning."

On Ann's seventeenth birthday in August, Clare gave her a
wonderful party for which her young friends came from all over
the eastern seaboard. The Luces themselves cleared out for dinner, leaving the young people chaperoned by Burney. It lasted until
dawn. Two days later Clare left for the Philippines to report the
situation there for her husband's magazines.

As Clare was about to take off, she paid Ruth Burns a tribute
she has never forgotten. "Before you came here," she said, "this was
just a house. Now it's a home. I could not be leaving my baby with
anyone but you." Then, turning to Ann, she said firmly, "Burney's
the boss!"

Back over the long familiar clipper route went Clare to Hawaii,
where she spent a night with Doris Duke in the Persian palace she
had built overlooking the sea beyond Diamond Head. Imported
parrots chattered and monkeys swung from the trees in her brilliant
tropical garden with marble pools and splashing fountains. They
had a swim in the swimming pool, and Clare did her swan dive from
the high-diving platform that rose up and sank back into the
ground on a hydraulic lift so it would not spoil the view. That
night Doris, "her long flaxen hair brushed up from her high brow,
and blue Siamese-cat eyes, danced . . . an exquisitely subtle hula,
for her guests." Then the native musicians strumming their steel
guitars sang a new song called "Love Her and Leave Her on the
Lava."

Then Clare took off in the clipper and flew along the desolate,
stepping-stone islands whose names nobody could remember until
a few weeks later when they tolled like bells in the news: Midway.
Wake. Guam.

There was an interesting group of passengers in the long body
of the clipper. The new Ambassador to Thailand, Willys Peck
and his wife; Mr. Duff-Cooper, en route to Singapore to coordinate
the Far Eastern defense of the Empire, and his beautiful wife, "with
the blue-crystal eyes and cameo profile." She was the former Lady

Diana Manners, who had also played the Nun in *The Miracle*.
There were also Duff-Cooper's British secretaries; an American
army engineer bound for Chungking; and two well-dressed, sophisticated gentlemen who turned out to be missionaries; two benign-
looking characters who were brewers from Manila; together with
oil men, army and navy officers, and a steam-shovel operator going
to build the new airport runways that later came in so handy for
the Japs.

In her hold the clipper carried aircraft instruments and other
military accessories, and, even at this late hour, New York wedding
gowns for Manila brides and polo balls for Manila sportsmen.

Of course, Clare talked endlessly to all her fellow passengers,
learning something from each of them. She noted the problem of
getting workers "to stick," at Midway despite salaries of six hundred dollars a month and the soldiers who *had* to stay for twenty-
one dollars, and she went swimming in the aquamarine water at
Wake. Her strategic sense made her write of Guam as being "like
a luscious plum lying in a hornets' nest of Japanese-held islands."
There were only about four hundred American soldiers on Guam,
but at the governor's cocktail party everyone was sure the Japanese
would go some other way. Clare, who had heard that sort of remark somewhere before, headed this section of her article in *Life*,
with a quote from an army engineer: *"Empire builders can expect
to be bopped."*

Clare arrived in Manila looking less lovely than usual—her face
was "a measle-mask" of mosquito bites contracted at Guam. From
the plane she looked down on the "tight little rock" of Corregidor,
and Cavite, our one decent naval base in the western Pacific.

She found Manila vibrating with the same frenetic gaiety of
other capitals on the eve of doom. There was an afternoon reception
at Commissioner General Francis Sayre's, with all the ladies in print
evening gowns. While admiring the orchids and the brilliant ma-
caws in the garden, everybody talked about "the danger from the
north." In the confusion of differing opinions, propaganda, half-
truths, and false hopes, Clare wrote helplessly: "Page Major Eliot
. . . Page Walter Lippmann, Dorothy Thompson . . . Oh ask Wendell Willkie for these people living under skies that may—or may
not—rain bombs are not prodigal of death-dealing facts . . . What

is wrong here in Manila? Just what was wrong in Prague, Warsaw, Amsterdam, Brussels, Paris, London, Moscow. 'They' have
the offensive. We have not . . . Well you can't expect to hold, even
in escrow, an island Empire like the Philippines and not get
bombed. Or can you?"

Clare tore around the island of Luzon as a good reporter should,
paying no mind to the humid heat, except to change her dress
when "the hemline began to trickle." She talked with President
Quezon in his beautiful Malacaña Palace, with High Commissioner Sayre, and Admiral Hart in the Elizabethean Suite of the
Manila Hotel; and under the churning fans in his hot little headquarters she interviewed General MacArthur, whose intense,
dreamy eyes were firmly fixed on destiny.

Then she flew home to tell the American people in articles and
on the radio that the Philippines were the gateway to the China
Seas, and that the gate looked pretty rickety. She also wrote an enthusiastic profile of General MacArthur, which with superb timing
—for which Harry Luce gets the credit—appeared in the issue of
Life dated December 8, 1941.

On December 7 there was a luncheon party at "The House" in
Greenwich. House guests included Vincent Sheean, Laurence
Steinhardt and Dr. Lin-Yutang. James Whittaker was there and
Maggie Case. Twenty-two people in all sat down to lunch at
2:35 P.M.

It was an ironclad rule of the Luce household that meals must
never be disturbed by telephone calls. The only time it was broken
was when one of Ann's beaux called and Harry Luce, seeing her
squirming unhappily, would say indulgently: "OK, Ann, go talk
to him. We mustn't let him get away."

Ruth Burns had just settled herself with a tray in her room,
when the telephone rang. It was C. D. Jackson calling from
Time, Inc.: "I've got to talk to Harry. The Japanese have bombed
Pearl Harbor!"

Even war could not shake Burney's perfect discipline: "Mr.
Luce is at lunch. I'll have him call you back," and hung up.

Burney scribbled on a piece of paper, "C. D. Jackson has called
to say Pearl Harbor has been bombed by Japs," and gave it to the

butler. The butler put it on a silver tray and after the dessert had been served he handed it to Clare.

Clare glanced at the note, still talking to her lunch partner, Dr. Lin-Yutang. Then, as her eyes focused, she raised her voice. "Harry," she called to the other end of the table, "it's come! The Japs have bombed Pearl Harbor!"

Mr. Luce jumped up to go to the telephone. All the other guests except Dr. Lin-Yutang headed for the radio. The Chinese said, "I will finish my dessert if you don't mind. You see, this is all so very expected."

From that moment on pandemonium was let loose at "The House." Broadcasting companies called for Sheean, Whittaker and Clare to make talks about the situation in the Pacific. Clare, preparing notes for her broadcast, was informed by a house guest that the radio said there was a rumor that the West Coast had also been bombed.

"Ann. She's out there!" Clare said. "I must get her on the telephone."

She got the long-distance operator. The operator said that the wires to San Francisco were overloaded. Clare begged, "Oh, please, when one is free try to get my daughter at Leland-Stanford. This is Clare Boothe Luce, her mother."

The operator was suddenly all sympathy. "Don't worry, Mrs. Luce," she said, "for the past hour I've been listening to a lot of admirals and generals talking. San Francisco is OK. But ohmygawd, Pearl Harbor!"

Clare, relieved, said, "What happened?" The operator gave her the score cheerfully. She broke off—another call. Censorship had not yet caught up with her.

Harry Luce called his father and told him the news.

"This is terrible," the old missionary said, "but there is one good thing in it. We will now all see what we mean to China and China means to us."

That was Harry's last talk with his father. Dr. Luce listened to Clare on the radio broadcast from New York. He said, "She has spoken truly and well." Then he turned off the radio and, as always, committed his soul to God. That night he died quietly in his sleep.

CHAPTER FOURTEEN

VENI, VIDI, EVACUI

WHEN THE UNITED STATES ENTERED THE WAR, CLARE LUCE WAS working on a biography of General Homer Lea, the strangely prescient student of Far Eastern affairs who thirty years before had predicted the war between Japan and America in *The Valor of Ignorance*, and the conflict between England and Germany in *The Day of the Saxon*. She finished this book in February, 1942, and immediately started out for India, Burma, and China on what turned out to be the most dangerous and arduous of all her missions as a war correspondent.

On an icy morning at La Guardia Airport, she boarded the Anzac Clipper, taken from the Pacific run and camouflaged with wavy lines of white and gray in the fond and futile hope of making it look like a cloud. This was still the era of stepping-stone flying and the clipper went by way of Miami, Puerto Rico, Trinidad, and Brazil, and then took the shortest possible overwater hop from the hump of Brazil's coastline to the jutting shoulder of Africa. Clare records that the first sight of Africa looked satisfactorily African with thick green jungle crowding down to a golden, wave-washed beach. She finally landed in a black lagoon near the mouth of the Congo.

In other smaller planes, DC2's and 3's, Clare beat her way across Africa to India, where she talked with Nehru. Then on Easter Sunday, April 5, she boarded a CNAC DC3 at Dum Dum Airport, Calcutta, for the five-hour flight to Lashio in Burma.

The plane was full of bales of money for Chiang in Chungking and six shaven-headed Chinese soldiers in khaki shorts. At dusk they landed on the big clay airport at Lashio. Colonel Haydon Boatner, in charge of CNAC operations, greeted Clare with a big, broad grin, and said, "You're the luckiest reporter in the Far East. Guess who's just flown in? General Stilwell and the 'Gissimo. Madame Chiang came, too."

At the two-story wooden building that was temporary headquarters, Clare cornered Stilwell on a narrow staircase. He wore an overseas cap on his grizzled crewcut, bit on a long black cigarette holder, and was chewing gum rapidly. He peered at her through his steel-rimmed spectacles and recognized her instantly—not too difficult, since it could hardly have been any other woman in the world. "Hullo, hullo!" he said crossly. "Burma's no place for a woman!"

"But I'm a war correspondent," Clare answered. "And it sure is the place for a war correspondent."

Vinegar Joe gave something between a snort and a laugh. "OK," he said. "Tomorrow morning at dawn I'm driving to Maymyo. If you can get up that early you can join me—on the Road to Mandalay."

That night Madame Chiang sent for Clare to come to the little house where she and the Generalissimo were staying. They all sat in wicker chairs on its high porch looking at Burmese farm fires on the circling hills, burning in the velvet blackness. Clare describes Madame Chiang as "dynamic, flashing-eyed, swift-speaking, charming, and utterly dedicated to the one increasing purpose, to lick the Japs no matter who, when or what folds."

But Madame Chiang was very bitter that night as the defenses of Burma crumbled before the long, snaking columns of Japanese: bitter about the lack of supplies and planes and men from America, bitter about the British loss of the great fortress of Singapore.

"But they ran out of water," Clare said.

"We Chinese have run out of water," said Madame Chiang, eyes blazing. "We drink from muddy puddles, get dysentery, get up, and fight on."

Chiang Kai-shek said through his interpreter, Hollington Tong, that his wife was worth ten divisions.

The next morning Clare had breakfast with General Stilwell at

four-thirty, and the general demonstrated his virtuosity by simultaneously smoking a cigarette, chewing gum, and eating a fried
egg with chopsticks.

After breakfast the general's aide, Colonel Frank (Pinkie)
Dorn opened up a small trunk full of American decorations, and
Stilwell put a Distinguished Service Cross and a couple of Purple
Hearts in his pocket. Clare quoted Napoleon's remark: "With
these bits of ribbon a man can build an empire."

"It's going to take more than bits of ribbon to hold our empires
together," said Pinkie Dorn.

For five hours on the temple-dotted road to Maymyo, Clare rode
with General Stilwell and Colonel Dorn in an ancient Ford driven
by a hooked-nose Persian civilian named Saidie. Behind them came
another sedan with the Chinese liaison officer, Lieutenant Richard
Ming-Tom Young, and four Chinese guards with tommy-guns. At a
curve in the narrow mountain road the second car shot ahead
with two of the guards leaning out of the window very carsick.

Maymyo, in the cool Shan hills, had been the summer capital of
Burma. Now it was Stilwell's last-ditch headquarters in the Irrawaddy Valley. The Japanese had already taken Moulmein, with
all its pagodas, and the great Burmese port of Rangoon, and were
coming fast up the river valleys, up the real Road to Mandalay.
When Clare arrived, she learned that Mandalay had just been
heavily bombed. Refugees were streaming back carrying cholera
with them.

The red-brick headquarters building was in a former missionary
compound, the Baptist Shirk Memorial Rest House. All around
it the flowers of the East and West met. There were roses, poin-
settias, larkspur, frangipani, and honeysuckle, all blooming at
once, making the air incredibly sweet. Clare was assigned a small
bedroom on the second floor, with a rickety iron bed under mosquito netting. The common bathroom consisted of "a row of
wooden-seated metal cans, a dented tin basin with one spigot out
of which a dark-brown, lukewarm trickle ran, and an iron tub,
also with one spigot, out of which no water ran at all."

After lunch *Life* photographer Dick Rodgers, just in from the
front, agreed to take Clare to Mandalay. She changed into black
slacks and a pleated white blouse and wore a little Puritan-maid

cotton bonnet to keep the fierce sun from burning right through her skull. In Rodgers' jeep they tore down from the hills to the level plain, where the heat enfolded them in a warm, wet blanket. Before they reached the city, its stench struck them like a blow, the stink of eight thousand decaying bodies in the ruins of Mandalay.

The city had been leveled by the bombs and the aftermath of fire. There were acres and acres of charred timbers and twisted tin roofs. It had been a city of one hundred and fifty thousand. On the day after the bombing Clare saw only twenty or thirty people on the streets: a group of Burmese rifles, some natives on bicycles, and a few Buddhist priests with shaven heads and saffron robes, carrying black umbrellas.

Those were the *living* people that she saw; the dead were everywhere, lying where they had fallen because only certain priestly castes were allowed to bury people. As they drove through the dreadful streets, houses were still smoldering. The long brick walls of Fort Dufferin were still standing. In the stagnant green water of its moat bodies of men and women and babies, "bobbed like rotten apples."

Vultures were wheeling in clouds over the ruins of the railroad station. "They didn't get much rolling stock," Dick Rodgers explained. "But there were fifteen hundred Prome refugees camped on the platforms. Shall we go in?"

"No," said Clare faintly. "Let's go home now."

They drove back to the Maymyo Country Club with its cricket fields and golf links green in the golden sunshine. Clare went to her locker room to freshen up. A girl in tennis shorts looked at the dusty apparition and asked, "Where on earth have you been?"

"To Mandalay," Clare said curtly, still shaken with horror.

The girl went on making up her face. "Oh poor, dear Mandalay," she said. . . .

In the officers' mess that night General Stilwell came in late from the great conference with Chiang and British General Sir Harold Alexander. Stilwell had dragged Chiang all the way from Chungking to straighten out the triple snarl of command: Chinese, British, American. The general was in high spirits. He had forced

Chiang to order his generals to do what he said, and Alexander had agreed to cooperate.

"That's fine, General, but will it last?" Clare asked skeptically—she knew a little about allied commands.

"Nope," said Stilwell cheerfully. "It can't last long. But at least we'll have a little time. . . ."

After dinner the general and his aides disappeared into his office to work. Clare went with the younger officers to the parlor of the mission, where they sat eating peanuts out of a scrapbasket in the fireplace and talking about the dissolving Irrawaddy front.

"It's not that the British don't fight," said a young liaison officer. "They've got so little to fight with. The tanks don't work. Mechanization's no good in a country with only one road. The Japs in their sneakers and shorts just flit through the jungle and cut 'em off. Oh the Sikhs and the Gurkhas and the British are putting up a hell of a fight. Boy, they're taking it! Guts. They've got that all right!"

Somebody strummed softly on the piano and sang, "We can't give you anything but guts, Baby, That's the only thing we've plenty of, Baby . . ."

Clare was in her room the morning of April 8, writing up an interview with General Stilwell, when the sirens wailed. She gathered up her papers and started putting the lid on her typewriter when General Thomas Hearn, Stilwell's chief-of-staff, stuck his head in the door. "We go out to the slit trenches in the compound," he said.

"How long have we got?" Clare asked.

"I don't know," said the general. "But don't fiddle," he added sharply as Clare sat down to load her camera.

All the American officers gathered in a little woods where the trenches were, except Stilwell, who was in another woods with the Chiangs. After about ten minutes of tension they began kidding around taking pictures of each other holding tommy-guns and looking warlike.

"What's the chance of this being a real raid?" Clare asked Colonel Frank Roberts, who was standing beside her.

"A hundred to one—on."

"Why?"

"Because the Japs have Burma loaded with spies. They know everbody's here. Stilwell, Alexander, the 'Gissimo and Madame Chiang. Knock those two out and Chinese resistance becomes— unpredictable."

Colonel Roberts was a little nervous. He said apologetically that he'd been through this before. Pointing to the skylarking officers he remarked, "See how differently they behave when it's over. It will be quite interesting for you."

Clare snapped her camera at General "Long Tom" Hearn who was sitting against a tree sucking his pipe.

"He'll let his pipe go out. Otherwise *he* won't change," said Roberts.

Then, sharply: "Down in. They're coming!"

As Clare climbed into the narrow, deep trench with Colonel Roberts, she could hear the pulsating rhythm of many motors. The colonel pointed to a blue patch of sky between the trees, and Clare saw the little white planes. They were not as high as the bombers at Chungking. They did not need to be. There was no antiaircraft here.

The colonel counted. "Eight, twelve, sixteen, twenty, twenty-eight. They're right overhead. Here it comes!"

The sound of the bombs began as a whistle and ended in a screech of death. Clare burrowed into the bottom of her trench "like an animal." Then the whole world rocked and shook and shuddered to blast after rending blast.

In silence broken only by the diminishing *thrum-thrum* of the motors, Clare crawled out of the trench. She was absurdly proud that her hands had stopped shaking and that nobody could see that her insides felt as though they had been in a Waring mixer.

They all walked solemnly back to the mission, which was untouched. Across the street some little houses were blazing, and a five-hundred-pounder had torn a great crater in the driveway, burying some people who had been in a shelter. They were dug out miraculously intact: two Burmese boys and a young English-woman in a gingham dress who said, "I'm quite all right, really," before she fainted.

Almost immediately the road was full of stampeding horses and cattle and natives carrying suitcases. The people of Maymyo were pouring out of their flimsy, stove-in houses, and beginning to load everything they owned on bullock carts, native carriages, and bicycles for the long trek to India.

In headquarters all the servants had taken off, except the cook. He began cooking and the officers brought the food to the table. Clare was right in the middle of lunch when General Alexander's spruce young aide arrived to take her to lunch at Flag House, the British headquarters. Clare explained that she thought the bombing had canceled the invitation.

"Not at all," said the aide. "Not unless the target is definitely achieved."

So an hour after she climbed out of her trench, Clare sat down to lunch with General Alexander at a table set with real silver and flowers. His servants had not run away—the British order these things better. The beautifully cooked meal, was served by a turbaned Indian bearer.

The bombing was only mentioned once. Then Clare and her dapper host, in his robin's-egg-blue bush jacket, talked strategy, not tactics. General Alexander was realistically optimistic. The British would hold Burma as long as they could: Alexander only had seven thousand men. Then they would hold India as long as they could. But it did not matter even if India and China, too, fell, so long as they won in Europe. They could retake them after they had disposed of "the Hun."

This was not what Clare wanted to hear. It was not what Stilwell had told her, for he believed that Burma was a key position. Her analytical mind realized that what Alexander said was probably true, but her emotions were too deeply involved, with China, and now with Burma, to be able to think of this as a secondary front. She knew from what Alexander did not say that Burma was lost, and the knowledge filled her with despair, even while she realized that this was illogical. She noted in her journal: "Is it because the stink of Mandalay, entering my civilized nostrils, has permeated every cell of my mind, clouding it with false intimations of inevitable disaster, corrupting, in short, my untried American valiance?"

On Friday, April 10, Clare started her long trip home. First to Lashio with Colonel Roberts in a jeep. They went to Colonel Boatner's cottage, and he remarked gloomily, "Nobody knows when a plane will be in. It wouldn't surprise me if the Japs took out Lashio Field tomorrow."

Pretty soon the telephone rang, and Boatner told them, "A CNAC plane has just landed. It's taking off in thirty minutes for Chungking."

Clare said, "I'll take it."

"But your ticket reads to Calcutta," Boatner objected.

"I'll either take it or go back to Maymyo," announced Clare.

"You'll take it," said Roberts firmly.

The plane was piloted by Dude Hennick of "Terry and the Pirates." His real name was Higgs, and his cargo was some sixty Chinese civilians—in a forty-passenger plane—there were lots of babies. Roberts said, "Good-by. Tell the American people the truth about this. They've got the right to know, haven't they?"

And Boatner said, "Oh yes, the story? If you know the story, tell me in three words. I'd like to know too."

Clare leaned out of the door of the plane. "In three words," she said, "*Veni, Vidi, Evacui.* Which means we came, we saw, we got the hell out."

"I think she's got the story," Boatner said, grinning.

So Clare, in what was said to be the last plane out of Lashio, flew the dreadful Hump, with its rocky fangs rearing eighteen thousand feet to trap unwary fliers, to Kumming, where she paused to take the only color photographs of Chenault's Flying Tigers, and on to Chungking. Then back to India and from there to Cairo, talking to everyone, high and low, whom she could reach; and she missed very few.

From Cairo she began the last lap homeward, across Africa. On that trip she pulled the very worst boner of her not faultless life. Occasionally, she can be persuaded to tell the story, though people cringe when they hear it, and so does she, even now.

Her plane put down at an army field on the west coast of Africa, and the pilot announced they would be there for six hours. Clare was hot and tired and covered with desert fleas. "All I want in the world is a bath," she said. "Do you suppose there is a bathroom anywhere?"

Yes, she was told. An elderly American shipping agent had just completed a small modern house, which had the only bathroom in town.

"It was a dear little house," says Clare, "and he was a dear old bachelor. He gave me a long, cool drink and told me how he had struggled to build his house, what with wartime shortages, the unskilled labor, and the need to be careful of money. 'I moved in only two weeks ago,' he concluded. 'Now I must go to my office. My house is yours.'"

Clare dashed upstairs, turned on her bath, and began to undress. The water running into the tub was the loveliest, coolest sound she had heard in weeks. Then the houseboy knocked on the door. The telephone, he said. Putting on a robe, Clare went downstairs to the telephone closet. It was the Pan-American boys, who said a VIP had just flown in on an army plane. He had pull enough in Washington, they said, to bump her and take her place in the plane. Clare protested—it might be a week before another plane came through. There was a long argument. Meanwhile she noticed a tropical storm had come up; she could hear the rain pouring down. At the end of forty-five minutes she won her argument and came out of the closet. Sheer horror gripped her.

That tropical storm was the bath she had forgotten to turn off. Water streamed through the ceiling, cascaded down the stairs. She ran up and turned it off, then ran downstairs, yelling for the house boy. "Mop it up," she pleaded. "Quickly!"

He fetched a tiny rag and began dabbing at the flood. "Get the furniture out!" she begged him.

Woosh! A big piece of plaster whizzed past her nose. Plop! Another crushed a delicate settee. Eventually the whole ceiling came down. The pretty drawing room was a sodden wreck.

Clare says that the hardest thing she ever did was to wait for the return of her host. When he came, she tried to break it to him gently outside, gave up, and led him in to see the ruin of his home.

"You know, of course, I will pay for it," she pleaded, "but I realize that's no reparation. All those years you worked for this . . . What can I say? What can I say?"

That was the old bachelor's finest hour. "Do not trouble yourself about the house," he said gently. "I never really believed I would have it, in any case."

Friendly Pan-Am boys assessed the damage, and Clare left a check and a letter on her departure. She felt a little better, but not much, when some months later he wrote her that the repairs had been completed, but that the story had made him famous throughout Africa. She still thinks that he is the greatest gentleman she has ever met on five continents.

CHAPTER FIFTEEN

CONGRESS

WHEN CLARE CAME HOME FROM BURMA, SHE WAS EXTREMELY restless. There was simply not enough for her to do to use up the consuming energy that was fired by her passionate convictions about what must be done for victory. It was no use trying to sit down and write; she was no Nero to fiddle around with plays while the world was ablaze. Of course there were speeches to make, and there was talk of her going again to China or to Australia for *Life;* but her candid dispatches had irritated President Roosevelt, who had not forgotten the sharp barbs she had planted in the hide of his administration during the Willkie campaign, and in many speeches since. So there were mysterious delays about a passport and finally a flat refusal from the State Department.

Then one day a letter came from Albert P. Morano proposing that she run for Congress as the Republican candidate for Connecticut's Fourth Congressional District.

Her stepfather, Dr. Austin, after being Health Officer of Greenwich for twenty years, had represented that district from 1938 to 1940, when he had lost by only nine hundred votes out of one hundred and eighty thousand in the Democratic landslide that engulfed Willkie. Morano had been his backer and political mentor, and had served him as congressional secretary during his term in Congress.

Dr. Austin had died on January 26, 1942, and Morano's letter suggested that Clare was the ideal candidate to take his place.

The idea was exciting. Here was a chance to take positive action to implement her ideas; and here a national sounding board to echo her ideals. She would not have been Clare had she not also seen the wonderful opportunity for further harassment of Roosevelt and his cohorts.

There were, however, serious objections. All her previous experience in politics had been in the nature of brilliant forays by a gifted amateur. To become a professional meant starting a whole new career, learning a new technique almost from the ground up. No doubt she could learn, after all she had already mastered three other professions: editor, playwright, war correspondent—but she had considerable misgivings about starting so close to the top. Knowing herself, she foresaw some spectacular bloopers. Also, she had very serious doubts as whether Al Morano was the voice of the people, or even the husky tones of the Republican party.

Morano says that she telephoned one night and asked him to come to "The House." Isabel Hill greeted him and told him that Clare would be with him in a few minutes, and meanwhile would he read a letter she had written to J. Kenneth Bradley, Chairman of the State Central Committee. In it Clare stated her reasons for refusing to run.

It was a blow to Morano. But you do not rise from the dumps of the Chickahominy District of Greenwich to become a political leader by giving up at the first rebuff. Nor do you rise without knowing how to handle people. In the service of her stepfather, Al Morano had become something of an expert on handling Clare.

When she floated into the room, looking enchantingly fragile, Morano fixed a look of impassive resignation on his square, expressive face.

"What do you think of my letter?" she asked.

"It's a very good letter, indeed," said Morano.

The faintest suggestion of a frown creased Clare's forehead.

"I want to be sure that it's right," she said. "Let's go over it together."

So they did, with Morano praising every sentence. Clare read aloud the final paragraph in which she stated her irrevocable decision not to run. "Is it all right?" she asked.

"Excellent," said Morano. He could not keep a spark of amusement out of his lively brown eyes as he observed that the lady was disconcerted by his lack of despondency. She had come girded for a whale of an argument; instead she was getting unflattering acquiescence. He knew the time had come to jerk the hook.

"Will you do me one little favor?" he asked. "Promise me to take just one word out of that letter."

"What word?"

"Promise first?"

Clare was a sportsman. "I promise."

"The word," said Morano, "is 'irrevocable.' "

It was not over as quickly as that; both Clare and the Republican party needed considerable further persuasion. Sam Pryor, Vice-President of Pan-American Airways, and George Waldo of the Bridgeport *Post-Telegraph,* added their voices to that of Morano, as did Kenneth Bradley. One of the most powerful pleaders was Niver W. Beaman, editor of Greenwich *Time.* He wrote a long letter to Clare, meeting all the objections she had raised. Among them was the fact that she was wealthy. "You made most of it yourself," Beaman said. "Nobody's going to hold that against you."

When Clare finally said she would run if they could convince her she had a chance, Morano and Beaman put on a subtle campaign to make her known to the party leaders and the rank and file. Few took her seriously at first, but as they were exposed to her unexpected combination of charm and common sense, they capitulated. After all, the Republican politicians thought, they had very little to lose; in that particular year of 1942 the Republican candidacy was regarded as a pretty forlorn hope. This fact was also a powerful incentive to Clare for that is the kind of hope she likes best to lead.

However, there was a stalwart core of Republicans who were appalled at the idea of a woman candidate. As Clare points out, there was still a lot of prejudice against women in politics: "Margaret Chase Smith and I were practically regarded as freaks. This is one thing," Clare adds, "in which Europe is 'way ahead of us. The presence of women is no unusual thing in the parliaments of many European countries—almost fifty per cent of the Dutch parliament are women. This is partly because the distances there are so much shorter that a woman can serve without neglecting home and husband. It is hard to find responsible women who are willing to do that. Those who do it easily are not worth having. Because Connecticut was so close, Harry could come often to Washington and Ann was in college, I was unique and fortunate in being able to arrange things."

Most of the men candidates for the nomination dropped out of the race in Connecticut with snorts of disgust, and in the end it was between Clare and Miss Vivien Kellems, a lady of reactionary opinions who owned and ran a factory and was the darling of the National Association of Manufacturers.

Clare was chosen by the Republican leaders to make the keynote address at the Republican State Convention. Her theme was that the administration was still fighting a soft war, and that the American people wanted no pampering, but an all-out effort for victory. So persuasive was her logic, and so inspiring her courage, that all opposition collapsed. She was nominated by eighty-four votes to two.

Then she rose to accept the nomination. If the members of the convention expected wisecracks and fireworks they were disappointed. Clare's speech was touchingly modest, which was really the way she felt in the face of this untried responsibility. She said that she had prayed to God in many different places, sometimes in church and sometimes "in slit trenches while bombs were falling. Sometimes in airplanes, flying over forbidding mountains and in cities on the brink of being socked by the enemy. . . . I am praying now, here in Bridgeport, that I will be as good in this job as a person may be. . . ."

Those words came from her heart, for although she had not as yet joined any church, Brussels and Burma and Chungking had quite cured her of agnosticism. In those terrible far-off places she had learned that man alone was not enough, and she had turned to God.

Then came the campaign. Clare threw herself into it with the incandescent zeal of a Savonarola trying to clean up Florence. There was nothing too arduous for her to do; no call that she would not answer; no place she would not speak if even six people would gather to hear her. She made a total of one hundred and sixteen speeches. In Al Morano's little, beat-up Chevrolet coupé she barn-stormed about the district, meeting virtually every shift at every factory as they came out from work, and talking to them from the traditional soapbox. She induced them to talk to her too. As George Waldo put it, "She listened as well as glistened at the factory gates."

Clare's opponent, Democratic Congressman Leroy Downs, had the double advantage of being the incumbent and of being backed by the Roosevelt's administration, which he had supported on virtually every issue. Clare went after him with bare fists, calling him "just another rubber stamp," and "one of the men in Washington without faces."

Though the big guns of the administration were trained on her, Clare had some heavy artillery on her side. Herbert Hoover backed her and Wendell Willkie at her final rally said, "She has a knowledge of world affairs which few people possess. . . . She is a person of complete integrity."

Most amazing of all, Dorothy Thompson, magnanimously forgetting the "cat fight" two years before, came out in a paid advertisement, backing her because she had so much greater knowledge of foreign affairs than her opponent.

Clare's campaign was based primarily on "Win the War." But she pointed out that patriotic criticism was a good thing, that we must "help the President think," and that the fundamental design of political liberty required two parties.

Clare's own reason of why she won the campaign is the women. "It is simply not true," she says, "that women prefer to vote for a man. Women will vote for a woman rather than a man provided they are convinced that she is competent. I went out to organize women—working women. For instance, I gave a big dinner for working girls in Bridgeport, told them my qualifications, and asked them to vote for me. In the end I cut down the big Democratic lead there by exactly the number of women I had thought could be changed."

Then she wryly tells a story of why one woman changed. "All through one of my first meetings I saw this woman nodding and smiling at almost everything I said. *Anyhow,* I thought, *I've got you.*"

When the woman came through the receiving line she said, "I'm going to vote for you."

"Are you an independent?" Clare asked.

"My family says I'm a very independent person."

"What made you decide to vote for me?"

The woman answered very seriously, "My father and brother are dentists. I know they would want me to vote for a candidate with such beautiful teeth."

Despite all the poise and assurance Clare showed facing the great mass meetings, and even dropping in to back-alley saloons in Bridgeport to chat with radical labor leaders, she was at heart uncertain and fearful. Almost every night she called up Al Morano at one or two in the morning to ask, "Am I doing all right?" And every night Al, steady as a rock, would say, "You can't miss." Now he wears a handsome wrist watch on which is engraved: *From CBL to APM Nov. 3, 1942. You can't miss.*

Clare became devoted to her stalwart, humorous, idealistic aide. In appearance he reminded her a little of her brother David, who had once again enlisted in the Marines and risen to be a fighter-pilot. "When are you going to stop calling me 'Mrs. Luce,' Al?" she asked.

"What should I call you?" Morano countered.

"It would be nice if you called me 'Sis,' " said Clare.

Once during the campaign they drove past Morano's small house. Outside a very dirty little boy was playing. "That's my son, Tony," Al said with pride in his eyes.

Clare said nothing then, but one day when the campaign was over she queried, "Al, will you get mad if I ask you something?"

"No," said Al.

"Promise?"

"Yes."

"I want to talk to you about Tony. I want to put him through school."

Morano says, "It was my burning ambition to give Tony the education I did not have, but I told Mrs. Luce I must ask Mrs. Morano."

Tony's mother agreed, and Clare sent the boy first to a private school in Greenwich and then to Canterbury Academy. When Al himself became a congressman he said to her, "Now I'll take over Tony's education."

Tony is only one of dozens of children Clare has helped to educate, according to Morano.

On the morning of Election Day it was anybody's race. Clare's campaign manager, Big Bill Brennan, figured she would win by five thousand votes, but managerial estimates are usually about one hundred per cent overoptimistic. Clare and Harry voted at the Greenwich Armory early in the morning and then made a mad, final dash to all the twenty-three towns and cities in Fairfield County. That night they listened to the returns at campaign headquarters in Greenwich. It was close, all right. Downs led at first as the voting machines in Bridgeport came in. Then paper ballots from the country, more slowly counted, put Clare ahead. Even when Leroy Downs conceded, she did not quite believe it. And when after midnight her victory was announced as official by over six thousand votes, wit for once failed her. All she could say was, "Whew!"

Early the next morning Clare telephoned Morano. "Good morning, Mr. Secretary," she said, which meant that she had appointed him to the same post he had held for her stepfather. Then she took a train to Hollywood to work on the script of a moving picture about China.

She spent Christmas on the Coast with Ann and returned direct to Washington. It is said that never had so many reporters turned out to meet a novice congressman. Feeling completely bedraggled by her three-day trip, Clare gave them the slip at the station—which infuriated them—and announced a press conference in her office the next morning.

Of course all the newshens came and many of the veteran Washington reporters. About fifty people tried to get into that small room already packed with photographers and newsreel cameras, and booby-trapped with writhing light wires. As Clare came in the riot began. Photographers were jumping on chairs and tables, while the flash bulbs exploded like summer lightning in the Catskills. A wire got crossed and shot a stream of sparks and smoke. Women reporters screamed and a deep voice said, "Must be the Japs." Everybody asked questions at once. Nobody could make any sense and hardly anybody but Clare tried. She at least got off one sensible remark. A reporter asked, "When are you going to make your maiden speech?"

"I wouldn't know," Clare replied. "Certainly not until I have something to say."

Before that time came, Clare had some of the misadventures she expected. The first day she went to take her seat, a grinning page-boy spoke to her just outside the chamber: "Do you want me to be your friend, Mrs. Luce?" he asked.

"Of course I do," said Clare with warm amusement.

"Then I'll say it, Ma'am. Your slip's showing."

By the rules of Congress no hats were allowed to be worn on the floor—this meant women as well as men. Clare usually wore a little bow of ribbon perched on her hair. One day some press photographers asked for a picture of her on the Capitol steps. The icy blasts of January wrecked her hair-do, so she tied a scarf around her head. That picture brought howls of anguish from the hat manufacturers of Danbury in her district. One apoplectic gentleman called her headgear, "that babushka!" Indeed, the most irate people in America that day were the mad hatters of Danbury.

Another thing the press chivied her about was the fact that she was located in the coveted New House Office Building. Since rights to such palatial quarters went by seniority, undue influence was hinted at. The truth was that after seniority was exhausted, the few remaining offices were given out to the first comers. Faithful Al Morano got into the waiting line early and acquired the last office in the building for Clare.

The third ruckus was about the traditional White House buffet supper for freshmen congressmen. Clare did not, at first, receive an invitation. Morano called the White House and was told that the President had had an attack of indigestion just as he was about to sign the letter inviting her. In view of Roosevelt's feelings about Clare it was probably psychosomatic.

When the invitation finally came, Clare accepted it in a six-page letter, informing the President that there were some things she wanted to talk to him about. Congress, she wrote, was "very much perturbed. There has been transferred to Congress, as if by swift contagion, the people's long-delayed fury against the swollen and wasteful Washington bureaucracies that have burgeoned through the years. . . ."

Steve Early replied irately through the press that the supper was a purely social affair and no place for politics. The President planted a sharper barb. When he met Mrs. Luce all he said was, "How's Henry?"

At her press conference Clare had said that she would like to be on the Foreign Affairs Committee of the House. This brought another attack from the press on the ground that she was "presumptuous," since such appointments went by seniority. Actually, Clare was merely expressing a preference, not an expectation. Joseph W. Martin, Jr., Republican Leader of the House says, "We looked around for a good place to put her, and decided on the Military Affairs Committee. Women were taking an ever more important role in the war, and it seemed right that they should be represented there. At the same time we put Margaret Chase Smith on the Naval Affairs Committee. Clare did very good work. She was a very effective speaker, for she always knew what she was talking about. In Congress she made good on her own."

It was no accident that Clare had the facts. She went out to get them with her usual single-minded purpose, studying reports and making many trips to inspect military installations. Thus she made herself an expert.

The appointment made the second first for Clare in three months. She was the first woman congressman ever elected from Connecticut and the first woman ever appointed to the Military Affairs Committee.

On February 9, 1943, Clare finally felt that she had something to say. Her speech was scheduled for late afternoon, a time when the House usually is virtually empty. On this occasion almost every Representative of both parties was in his seat, and the galleries were packed.

The subject of the freshman congresswoman's speech was "America in the Post War Air World." It was inspired by an article by Vice-President Henry Wallace in which he called for Freedom of the Air, as well as Freedom of the Seas. With clear, incisive logic Clare demolished the Utopian theory that any nation would, or should, permit unregulated traffic in the air above its cities and farms, its rivers, water works, and military installation. She went on to say that America must not lose its leadership in civil aviation as it had neglected its merchant marine. Her closely reasoned argument was that America must keep leadership in the air—not monopoly, but leadership—for the sake of its safety in war and prosperity in peace.

There was only one wisecrack in the whole speech: "[Mr. Wallace] does a great deal of global thinking. But much of what Mr. Wallace calls his global thinking is, no matter how you slice it, still globaloney."

That word rang around the country. Her intelligent and far-sighted aspirations for American civil aviation were ignored as radio and press had a field day with "globaloney." It almost leads one to believe that the greatest handicap a politician can have is a sense of humor.

Though the public received a smart-alecky impression of her speech, those who heard it did not feel that way. As she concluded with the exciting phrase: "The sky's the limit. The time is now," Democrats and Republicans alike paid her the unusual tribute of a standing ovation.

This was only the first of many speeches Clare made in her first term. Not only did she throw her splendid energy into the immediate problem of winning the war, but she worked for long-range planning of America's defense. In addition, though her party was in the minority, she initiated and took a powerful part in the passage of legislation for protecting the rights and health of the citizens of this country, its children, and the children of less lucky nations. She constantly called for means of alleviating famine and hardship abroad, and, on the basis of sense and enlightened self-interest, she foreshadowed the Marshall Plan six years before it was thought of by plugging for comprehensive legislation for rehabilitating Europe and Asia economically.

Nor was she always opposed to President Roosevelt. Because of her belief that we should fight a hard war, she supported his plan to put an absolute ceiling of twenty-five thousand dollars a year on individual incomes.

She paid no mind at all to the roars of amazement, rage, and anguish that issued from the elegant houses of her more affluent constituents from Greenwich to Bridgeport. For her money, it was the right thing to do.

CHAPTER SIXTEEN

UNDER THE LIVE OAKS

THROUGHOUT HER POLITICAL CAREER CLARE HAD DETERMINEDLY
and successfully kept her daughter away from the blazing publicity
that lit her own life like a million-candle-power magnesium flare.
Certainly it would have been an advantage to Clare with the voters
to be known as the devoted mother she really was. But Ann was so
dear to her that she could never trade on that devotion or subject
her daughter to a possibly unfortunate influence. "I hate people
who exploit their children," said Clare.

The bond between these two was by now unusually close.
Though Clare had come to believe again in God, she did not believe in life after death. But since man so desperately needs some
sense of personal immortality, Clare, like her own mother, who
often said, "I live in my children," compensated by deciding that
she would live again in her daughter. Ann, so sweet and pure and
gifted, was to be her only immortality. In the "Real Reason," published in *McCall's* magazine after her conversion, Clare wrote: "I
would seek my justification, my salvation, and the meaning of Life
itself in the joyous, fruitful and meaningful life my own daughter
would have. . . ."

During the Christmas recess of 1943 Clare and Harry traveled
to California to see Ann. They had a completely joyful week together in Palm Springs, hot and tranquil in its desert bowl of mountains. Ann was particularly gay. She had won high academic honors
at Leland-Stanford. Her professor of senior philosophy had particularly praised an essay she had written just before vacation. It
was headed:

"Personality Integration East and West."

Under that was the Oriental symbol of Yin-Yang (the all-embracing, ever opposed, ever joining duality of all things) and the Western Scales of Justice.

The essay was an amazingly mature, brilliant, and spiritual development of her theories of what she termed the "Oneness of Life and Reality." Ann was indeed growing up into the sort of woman of whom any mother would be proud.

Nor was Ann content any longer to be banished from her mother's public life. She had always been an ardent partisan, going to as many of Clare's meetings as she was permitted, raging impatiently, if silently, against those who opposed Clare or even backed her with less than what Ann considered her due meed of enthusiasm. Now she insisted that she be allowed actively to help—she knew well that she could. So Clare consented, and on January 10, 1944, they posed for what was intended to be the first publicity picture of them together.

Then the three of them left for San Francisco where Clare was to deliver a speech the following evening.

The next morning, January 11, Harry caught a plane for the East. Ann and her mother had a gay lunch together in the hotel suite, and then she left to motor down to Leland-Stanford with a classmate, to register for some courses. She would be back for dinner.

It was very quiet in the suite: Harry was gone. Clare's temporary secretary had taken some typing to her own office; and her maid was out shopping. For one of the few times in her life since she had married Harry Luce, Clare was absolutely alone.

She was working on her speech for the evening. Writing in longhand, crossing out, revising, rewriting with infinite pains, as she always did. The telephone shrilled through her concentration. For a few moments she did not answer, thinking somebody else would. Then its insistence made her realize that no one was there. She lifted the receiver.

The voice on the wire was flatly impersonal. "This is the Associated Press. We are calling to confirm the death of Ann Brokaw in an automobile accident."

The accident in which Ann Brokaw lost her life was one of those tragic, needless, unforeseeable, unavoidable things. Her classmate was driving the open convertible down the main road to Palo Alto, when a professor from the university turned in from a side road and hit the rear of the car. Ann was thrown out, and the car fell over on her.

To Clare the news was the end of life, here and hereafter. The shock was so great, her grief so deep, that it seemed she might lose her mind. Throughout the next dreadful days she was alternately barely conscious and bitterly, searingly alive to the pain of her loss.

Harry Luce came back immediately to strengthen and support her. They decided that Ann should be buried at Mepkin, which she had loved so much. So they began the long train trip to South Carolina. In Washington, Dorothy Holloran, Ruth Burns, and the Tex Moores joined the train. Clare asked where Ruth Burns was and, going to her, put her arms around her in comfort. "Poor Burney," she said.

Ann was buried on an unbearably beautiful, spring-in-January day in South Carolina. In Strawberry Chapel, a tiny one-room church close to the boundary of Mepkin, a big potbellied stove glowed with the effort to give warmth. Sunlight streamed through the clear glass windows and lighted all the gay flowers of spring.

After the service the little group of people walked slowly to the old burying ground under the live oaks dripping with soft gray moss. A cow with its head over the fence mooed at them, and birds sang ecstatically all around. The camellias were in full flower. If there were consolation possible for Clare, it was in the beauty of the day . . .

Bernard Baruch begged Clare to go to his lovely South Carolina home, Hobcaw Barony, to rest and revive her spirit. Alone with Harry, who gave up everything to be with her, she spent many weeks there fighting despair. There was no telephone at Hobcaw and the nearest post office was several miles away. They spent the long days very quietly. In the mornings Clare answered the thousands of letters that brought messages of affection and consolation from all over the world. Harry read aloud to her a great deal while she did her exquisite needlepoint. There was a hush over all life.

But it did not bring tranquillity to Clare. Outwardly she was for the most part quiet. Indeed, for many years she was too quiet. Her friends say that the inner radiance which had lighted her was gone, and although beauty remained, it was the beauty of a marble effigy upon a tomb.

Inwardly Clare was a raging conflagration of despair and anguish. Years later she wrote of Ann: "She was my true love, where was she? And where were the true loves of many an English, French, and Chinese mother I had known; and many an American son of a dear friend . . . were they sleeping or merely rotting?"

At Hobcaw, Clare found a book that gave her brief though spurious comfort: *A New Model of the Universe,* by a Russian mystic called Ouspensky. It was filled with Oriental theories of the transmigration of souls, supported by allegedly modern Western "scientific proofs." To these Clare added a strange farrago of her own theories of relativity and the simultaneous interpenetrations of souls and bodies in "a spiral time-track." Although this was merely a temporary measure to find peace, it served a purpose. She recovered sufficient strength of mind to go back to Washington and her job through her belief in this ersatz immortality.

In Washington her closest friend became Olive Clapper, whose war-correspondent husband, Raymond Clapper, had been killed in the Pacific two weeks after Ann's death. Clare had known Raymond well for many years and had become very friendly with Olive when she first came to Congress. Olive admits being prejudiced against her at first by the fact that her husband spoke so often of Clare's brilliance and beauty. But as soon as she got to know her well, she changed her mind. "Clare has the quality of giving friendship," she says; and adds, "she has an emotional intellect."

The Luces and the Clappers often dined together, and the conversation of four such thoughtful people in those tremendous days must have been something to hear.

Olive Clapper lived in a big, secluded house in Washington, and her home became a refuge for Clare. She could leave Capitol Hill and go there, sure of warm understanding and affection. And there importunate people could not find her.

Speaking of Clare at this time, Mrs. Clapper says, "She did not eat and was consumed by a terrible, restless energy. She used to take long, furious walks, and her health was very poor. I did not think she would survive.

"In addition Clare worried for fear she was no longer able to do her job in Congress. She wanted to give up active political life. I did not want that to happen. Although I am a Democrat and opposed to Clare's ideas nine tenths of the time, I felt that there were too few people of ability in Congress for us to be able to spare such as she."

Olive Clapper cast about earnestly for something that would revive Clare's interest in politics. By chance the thing happened at her house. A message came from the Republican National Committee that they wanted Clare Luce to give the keynote address at the National Convention of 1944. No woman had ever been invited to do this before.

Olive says, "I knew this might be the spark that would fire Clare's interest."

However, Clare was so depressed that she did not want to accept. Olive went to work on her, using the argument that it was Clare's duty to do it; that for a woman to have so prominent a part in a national convention was an opportunity that must be taken for the sake of women everywhere.

In the end it was Ann who decided. For Clare's criterion was, Would Ann want me to do it?

There could be no doubt as to the answer, Ann most certainly would have said, "Yes!"

CHAPTER SEVENTEEN

FROM CHICAGO TO BUCHENWALD

THE REPUBLICAN CONVENTION OF 1944 WAS HELD IN CHICAGO. It was not exciting from the horse-race point of view, because Governor Thomas E. Dewey of New York came into the convention with such a vast preponderance of delegates that there was no other possibility. But it was an extremely delicate business for the Republican party. In the midst of a great war, with Eisenhower's men fighting on the beaches of Normandy, American ships and men battling from island to island against enormous odds in the Pacific, and ten million American families praying for their sons overseas, the question was how to campaign against the President-Commander-in-Chief, without seeming unpatriotic. On this touchy subject the keynote address would set the tone and character of the campaign.

Clare was vividly aware of the enormous responsibility resting on her shoulders. In making her their keynote spokesman, the Republican party had, in effect, entrusted her with its very life, for in a single ill-judged sentence she could do it irreparable damage.

More important by far to her spirit of burning patriotism was that she might help or hurt America itself by what she now said. She was ablaze with indignation at what she had seen of waste, inefficiency, and callous politicking in Washington which she called, "a sight more strange than pleasing." She felt with all her heart that the drift toward a single party as Democrats won election after election must be checked if liberty itself were to be saved. Yet she must not shout too loudly of the administration's blunders or voice her greatest fears, lest the confidence of the nation in its leaders be shaken and the enemies of America find comfort in her words.

What wonder if Clare was nervous that hot, humid night in Chicago? She had worked on her speech with a tremendous concentration, unusual even for her. In an hour or two the words would be said, flung through the air to fifty million listeners, printed in ten thousand newspapers throughout the world, said and recorded beyond recall.

Clare had dinner in her sitting room at the Drake Hotel that evening with Harry and Olive Clapper. She had not dressed for glamour but, with her acute sense of good taste, wore a little dark blue dress. "She looked inexpensive."

Mrs. Clapper says that never before had Clare appeared nervous on the eve of a speech, no matter how she may have felt inwardly. Even that night she had herself in hand, but one could feel the strain beneath her poised exterior and her calm speech.

When dinner was over she said to Olive, "I don't want either you or Harry to go to the Convention Hall with me. I want to go all alone."

And so she did. Olive Clapper, who was commenting on the convention for Dumont, followed a few minutes later. She reached the door of the hall and struggled through a trampling, jostling throng of delegates and spectators. Just inside stood Clare, buffeted by the surge and eddy of the crowd, with the look of a little-girl-lost on her face. Olive struggled toward her and half humorously, half maternally said, "Can I help you?"

Clare turned bemused eyes on her. "Oh, yes," she said. "I'm lost. Could you show me how to get to the platform?"

Olive took her arm and piloted her firmly toward the passageway reserved for the elect.

In the blaze of the platform lights Clare came back to life, more completely alive than ever since Ann had gone. Olive Clapper says, "Her beauty was much more than a perfect face. It was a glow, the quality of a great actress in a noble role."

When the cheering stopped, Clare began to speak in her clear, amber tones which seemed, as feminine voices seldom do, to have been designed by her Creator especially for electronic transmission. Her speech was far more emotional—less logical—than was usual with her, for her own emotions were so deeply stirred. She began by saying that she supposed she had been given the honor of speaking because, "through one woman's voice our party seeks to honor the millions of American women in war industries, in Red Cross work, in hospital and canteen and volunteer work . . . the women in the armed services and our truly noble Army and Navy nurses."

She said that American women were not thinking of themselves at this time, but of their men in service, of "GI Joe [whose] last name is Legion . . ." And even more, perhaps, of GI Jim. "Who is GI Jim?" she asked. "Ask rather, who was GI Jim? He was Joe's pal, his buddy, his brother. Jim was the fellow who lived next door to you. But, 'he shall return no more to his house, neither shall his place know him any more.' . . . He was the grandson and great-grandson of many nations. But he was the son of the United States of America. He was the defender of the republic, and the lover of liberty, and he died to make a more perfect union. . . .

"We are come here today to nominate a President who will make sure that Jim's sacrifice shall not prove useless in the years that lie ahead.

"For a fighting man dies for the future as well as the past, to keep all that was fine of his country's yesterday, and to give it a chance for a finer tomorrow. . . ."

Then Clare spoke bitterly of past mistakes of the Democratic administration, which, she said, had led us unprepared into war. But, she added, "Jim did not complain too much about his government. . . . Jim figured that anybody can make mistakes. . . . If Jim could stand here and talk to you he might say, 'Listen, folks, the past wasn't perfect. But skip it. Get on with the business of making this old world better. . . . Take off your hats to the past, but take off your coats to the future!' "

She went on to say that Jim would want this convention "to raise here 'a standard to which the wise and honest can repair.' [He] knows that the event, today as yesterday, is in the hands of God.

"And this we will do here, for Jim's sake. . . ."

At the end she spoke again of Jim's living buddy, GI Joe, saying, "Yes, we Republicans, men and women, are here to build a greater, freer America, not only for, but with the millions of young, triumphant GI Joes, who are fighting their way home to us."

As she finished, the convention's many-throated voice shouted approval and appreciation and personal tribute. For those long moments Clare, standing in the blaze of lights with her arms outstretched to them, seemed the shining embodiment of feminine beauty and spirit, of the hope of tomorrow, and of the compassion of women.

Clare still wanted to quit politics. The excitement of the convention was only a respite from unhappiness. But to do so at such a time as this would obviously make her a quitter. Again, Ann would have answered the question of whether her mother should run again in 1944 with a resounding "Aye." So Clare became a candidate to succeed herself. The election was her hardest fight of all.

The entire Democratic administration hated her with a kind of holy fervor. Though her wit and logic had not been a lethal dagger, it had been a very disagreeable thorn in their sides. Particularly embarrassing to them had been her tactless linking of many of their leading spirits such as Sidney Hillman, and Vice-President Henry Wallace, with the Communist party line. President Roosevelt and his colleagues decided to get rid of her if it took the whole gang to do it. The forces they massed against her were like sending an armored division to take an African kraal.

In a very amusing record of the campaign prepared for Clare by George Waldo and Tere Pascone of the Bridgeport *Post-Telegraph*, the big brass sent against her are enumerated under the following heads:

Red Dragons	Pink Scorpions	Budinskies
Earl Browder	Sidney Hillman	Quentin Reynolds
Rex Stout	Samuel Gruber	Harold Ickes
Leigh Dannenberg	Clifton Fadiman	Orson Welles
	Max Lerner	F. P. A.
	Henry Wallace	

On the side of "The Queen who lived on King Street," as George Waldo called her, were: Bill Brennan, George Waldo, Al Morano, Tere Pascone and J. Kenneth Bradley.

Under that list is the quote: "The odds were great, but not great enough."

The Democrats decided that the Fourth Election District liked to vote for women, so they picked Maggie Connors to oppose Clare. She was long-faced and humorless, but she had an unblemished record of left-wingism. Things did not really get hot until Clare made a broadcast address in Pittsburgh warning Labor that the Communists were trying to take over American labor unions, citing chapter and verse. She pointed out that Sidney Hillman of the CIO was collaborating closely with Earl Browder, who was admittedly America's No. 1 Communist. And, finally, she accurately described Communist methods of government as similar to those of the Nazis. She called it "German sauerkraut with Russian dressing."

At this insult to our noble Russian allies, everybody howled blue murder. Even Clare's friends asked, "Aren't you going a bit too far? After all, they *are* our allies."

Clare simply said that she hated totalitarianism in any form. And the New Dealers swarmed into Connecticut to purge her. The Vice-President of the United States made no less than twenty-two speeches in her district. President Roosevelt ordered his campaign special stopped in Bridgeport, and stood for five minutes talking to a great crowd, with his arm around Maggie Connors.

The Republicans were too busy fighting a rear-guard action for Candidate Dewey to send much help. Clare fought back alone.

It looked bad election night in Greenwich. Clare and Harry Luce listened to the returns on the radio at home. They were not good hearing. Bridgeport's voting machines gave Maggie Connors a thumping lead. At eleven o'clock, Clare telephoned Al Morano. "I've lost, haven't I?" she asked.

"You're going to win," said Al.

"Then Harry took the phone. "You can tell me the truth, Al," he said. "She can't catch up now, can she?"

"She'll win," said Al.

Listening to the returns on his porch overlooking the Hudson at Hyde Park, President Roosevelt sighed contentedly. "It's a good thing for the country that she is beaten," he said.

His observation was slightly premature. As the country ballots were counted, Clare crept up. By two o'clock it was neck and neck; by three she had won—by two thousand votes.

Clare had hardly gotten back to Washington when the Pentagon called her. Members of the House Military Affairs Committee were going to the various fronts to see conditions for themselves. The army was particularly anxious that Mrs. Luce should go. Would she? Would she not!

Clare had forty-eight hours to get ready. All she took along was a black silk suit, a regulation WAC uniform, minus insignia, but with a St. Christopher's medal for luck, and a pair of fleece-lined ski boots. The press later described her visit to a front-line hospital in the following terms: "Like an exotically scented zephyr, she drifted through the gloomy sickbays, and her costume, something right out of the top drawer in military raiment, had the GI's eyes bulging. Her military green jacket was fitted at the waist like a glove. Faultlessly creased green trousers were neatly tucked into brown woolen socks that emerged snappily from tan fur-lined boots. . . ."

Actually, it was just that old WAC uniform, which, according to Clare, smelled anything but exotical by that time. But it must be admitted that she filled it better than most WACs.

The Congressional Committee's army transport plane with bucket seats took off on November 20, for London, which was under constant bombardment by buzz bombs and the terrible new V-2 rockets.

In England, while the rest of the committee were being briefed at an air corps field, Clare had a ride in a Flying Fortress "on a routine mission." In France she met General Eisenhower at his headquarters in Versailles and with the committee visited General Patton's Third Army in the frozen mud of the Saar Valley. While the other committeemen were being briefed on the military situation, Clare felt it her duty to visit the forward hospitals, where the wounded men lay limp or twisting with the pain of their terrible, fresh wounds. It was a heart-wringing experience which took more courage than facing bombs or artillery fire.

After that it was a relief to go to the very front lines and look through the trench periscope at the somber, gutted, rain-drowned land that was still Nazidom. When an artillery colonel offered to let her fire a 155-mm. howitzer, she pulled the lanyard with a will; and the crash of the great gun woke echos of savage satisfaction in her heart.

It was inevitable that she should get along fine with Third Army's prickly commander, General George S. Patton, Jr. They had just the same all-out, neck-or-nothing will to victory, and the same ruthless, logical type of mind that cuts straight through the layers of soft thinking to the hard realities of what must be done.

After their return to Paris, the committee flew to Rome over the battlefields and ruined villages of Italy. From the air Clare said, "The earth looks as though it had a hideous case of smallpox with its shell holes and the swollen, muddy craters made by bombs."

In Rome, Clare put on her black suit and went with the committee to a reception given by American Ambassador Alexander C. Kirk, where she met Premier Bonomi of liberated Italy. The feminist in her got the better of diplomacy, and she asked point-blank, "Are you going to give the vote to Italian women?"

"But, yes," said the Prime Minister politely.

Clare's eyes bored through him like blue augurs. "Will you promise me that, so I can tell American women?"

"Yes, I will promise," said Bonomi. And they shook hands on it, American-style.

Exactly seven weeks later Italian women were able to vote for the first time in history.

The committee did the routine inspection chores and then hurriedly emplaned for Christmas at home. Clare asked if she might stay on and spend Christmas with the troops.

The Italian front was held by the British Eighth Army and the American Fifth Army. The latter was perhaps the toughest and bitterest of American armies. They had been fighting, some of them, for over two years in Africa and Sicily, and slogging over the whole mountain-crossed Italian peninsula. They were tough because they had to be; and bitter because they considered themselves the Forgotten Army, while the American press wrote of Patton's brilliant victories in France and called Italy "a secondary front."

On the day before Christmas, Clare went up to the front lines in the Apennine Mountains between Florence and Bologna. The jeep she rode in slid and bucked over the icy mountain roads while the wind whipped the dry, stinging snow in her face, and the temperature dropped to twenty-five degrees. That night she slept in a pup tent in the snow and the next day toured the front lines, looking especially for men from Connecticut who wanted to send messages home.

She described it two days later in a broadcast from Rome: "All along the roads was white loveliness. . . . The snow mercifully hid the bomb rubble and the ruin of towns . . . and in every valley on the road there were the myriads of pitch-black tents of our army, with their rotund icicles like Christmas trees, with short gusts of black smoke puffing from stove pipes. . . ."

In one of the villages the men had rigged up a Christmas tree, "trimmed with the likes of which have never been seen on any American tree. Yet there was all there was to be found in the way of color and festoon. The tree was trimmed with an old pack of playing cards and streamered with a roll of bathroom paper. And there were a few Italian children standing admiringly about it, learning to say 'Merry Christmas!' from the GIs. . . ."

Nearer the front there was no symbol of Christmas at all, "but we never came, nor do I think we ever will, even in the foxholes, to a man who had forgotten that this was Christmastide . . ."

Most impressive of all to Clare were the Christmas services being held in the fields behind the front with thousands of soldiers kneeling reverently in the snow.

Back in Rome, Clare put on her black suit again and went for an audience with Pope Pius XII. The Holy Father gave her leave to speak what was in her mind, and she told him that women had less faith than men in keeping the peace by military might, and that, "We believe that justice, charity, and love must be the foundations of true peace."

After the audience she went to see how the Vatican was caring for hundreds of refugees, Protestant and Jewish as well as Catholic, to whom the Pope had given sanctuary and succor. Then she fell in love. His name was Augusto, and he seemed to be about eight years old, a very gaunt and dirty golden-haired cherub such as Raphael never painted. She watched him eat his breakfast—a hunk of bread washed down by water—there was no milk to be had. She went back to her room at the luxurious Excelsior Hotel, and she could not stop thinking about him.

Finally she made up her mind. "We can't help them all," she rationalized, "but if each of us helped one, that would, at least, be something." So she went back to the Vatican and got Augusto and brought him back to her hotel room. She gave him a bath, which he thought was wonderful, scrubbing him until the dirt of years peeled gradually off. Then she pulled her rank and ordered an American army doctor to come over and give him a shot of the then-rare drug, penicillin, to cure his dreadful cough. Finally she put him to sleep in her own bed, and rolled up on a sofa.

The next day she brought him a complete outfit of clothes and arranged that when she left Rome he was to be educated in a boys' school supervised by priests until he was eighteen. Years later, when she was again in Italy with Buff Cobb, the latter recalls that they were invited one day to lunch at the famous Colonna Castle outside of Rome. Clare said, "No. I have a more important engagement."

Buff was both irritated and mystified as they drove through the narrow alleys of the old city. Finally they came to the school. Augusto was waiting by the gate. When he saw Clare, he flung himself on her, exclaiming, "My beautiful American mother!"

Clare got home in time to spend New Year's Day with Harry in Connecticut. Then she went on to Washington for the opening of Congress. Almost the first person she saw at the Wardman Park Hotel, where she lived, was Olive Clapper.

"What's the gossip?" Clare asked her newspaper friend. "Who am I supposed to be in love with now?"

"Plenty," said Olive grimly. "You're supposed to have had a romance with Mark Clark. Then an American pilot is mentioned, and some Englishman in the diplomatic service. What's the truth?"

"I'll tell you the awful truth," said Clare rapturously. "I'm in love with the whole Fifth Army!"

At her first news conference on her return, Clare made a plea that we send more food to the Italians. "[They are] dying by the thousands from cold and hunger," she said, "and we have failed miserably to keep our pre-election promise to supply them with 300 grams of food a day."

She also announced her intention to reintroduce her bill to draft 4Fs into a work corps, which Democrat James Byrnes, Director of War Mobilization, had suddenly announced was a good idea.

On January 10, as she was leaving for Mepkin to observe the anniversary of Ann's death, she received word that David Boothe had been seriously wounded in the Philippine theater. However, later reports announced that he would recover.

Clare came back to Washington to find that her Democratic colleagues were trying to purge her from the Military Affairs Committee. Some of them were frankly "mad as all get-out" because the reporters in Europe had given her more space than they, and had even—horrendous error—referred to "the Luce Committee." But Joe Martin stood by her stoutly, and she kept her place.

Democratic Senator Francis Maloney of Connecticut died on January 16, 1945. Strong pressures were put on Governor Raymond E. Baldwin to nominate Clare Luce as the Republican candidate to succeed him; but Clare said, "No," because that would mean another bitter campaign.

Two days later she made her report to the House on her Italian trip. In a long speech, informed by firsthand knowledge and passionate conviction, she traced the hard history of the "forgotten" Fifth Army; told of their needs as expressed by hundreds of GIs with whom she had talked, and made a heartfelt plea for a system of fixed-tours duty, such as the air corps had, for infantrymen. "There is no more heroic army . . . than the Fifth Army," she concluded, "and today, despite all they have endured and are yet to endure, General Truscot says—'Their tails are up!' Their morale is good. . . .

"We have won great victories—they have managed it. We will win a great peace—they have purchased it."

Clare was in Washington just two months before she was unexpectedly called overseas again. During that time she came out for universal military training, backed the "Work or Jail" act to mobilize manpower, and combated the Yalta pact on Poland as violating the Atlantic Charter. On March 5, at the special invitation of her old friend from Burma, Field Marshal Sir Harold Alexander, now commanding Allied Forces in the Mediterranean theater, she flew again to Italy.

Clare did not want to go. To face so soon again the tremendous strain and the real hardships of such service was asking more than she felt her physical strength could bear. But she did not hesitate a split second.

The field marshal, who had noted the superb job she had done in bringing the story of Fifth Army back to the American people, had invited her to get some good publicity for his beloved Eighth Army and to tell the story of British-American cooperation, which was far closer in Italy than on the Western Front. Knowing this, Clare volunteered to write a series of articles for the combined American press.

Alexander was not disappointed. Clare's sparkling dispatches, which alternated between the human story and brilliant evaluations of military strategy, were played up by newspapers all over America. The Italian fighting began to emerge from the penumbra of silence cast by the more dramatic events in Germany.

To get her stories, Clare drove herself so hard that only the constitution of a horse, with which she credits herself, could have stood it. She appeared on every part of the Italian front and visited troops of every nationality in that curiously polyglot army that was fighting so desperately in that "secondary" battle.

Perhaps the thing that touched her most was her visit to the barracks of the Polish Women's 316th Transportation Company. These two hundred and thirty-two women drove three-ton supply trucks up to the lines. "I call them women," Clare wrote, "but most of them were girls in their teens."

She asked the matron in charge, Madame Gylinska, why almost all the camp cots in those long, bleak wooden buildings were decorated with either a small pillow or a doll. "The girls must have something to cuddle at night," Madame Gylinska replied.

Clare burst into tears.

But she was dry-eyed and burning on a more awful occasion. By the logic of her do-or-die nature she could spare herself nothing. So when Patton's Third Army captured the Nazi charnel house of Buchenwald, Clare was early on the scene. When she came into the dreadful camp, the wagons with shriveled bodies stacked like firewood were still standing before the crematorium. Inside, skeletonized prisoners too weak to move were lying on mattresses on the floor, or in their shelflike tiers of bunks. A prisoner-guide took her to the basement where in a white-walled room thousands of men had been hanged from iron hooks. She saw the furnaces, still half choked with charred bones. All this she wrote and broadcasted to America.

Then she flew home. In Miami someone handed her a newspaper that said Hitler had killed himself, and she said, "Golly! Then it's true! It's like the end of a nightmare."

In Washington she made a speech demanding that if Germany were not occupied after the war, it should be divided up into small states, as it had been before Bismarck. If the tone was a little hysterical and her logic knocked cockeyed, who can wonder?

There is no space to write of Clare Luce's multiple services during her last term in Congress. She continued constantly to hold to her beliefs, which were neither rigidly conservative nor even strict Republican doctrine. One of the many things she proposed was a bill to authorize a survey of practical experiences in profit-sharing by industrial concerns, and another to set up a bureau in the Department of Labor to insure that every worker would receive equal pay for equal work without regard to race, creed, or color.

Clare continued to work steadily for American cooperation with other nations for peace and to liberalize the immigration laws to permit the entry of people of all races, and especially to take care of refugees from Europe, displaced by either Nazi or Russian totalitarianism.

After the atomic bomb ended the war in the Pacific, she helped as a member of the Military Affairs Committee, to write the Atomic Energy Act, and fought successfully to keep the bomb under civilian rather than military control. She became a member of the Joint Committee for the Control of Atomic Energy.

Most consistent of all was her violent opposition to communism. Long before Winston Churchill made his Iron Curtain speech warning against Communist plans for world conquest, Clare had told the same story, not once but fifty times. In addition to her regular congressional office, she had a spare office in the Old House Office building, presided over by Blair Taylor, where anti-Communists from all Russia's satellite countries were welcomed and helped and, above all, listened to.

In the days before Japan fell, Syngman Rhee often came to her for comfort and advice. "He was a pathetic figure," says Morano.

Indeed, virtually every one of the people exiled by communism came to Clare for help. One of her last acts as congresswoman was to put in the *Congressional Record* a series of speeches entitled, "Leaning Over Backward" and "Not Unduly Exacting," exposing Communist methods and American appeasements in Austria, Poland, Hungary, Yugoslavia, etc. These are but a few of her services in the 79th Congress.

On January 30, 1946, Clare announced that she would not run again for Congress, and added mysteriously, "My good and sufficient reasons for this decision will be abundantly clear in time."

CHAPTER EIGHTEEN

"ON THIS ROCK"

THE BLINDING FLASH THAT KILLED A HUNDRED THOUSAND PEOPLE in a hundred thousandth of a second and ended the Japanese war, seemed to scorch Clare's soul. The atomic bomb was so hideous an instrument for man's inhumanity to man that she thought it made the future of the human race appear dark, even quite improbable. In the face of such a potential of destruction, her puny efforts to alleviate human suffering and try to make a better world seemed to her ridiculous.

In addition, these efforts had been frustrated in every direction. Helplessly she had watched what she considered the cynical jettisoning at Yalta and Potsdam of the great ideals for which the war had been fought—Poles, Chinese, and millions of other people, who had put their faith in America, sold down the Russian river. It seemed to her that we had abandoned principle for power politics—not very intelligent power politics. The Russians had bamboozled us into trading our birthright of idealism for a very odoriferous mess of idealogical pottage.

Throughout the past years Clare had been tremendously preoccupied by the thought of death, not only because of her personal bereavements but by reason of the horrors she had seen from Burma to Buchenwald. In *The Real Reason* she wrote: "Death by accident, Death by design. Death by bomb, bullet and torture. Death by fire and cold and disease and famine. . . .

"The awful, sickening abundance of it at last made the Great

Question inescapable: What was the meaning of Death?" The bomb was death on a global scale.

As she watched the things so many men had died for being traded away, and as she noted what she called, "the growing malaise in America about the peace," she could find no meaning in death. And if there were none, and if death were only the inglorious end of everything, then life had no meaning either.

During the war her fervent patriotism had kept her going—the will to victory, the fight for another chance to remold the world and do it better, had been enough. But the chance to do so that had been won at so great a cost was being frittered away. And nobody seemed to care very much. Logic asked, then why should she? Finding no answer, the mainspring of her spirit came unwound, and all the sorrow she had held at bay by furious activity and her sense of accomplishment flooded back to drown her soul. Now, when she thought of death it was of the gift of oblivion; and as a person in pain too great to be borne will seize the ether cone, so, many times, she longed for death. And sometimes considered means to embrace it.

One night in September, 1945, when Clare was alone in her room at the Waldorf in New York, she reached the bottom of the black shaft of despair. All her personal frustration, bitterness, and sorrow, combined with her disillusionment and hopelessness, her horror of and pity for all humanity, converged upon her in a flood-tide of dolor. She, who had never lost her nerve in physical danger, was terrified that she was losing her mind. She summoned all the power and logic of that fine instrument of which she had always been far more proud than of her beauty. It failed her utterly. Then she knelt beside her bed and prayed—a little amateurishly, for she was not used to praying, but fervently for help.

When she got up from her knees she noticed an unopened letter lying on her table. It was, she saw, from Father Edward Wiatrak, a Jesuit priest who had first written to her years ago about a speech she had made for Madame Chiang's war orphans. She had answered it, and he had written again and then again when Ann had died, and often after that. Sometimes she answered him, more often she did not. And lately she had become a trifle bored with

Father Wiatrak's little homilies and Latin tags. But she opened the letter.

Father Wiatrak almost seemed to have had a prevision of her travail. For in his letter he asked if she had ever read the *Confessions of St. Augustine,* and described how the saint had suddenly, on a beautiful day, burst into violent weeping in overwhelming grief at his own shortcomings and the vileness of the world. And how he had heard a child's voice saying, "Take and read." Father Wiatrak wrote that he was praying for Clare.

She searched the room for a Bible, but the Gideon Society's offering had long since been removed. So she turned to the telephone book and looked up the Jesuit Mission House from which Father Wiatrak's letter was addressed. Though it was two o'clock in the morning, she called the number.

The very sleepy novice who answered her said, "I will call the father." While she waited, Clare suddenly felt foolish, and all the prejudice against "Catholic bigotry" rose in her mind. She hung up the receiver. Then she picked it up again before the connection was broken.

Father Wiatrak's voice sounded strong and serene, and not at all surprised. When Clare told him that she was in great mental trouble, he answered, "We know. This is the call we have been praying for."

"When may I see you, Father?" Clare asked.

Wiatrak answered, "We are not the one you should see; we are only a simple priest. You must see Monsignor Fulton Sheen, who also lives in Washington. Your trouble is really spiritual, not mental. We will write to him, and he will talk with you. Now have a good sleep—and God bless you!"

It seemed to Clare that she felt God do so. She knelt to thank Him and then, like an obedient child, fell asleep.

A few days later Monsignor Sheen telephoned Clare in Washington and invited her to have dinner with him in the little house he shared with two other priests, who were, like him, teaching at the Catholic University. There she met him for the first time: a remarkable man, lean and quick in his movements, with deep-set, glowing, ever-changing eyes, like small gray seas of infinite depth.

The sense of his dedication to God informed his person, but did not overpower her, for he was saved from austerity by his quality of warm humaneness, and by his wit. If you could imagine Saint Patrick with the logical brain of Socrates, plus a sense of humor, you would have Monsignor—now Bishop—Fulton J. Sheen.

That first night Clare, supercharged with theological excitement, began to talk about it as they sat down to dinner. With his engaging grin Monsignor Sheen said, "Let us not talk religion at the dinner table."

After the meal they went to the monsignor's library-office, and there he took firm direction of the proceedings. "We cannot cover the whole subject of religion in an evening," he said. "Therefore, in order that our discussion may be decorous and orderly, let us talk about one subject tonight—we can talk about the others next time we meet.

"First we will consider the existence of God. I should like to talk for fifteen minutes without interruption. After that you may say anything you please, and ask as many questions as you like, for two or three hours, or all night if you wish."

When Bishop Sheen described this interview, he smiled and said, "Of course I was a fool to think I could talk to Clare for fifteen minutes without being interrupted."

The priest began by pointing out the philosophical necessity of finding a First Cause for the universe. It could not have leaped out of nothing by accident, he said; and since the universe is finite, and therefore has been created, we must look for an infinite, a transcendent Power as its Creator. "Since existence does not belong to things by their own nature, the reason for existence must be sought extrinsically and transcendently to the things themselves . . . They are caused by one First Being, Who possesses being most perfectly. This Being is called God."

But Monsignor Sheen said that God is also immanent in this world. "God is in the universe but not shut up in it; God is outside the universe but not excluded from it." In other words He did not create the universe and then wash his hands of it. Rather, he is immanent in the world by His wisdom, by His goodness, and by His power.

Monsignor Sheen talked first of the divine order of things. God is present in things as the Wisdom which planned them, and His Wisdom participating in things explains our own intelligibility. "God made things intelligently. We know, not because we invent, but because we discover—discover the Wisdom of God hidden in the things which he made."

God is also immanent in the universe because of His Goodness, Monsignor Sheen explained. He has placed in all beings a desire to strive for their own perfection and thus to share in some way His own perfect Goodness and Love. "We are attracted to God by the immanent gravitational pull of Goodness and Love."

It was at this point that Clare erupted. She jumped up and shook her finger under Monsignor Sheen's nose. "If God is good," she cried, "why did he take my Ann?"

Very gently the priest answered her, "Perhaps it was in order that you might become a believer. Maybe your daughter is buying your faith with her life."

Bishop Sheen believes that "This was the turning point."

Many non-Catholics think that Clare Luce's conversion to Catholicism was an emotional thing—a frantic leap of faith. This is not true. "We do not allow a leap of faith," Bishop Sheen says. "Before anything else there must be conviction. You cannot start with faith. It is like credit, there must be a reason for giving it—a motive for accepting the truth.

"In the Catholic Church no one is ever told, 'You must believe this.' If they do not believe, it may be because we do not explain it right. Like the woman to whom I tried to explain the mystery of the Holy Trinity. She said she understood it perfectly. 'If you do,' I answered, 'then I have not explained it right.'

"For the existence of God is susceptible of proof; but the Trinity is a mystic conception that must be taken on faith.

"Instruction in religion is like teaching any other subject—algebra, Latin, philosophy. You take nothing for granted. For example, you do not say, 'Of course you believe in God.' You prove the existence of God. It is systematic; nothing is left out."

Many people believe they have a message from God, the bishop says. But they must show their *bona-fides* before we can accept them. This is done by three things: 1. Prophecy, 2. Miracles,

3. Consonance of doctrine with the natural aspirations of the human heart.

1. Of all the great religious leaders—Buddha, Lao-Tze, Mohammed, Christ, only Christ's coming was foretold. The bishop cited the many prophecies of His coming from the Old Testament. It was recorded in Persian and Babylonian history; that is why the Magi, who were Persians, came to Bethlehem.

2. "Miracles must be performed not just to excite wonder, but used as a seal or attestation of the *bona-fides* of the worker of them," says Bishop Sheen. "If you are from God the least you can do is to let me know you are coming. If General Motors sent an agent he would present his credentials. So God should have the power to prove He is the bearer of a message."

3. Finally, the Christian doctrine is clearly in accord with man's natural aspiration to be more perfect.

Reason, implemented by history, is the basis of the proof of these three arguments. They are known to churchman as the *Apologetics*.

After thus proving that it is logical to accept Christ as Authority, you are ready for faith. "But Faith, complete faith, comes as a gift from God."

Thus did Bishop Sheen prepare Clare's mind to accept faith. It was no easy task. Her first attitude, he says, "was that of the sophisticate." Her first question was, "Do you know about the Yin-Yang philosophy?"

Sheen, a professor of philosophy, knew far more about Taoist mystic doctrine than Clare did. So she began to respect his mind, and he learned to respect hers. "Clare has a brilliant mind," he says. "She is a wonderfully stimulating person to talk to. There is in logic a thing called sorites, a form of argument like a chain with something dangling at the end—a conclusion. Sometimes it is a tremendous conclusion. Clare used sorites better than any other person I ever met. There is no quality of bludgeon about her mind. It has the quality of a rapier and cuts like the sword of truth. Sometimes it was an almost intuitive flash of truth. Like a sword, her mind cuts away all the merely incidental things that are not to the point.

"Our discussions were a battle of wits on a very high philosophical plane. She raised difficulties the like of which I have never known before, although my life has been devoted to giving instruction in the Church. *I believe I got more out of that course of instruction than Clare did.*"

One of their hottest arguments came the night Clare opened the discussion by saying, "I don't accept hell."

The bishop says, "Then she spoke for an hour straight, giving the most beautiful unfolding of the argument of the mercy of God I have ever heard."

Monsignor Sheen spent an hour and a half in his rebuttal. Using such arguments as he later wrote in his book *Preface to Religion,* he proved the existence of a personal devil—not a comic figure in red with a pitchfork, but Lucifer the fallen angel; and of the existence of hell, not because God wills suffering but because having bestowed on His creatures the gift of free will, His justice allows them to create their own hell if they refuse His gift of Love. "Hell is loneliness," he said. "Because we turn away from God we feel the absence of His Love, His Beauty, His Truth—and that is called the pain of loss. Because we turn to creatures and pervert them to our sinful purpose, we are punished in some way by the creatures we abused. Hellfire is one of the aspects of this sense of pain. . . .

"The lost souls could have loved God freely, but they chose to rebel against that love, and so came under Divine Justice. Justice forces them to *love* God, that is, to submit to the Divine Order; but to be forced to love is the very negation of love. It is hell!

"You ask, 'How can God be so wrathful as to sentence souls to hell?' Remember that God does not sentence us to hell as much as we sentence ourselves. When the cage is opened, the bird flies out to that which it loved; when our body dies, we fly out either to an eternity of love of God or to a hatred of God . . .

"God is a loving Father indeed, and He accepts us back as He did the Prodigal, but only on condition that we are repentant.

"Hell is at the foot of the Hill of Calvary; and no one of us can go down to hell without first passing over the Hill where there is a God-man with arms outstretched to embrace, head bent to kiss, and heart open to love."

When Monsignor Sheen concluded his long, brilliant exposition of which these sentences are but a shadowy outline, Clare threw up her arms. "Oh, God," she said, "what a protagonist You have in this man!"

Clare's course of instruction lasted approximately five months. It was the longest Bishop Sheen has ever given—usually from thirty to fifty hours are sufficient. During it, many of Clare's friends argued against taking such a step. Among them was Buff Cobb, who came frequently to the Wardman Park to beg and argue against Catholicism. Later Buff took instructions from Bishop Sheen, and Clare was her godmother when Buff joined the Church.

Many people wonder how so ardent a Presbyterian as Clare's husband felt about her conversion. Harry Luce was devout, but he was no bigot. He was glad that his wife had come to believe in God, even though she had taken a different course than he. He often goes to mass with her, though this does not imply that he is wavering. On this subject he once said, "Of course Clare would like me to join her Church. But," he added, smiling, "I have what is known as 'the Presbyterian's invincible ignorance.' "

There is no question that Clare's conversion was the result of intellectual conviction. Her instructor's lucid arguments brought her to agree with him "That we [the Church] are the great defenders of reason—reason and history combined." On the acceptance of Divine Authority, Sheen says, "Everybody accepts some kind of authority. Most people accept an anonymous 'They.' Others accept Karl Marx. That's better. At least he's a person. We accept Christ, prolonged in the mystical body of His Church. There is the direct authority of Christ when he chose Peter as his Rock. Three times he asked, 'Lovest thou me?' When he was sure, he delegated the authority."

Clare herself wrote: "Upon careful examination Catholic doctrine seemed to be the solid, objective truth. And when I say the solid, objective truth I mean just that, and not . . . one of the best aspects of the truth."

With intellectual conviction came God's gift of faith. Of it she wrote in *The Real Reason*: "The glow of conviction certainly can only be formed in the fire of faith by the breath of God's grace, as one opens one's heart as well as one's mind to it. It is not that you abandon your reason at this point, but rather having gone as far as *your* reason will carry you, God, at your prayerful request, carries it into the realm of Faith. And Supernatural aid lifts and illumines earthly reason."

So, on February 16, 1946, Clare Luce was received into the Catholic Church. Monsignor Sheen performed the ceremony at Saint Patrick's Cathedral in New York. There were no more than half a dozen people present. Clare's devoted friend Dorothy Burns Holloran was her godmother in this simple ceremony which consisted first of baptism, as one baptizes a child, followed by her first communion and confirmation.

After Clare became a Catholic she was the object of constant attack for "her irrational act," both by friends and strangers. An amusing coincidence occurred one night when she was sitting next to Erich Remarque, author of *All Quiet on the Western Front.* Remarque challenged her by saying, "Do you really believe in the devil?"

"Oh yes," Clare answered.

"How can you?" Remarque pursued. "It is an absurd conception. What could the devil do if he did exist?"

"Well for one thing," Clare answered, "he could tempt me. Or he might do all sorts of things. Even cause a disturbance."

"How silly!" the novelist commented.

At that precise moment one of the waiter's tripped and dumped a complete baked Alaska down Remarque's neck.

"You see," laughed Clare.

Harder to bear than the gibes of strangers or the thousands of letters condemning her act—of course, there were more thousands approving it—was the real concern of many good friends, who felt that she was totally irrational and even traitorous to her Protestant upbringing. Her devoted secretary, Isabel Hill, was one of those who simply could not understand it. And one of her best friends talked as though Clare had chained herself in a dungeon to die of intellectual starvation.

The results were hardly as dire as these well-meaning people foresaw. For the first time in her life Clare felt serene. The tremendous nervous energy that had driven her to height after height was still there. But it was channeled now to a high purpose. No longer did she restlessly seek something, she knew not what. For she had found the things that she was seeking: a sure knowledge that her sins and inadequacies were forgiven, and the wonderful, warm sense that she had found the love she had always craved in the overflowing all-embracing, comforting, and inspiring love of God.

Recently one of her Protestant friends said, "Clare always had the capability of being great. There was her wonderful brain, her beauty, and her real desire to serve her country and all the peoples of the world. But there was something lacking. Her conversion to Catholicism has given her the humility, the gentleness and warmth, a love of individual people as opposed to a sense of duty to humanity. These were the things she needed to make her the really great woman she now is."

As to the quality and stanchness of her faith, let Bishop Sheen speak the last word: "Clare's motivation for doing good things is now quite different. Her spiritual Christian motivation is now apparent. There is something in Clare that no biographer could see unless he had undergone some similar transformation. You cannot realize the depth of her, the spectacular sublimity of her motivation, which I know about and which endures."

CHAPTER NINETEEN

ENERGETIC RELAXATION

CLARE'S "GOOD AND SUFFICIENT REASON" FOR RETIRING FROM politics was, of course, her conversion to the Catholic faith. She did not want there to be any thought of advantage to her politically in that decision. Since her district had a very large Catholic vote, some people might have said that she was seeking to influence them. This she would not risk. However, she did not slow down but rather intensified her activities. Right up to the last minute of her term she worked as though she were going to remain in Congress forever.

Those were the days of her most ardent fight against communism. She joined with Natalie Wales Latham, Russell Davenport, Anne O'Hare McCormick, Jim Farley, and others of all parties and faiths in founding "Common Cause," the first American organization to fight communism on a global scale. John Foster Dulles was their unofficial adviser. Mrs. Latham, now Lady Malcolm Douglas-Hamilton, says that "Clare's penetrating understanding of communism, her knowledge of American institutions and politics, and the dynamic thinking she gave to Common Cause were extraordinary."

As early as 1946 Common Cause established liaison with the mysterious NTS—the strongest anti-Communist underground in Russia. Here was where Clare's personal friendship with virtually all the more important exiles from Communist tyranny in Europe proved useful. Her spare office in the old Office Building became a sort of clearinghouse for information from Russia and her unwilling satellites.

At a Christmas party for Common Cause at the Waldorf Clare was unexpectedly called on to address a group of exiles. On the spur of the moment she roused them to new courage and hope by quoting "The Ballad of Sir Andrew Barton":

> "Fight on, my man," Sir Andrew says,
> "A little I'm hurt, but not yet slain.
> I'll but lie down and bleed a while
> And then I'll rise and fight again."

In 1949 she helped to bring all the heads of the governments-in-exile together to lay the groundwork for the Free Europe Committee.

An interesting light on her later activities is the fact that, under Clare's influence, Common Cause called for the return of Trieste to Italy as early as 1947.

While still in Congress, Clare also jumped into the fight against racial prejudice. In a speech at a Lincoln's Day banquet she so deftly dismembered that ardent champion of segregation, Senator Bilbo of Mississippi, that he hardly realized what had happened to him. And when the Daughters of the American Revolution refused to allow the Negro pianist Hazel Scott to play in Constitution Hall, Clare in a flaming fury resigned from the Greenwich Chapter and practically started a revolution in the DAR.

Long before her conversion Clare had proposed a resolution in Congress that she personally regards as one of the most important of her actions there. It asserted that, Congress reaffirms, "the faith of its founding fathers to the people of the United States, to all other governments, nations and peoples, namely: That the inalienable rights of man, among which are life, liberty and the pursuit of happiness, and his birth in equality are the endowment not of government or men, but of the Creator. . . .

"Our government relying on the divine protection of Providence shall continue to seek all national and international solutions in the belief that the only proper guide and sanction for the laws and actions of men are the laws and authority of God."

This simple restatement of a fundamental American belief

caused considerable confusion in Congress. Nobody quite knew
what to do with it. Finally it was decided to refer it to the Foreign
Relations Committee for decent burial. Clare wondered aloud in
the press if this was because Congress considered God a foreigner.

Clare's retirement from Congress in January, 1947, brought her
temporarily, to a more homey sort of life. Now there was time to
do many things that had been squeezed out by the press of politics.
There was time to write again, and time for homemaking, and,
above all, time for companionship with Harry.

Certainly during the years of their marriage Clare had changed
and grown from the bitter wit of *The Women* to her statesmanlike
preoccupation with world affairs and increasing gentleness in her
personal relations. This was in considerable measure due to her
husband's influence. Harry Luce was an extremely well-informed
man, understandably, with Time, Inc.'s great fact-gathering organization funneling their findings to him. Neither was he a small
thinker. Agree with him or not, one acknowledges that his opinions
are based both on knowledge of the facts and on a good-will-toward-
men interpretation of them. Clare frequently did not agree with
the gospel according to *Time*, but she respected her husband's intelligence and learned a lot from him.

Harry Luce, too, had changed for the better. When he married
Clare he was still an awkward, brusque young man, rushing up the
road to success, knocking people out of his way, not from ill will
but because, in his single-tracked concentration, he did not notice
them. The shyness he had brought with him as a youth from China
was partly responsible for his gruffness. At times it was so painful
that he would stutter badly. Olive Clapper describes an evening at
her house in Washington when Harry's stuttering reached a point
where everybody was dying to help him out. Only Clare sat as
though she noticed nothing, with her head turned expectantly
toward her husband, waiting interestedly, but without impatience,
for him to finish his sentence.

It was just the way to handle him. Clare's social ease, her skill
at mixing with people, and her bubbling sense of fun was not lost
on Harry Luce. By association he acquired an important attribute

of greatness: the ability to take it easy, which comes from self-assurance.

In the matter of homemaking the Luces did considerable re-arranging of their lives at this time. The proximity of a new airport in Greenwich forced them to sell "The House" which was right at the end of the take-off strip. They then bought their present place, Sugar Hill, at Ridgefield, Connecticut. With Gladys Freeman advising her, Clare proceeded to put the stamp of her own and Harry's personalities on the place.

As it now is, you approach Sugar Hill on a sandy gravel drive that winds and swoops for three quarters of a mile up a wooded hill. The house is squarish and slightly austere, built of very dark red bricks in a vaguely Georgian style. But to the south it is all open and sunny, facing putting-green lawns in a glade of young white birch trees. The tennis court and the swimming pool, with its brick bathhouse and terrace, are some distance up a hill. In it Clare taught all the children on the estate to swim. There are usually quite a lot of them, for not only does the gardener have a cottage, but there is a guest cottage which Clare invariably lends for the summer to some friend from New York who has not the money to take her children to the country.

Inside, the house is classically formal. You come into a small white foyer decorated with an alabaster bust of Clare on a pedestal. To the right is the big drawing room, designed around Jean Brockhurst's portrait of Clare in green, which hangs over the mantelpiece. The walls are of dark hunter's green and the room is furnished in an unexpected but pleasing blend of Empire tables and chairs, beautiful ancient Chinese pieces collected by Luce, and, as a catalyst, some fine Chinese Chippendale. On the floor is a superb Chinese rug in bold, brilliant colors.

The small library, with a bow of French windows facing the lawn, is furnished in comfortable modern style; but the Chinese motif comes through strongly again in the dining room, which has cream-colored walls. Around the spacious table stand authentic mandarin chairs, high-backed and stiff with the dark patina of age, with bright yellow cushions, they are fit thrones for sages. There are tall, intricately carved Chinese cabinets against the wall. This room is mainly for state occasions. The Luces love to eat outdoors, and do so whenever possible, either on the terrace or under a magnificent oak tree on the lawn.

Another move the Luces made at this time was to give up their apartment at the Waldorf and buy the triplex on the East River.

Finally, in 1949, Clare and Harry gave Mepkin, whose memories were too poignant, to the Trappist Fathers for a monastery. Ann and the first Ann Clare are now buried there. The "Lady Foundress," as the fathers call her, visits Mepkin every year on January 11.

Of course Clare did not stagnate or even relax very much after she left Congress. She began writing again and was in great demand as a lecturer. She particularly liked talking to college girls, and made great efforts to accept every invitation to do so. Sometimes the lecture dates led to very amusing experiences. She tells of the occasion on which she gave a very serious and—she hoped—inspiring talk at Rochester on what makes men and nations great: the quality of leadership. "When I walked out on the campus afterward," Clare says, "a lovely kid about eighteen years old came up to me. She was scared to death but determined. 'I want to ask you a very important question—*very* important,' she said. 'I hope you will tell me because your answer may change the whole course of my life.' "

Clare says, "I braced myself to give profound advice about writing, the theater, politics, or what-not. Then the girl got her question out: 'Would you tell me how to make the kind of contacts you have had throughout your life?' "

On another occasion the chairwoman of the reception committee introduced Clare with an exceedingly flowery speech ending with the remarkable statement: "And, of course, Mrs. Luce will always be remembered as the author of that immortal classic *Little Women.*"

Hoping that Louisa May Alcott would not mind too much, Clare ignored the whole thing and went into her speech. After it was over a wide-eyed young thing came up to her and said, "Mrs. Luce, I thought the author of *Little Women* would be older and grayer than you look."

Dead-pan, Clare answered, "I am."

On a trip to Europe they made in the autumn of 1949, Buff Cobb found that, though Clare was now emotionally serene, her internal dynamo was still running at maximum rpm's. Their plane bounced and jounced through storms all the way across the Atlantic, and they got no sleep at all. Despite this, the moment they landed at Lisbon they were swept into a whirl of engagements which Clare had made by cable and transatlantic telephone that ended with a state dinner at the embassy lasting until after midnight.

The next morning at six o'clock Clare hauled her friend out of bed for the long tourist trek by automobile to Tomar and Thadema. For once Time, Inc.'s, staff work was inefficient; their automobile was a miserable vehicle which limped so painfully over two-hundred-odd miles of dubious roads that they just reached the Lisbon airport in time to make their nine-o'clock plane to Rome.

Buff Cobb says that she seldom sleeps in planes, but that night she dropped right off. It seemed no more than a second before Clare was poking her: "Wake up! Wake up! I have just met the most fascinating man, a wonderful old monsignor. He knows everything and is very wise."

Buff says that the priest was indeed brilliant but that she was too tired to enjoy him. Just as she was getting to sleep again, Clare jabbed her once more: "Wake up! Wake up! I want you to talk with the pilot. He has a matrimonial problem, and we need your advice. Besides, he's going to let us sit in the control cabin when we land in Rome."

Clare seemed not to feel tired at all as they sat in the navigator's place behind the pilot and watched the Italian peninsula, no longer pitted and pocked by the scars of war, brighten in the dawn. Soon after sunrise they saw the rosy bubble of Saint Peter's Dome. The pilot put his plane into a left bank, and they wheeled around the circumference of Rome almost over Emperor Aurelian's great wall. Underneath them the familiar rainbow-fountained squares and the ancient buildings spun like a huge diorama. The Campidoglio on its hilltop, the Forum, the broken arches of Caesar's Palace, and the Colosseum, rose-yellow in the rosy light. Icy white were the marble colonnades of Victor Emanuel, and then the area of parks and gardens, modern apartment houses, and the great historic villas under their stately trees: Villa Torlonia, Villa Taverna, where American Ambassador Jimmy Dunn lived; the Borghese and the Medici. Then around again, past the fat, round column of Castello Saint Angelo with its angel trumpeting the sunrise; and the great gleaming Dome, with Bernini's colonnades making geometrical patterns of shadow on the square. Three times they circled the city, lying within a bight of the looping Tiber. Never before had Clare felt the wonder of Rome so sharply.

As soon as they landed, Clare took Buff to mass in an ancient church where there were no pews and only the worn, uneven stones to kneel upon. When mass was over, Buff found she was so fatigued that she could not rise from her knees. Somehow Clare hoisted her to her feet, and they reached the Excelsior, where Buff fell into bed, saying, "Clare, if you wake me up, I'll slit your throat."

Despite that dire threat Clare was shaking her again in the late afternoon. "Wake up! Wake up! We're going to a most interesting dinner."

Buff says, "Never once did Clare stop. She had that list of engagements made by telephone. Every waking moment was taken up, and there were mighty few sleeping ones."

One of their engagements was a private audience with Pope Pius XII at gray, old Castel Gondolfo in the country south of Rome. With the Papal Guards in the multicolored baggy-trousered uniforms of Michelangelo; and the crimson vestments of the cardinals in attendance, the scene was wholly medieval; but the Holy Father was anything but archaic in his thinking, which was based on an expert's knowledge of European diplomacy. For the most part the talk was on the problems of world peace, but at the end Clare irrepressibly asked, "What do you do for fun?"

The Pope smiled broadly. "Well," he said, "I have my little canary, who sits on my shoulder and sings while I'm eating."

They paid a visit to Augusto at his school. He wanted a new bicycle, which went to him forthwith. The fathers told Clare that the boy's intelligence tests were only medium but that he had a gift for machine work. She arranged to have him trained as a mechanic, planning to bring him to America and set him up with a service station when he grew old enough.

From Rome the two friends motored to Florence, stopping at some of the hill towns. On the way Clare propounded one of her favorite Socratic questions. "Buffy, if you were stranded in a really desolate place like Siberia or Point Barrow, and were thrown in on yourself, what would you do?"

Buff thought it over and answered practically, "I guess I'd learn to cook; it always comes in handy."

"I'd learn Greek," said Clare.

"Why?"

"Because Harry says that no one can think clearly unless he knows Greek."

Buff giggled. "Clare, if you thought any more clearly you'd be incandescent."

In Florence they went to the Uffizi, where Buff, an old hand, took command. "There's a lot of junk here, and we haven't much time," she said. "We'll head straight for the gallery where they hang the primitives."

The lovely pictures, touchingly stiff and archaic, their golds and blues and deep wine reds glowing as brilliantly as though they had been painted yesterday, moved Clare to intense happiness. But Buff could not enjoy them. A small, dark man in corduroy pants was following them around. "Clare looked awfully expensive with lots of diamonds and a light mink coat," Buff says, "and I was worried."

Presently the man spoke to them. Buff froze, but Clare, "who is a real adventurer," began a conversation. "Have you seen the Botticelli Room?" the man asked.

Clare had not and accepted his offer to guide them. He talked brilliantly about the pictures, and Clare finally told him who she was and where she was staying.

As soon as they were alone, Buff burst out, "Clare, I could slap you! That was a stupid thing to do. How do you know he won't follow us and rob us, or else break into our hotel room?"

"Anybody who loves beautiful pictures as much as he does can't be bad," Clare said.

Buff snorted that it had nothing to do with the case, and acidly recalled a number of blackhearted historical characters who loved beautiful pictures.

The end of the story came six months later when Clare and Harry went on a trip to Mexico. The President of the republic sent a car to meet them at the airport. A brilliantly uniformed aide swung back the limousine's door, emblazoned with the presidential arms. Out of it stepped the small dark man from the Uffizi.

CHAPTER TWENTY

THEY LIKED IKE

ODDLY ENOUGH, CLARE'S FINEST PIECE OF WRITING DURING HER retiring era was never printed. It was not meant to be, for it was a motion picture.

In the winter of 1947-48 Darryl Zanuck of Twentieth Century-Fox engaged her to write the screen play of *The Screwtape Letters* by C. S. Lewis. Screwtape is, of course, the devil, and Zanuck must have figured that Clare would do a job on him.

However, the Mogul of Moviedom was doomed to disappointment. Clare did not pull it off. She could not concentrate, nor would the story live or words flow. It was a dismal failure, and Clare finally threw up her hands. "The devil undoubtedly messed it up," she said. "He doesn't like publicity; it spoils his plans."

But she had another and finer inspiration. In the little town of Bethlehem in Litchfield County, Connecticut, the previous summer, she had met the Reverend Mother Benedict Duss and Donna Mary Aline Trilles de Warren, two Benedictine nuns who had come from France with a call to found an abbey in America. They had no money and no influential friends, but they did have faith, courage, and a sense of humor. Starting appropriately in a stable, by their very goodness and simplicity, they prevailed on the cantankerous Connecticut Yankees to donate land, money, and personal labor to their undertaking. When Clare was in Bethlehem the abbey had become an accomplished fact.

Clare conceived the idea of writing a fictional account of their adventures for the screen. When she told her story to Darryl

Zanuck, he was so enchanted by the idea that he said, "Don't bother to submit a story line, go right ahead with the script."

Come to the Stable was the result. Clare wrote it with a combination of deep religious feeling and high comedy. The adventures of her two fictional nuns, played by Loretta Young and Celeste Holm, rattling down to New York in a borrowed jeep to interview the racketeer who owned their stable were hilarious.

Clare went back to Hollywood to attend to the casting. When she proposed the part of Sister Margaret to her friend Loretta Young, the latter is said to have exclaimed incredulously: "Me, a nun!"

Come to the Stable was nominated for an Academy Award in 1949. Though it did not win an Oscar, it was a tremendous hit. Clare gave all the money she made out of it to the Regina Laudis Monastery of Bethlehem.

Greater love hath no man than to give up a good secretary to a friend. This is what Bishop Sheen did for Clare in June, 1948. When Isabel Hill finally left her after twelve years of faithful service, the bishop sent her Dorothy Farmer; and his final injunction to her was, "Take good care of Clare." Oddly enough, the Pope used exactly the same words to Dorothy when she had a private audience with him in 1950.

Clare went West on a lecture tour with Dorothy in 1949. A new play was boiling in her brain, and after a lecture at Aspen, Colorado, she and Dorothy holed up in the Brown Palace Hotel in Denver where Clare wrote *Love Is a Verb,* in forty-eight hours of solid work.

They then went on to Hollywood, where Clare talked with Howard Hughes about an idea for a movie to be called *Pilate's Wife.* It was based on the fact that Claudia, the wife of Pontius Pilate, had tried to persuade her husband against the crucifixion. In the screen play Clare made her the first Christian convert.

Hughes was delighted with the idea, and Clare went to Hollywood again in 1951 to work on the script. She usually stayed at the Beverly Hills Hotel, but this time she took a pretty modern house in Benedict Canyon. It was, however, strictly for work and not for play. Dorothy Farmer describes a typical day as follows: "Betty Stewart of RKO would arrive at nine-thirty in the morning. First we'd type up a draft of the stuff Clare had written the night before. Meanwhile, Clare would be having her breakfast in bed and writing at the same time. She would often redo a scene five or six times. Later in the morning the three of us worked as a team, writing, discussing, rewriting. With time out for a quick bite of lunch, we'd keep on until dinnertime, which was at eight o'clock. After dinner we'd start again. Sometimes we'd work on the play, or talk about it, until late at night. Then Betty and I would tuck Clare into bed and tell her to get some sleep. But every morning there would be a big batch of new stuff she had written during the night."

On Valentine's Day Dorothy and Betty gave the Boss, as Dorothy always calls her, a parakeet named Philo. "We had a lot of fun with that bird," Dorothy says. "The Boss could always stop right in the middle of serious work, for ten minutes of hilarity, and go on refreshed. She finished the shooting script in five weeks."

This time schedule included several interruptions. One was the big social event of Clare's Beverly Hills season, a fifteenth birthday party for Mimi Hutson, which Clare gave in the lavish Hollywood manner, with children of the stars present, and generally high-jinks in Benedict Canyon.

The final break in their routine occurred when Dorothy woke one morning at five o'clock to find the house rocking and lurching like the Deadwood coach on a downhill run. She rushed into Clare's room and demanded, "Are you going to sleep, through an earthquake?"

Clare woke, instantly alert, and, as usual when in doubt, telephoned Harry in Ridgefield. It was eight o'clock in Connecticut and he was just starting for New York. "We're having a bad earthquake, Harry," Clare said.

Absent-mindedly he answered, "That's fine. Now go back to sleep, dear."

When he reached Time, Inc., and was greeted by the news that there really was a bad earthquake in California, Luce went wild. By that time it was pretty hard to get a call through, but Harry exerted the full force of prestige to demand a wire. His voice sounded satisfactorily overwrought as he asked, "Are you *sure* you're all right, Clare?"

Betty Stewart became Clare's great friend. Some time after the latter returned to New York, she got a sad little letter from Betty saying that she had cancer of the eye and that the doctor said it must come out. Clare went into what Dorothy describes as "a tizzy," telephoning several of the great eye doctors and cancer experts of the country to see if something could not be done, money no object. But even unlimited resources and all the knowledge in the world could not save Betty's eye.

On their next trip to Hollywood in 1952, Betty was back on the job, and they often worked until after midnight. One morning Clare said to Dorothy, "Do you realize how unkind we've been to Betty? Last night I tried writing with one eye covered. It was a terrible strain. We must slow up for her sake."

Less successful than her movies was Clare's next try at a play. *Child of the Morning* was the story of a fifteen-year-old girl who had a vocation to be a nun, and the difficulties she faced and overcame. It was written in Clare's wonderfully breezy mixture of religion and wit and delightfully played by Margaret O'Brien. Somehow it failed to click. After opening in Springfield, Massachusetts, and playing for two weeks in Boston to enthusiastic audiences and poor reviews, Clare withdrew it for revisions which were interrupted by the campaign to make Ike President in 1952 and the great events that followed.

Clare and many of her friends lost a sizable piece of their shirts when it folded. She had put up five thousand dollars; Producer John D. MacArthur twenty-two thousand five hundred dollars; Bernard Baruch five thousand dollars; Joe Martin five hundred dollars, and Bishop Sheen two thousand dollars. Ironically, this was the only play in which Clare herself ever invested money—or permitted her friends to do so—and the only one she ever wrote that did not make money.

It was on an earlier trip to the West coast that Clare decided on the perfect memorial for Ann. At first she had wanted to give Leland-Stanford a music room for her daughter, who loved music so much. Some difficulty arose, and Clare then proposed to endow a chair of philosophy. It was while this was being discussed that Kathleen Norris, the novelist, telephoned her to say that she had given the Newman Club her little house at Stanford, but they had no chapel. Would Clare consider giving one in memory of Ann?

Clare caught fire at the idea. Then came the discussion of what the chapel would be like. Clare, who believes in the validity and beauty of modern art and architecture, favored such a design. Father John Tierney, who headed the Newman Club, did not like the idea at all. Eventually Clare ordered two plans drawn. One was conventional, the other a brilliant architectural *tour de force* by André Girard.

At the final discussion with the authorities both plans were carefully studied. You could see that the priest was actually praying that the conventional design would be adopted, but Clare's enthusiasm for Girard's work prevailed, and it was decided to go ahead with that.

Now there is no greater enthusiast for his church than Father Tierney, who proudly tells everyone that it is the only modernistic Catholic chapel at any university in the country. And he has a right to be proud of it, for Girard, who is a master of modern technique with stained glass as well as religious painting, produced an exciting combination of modern design with medieval veneration. Writing of the chapel, Jacques Maritain, an authority on religious art, says: "What struck me first upon entering the mystery of this chapel was the all-pervading life and vividness; and, then, the mastery with which the frankness and the power of affirmation of color is tuned to the infinite delicacy and sweetness of the nuances of light.

"On your left, all along one of the sides of the chapel are the stations of the Cross, a series of large pictures which advance in tiers; for the wall is composed of oblique segments that overlap one another. . . . On your right are the windows—a continuum of light which constitutes the whole other side of the chapel . . . the fluid harmony of lines and the fineness, the tenderness of the hues and embroidery of light of which their glory is made. . . .

"Both in the stations of the Cross and in the windows one feels the rare and invaluable conjunction of genuine religious inspiration and genuine artistic mastery. . . ."

Clare first visited the Chapel of St. Ann in the summer of 1949, while it was being built. Afterward she went to the Newman Club where about twenty of the students were gathered. Clare smiled at them radiantly and simply said, "How wonderful you look. You all know why I am here. Any one of you could be just like my Ann."

Clare had retired from Congress, but she could not get out of politics. In the first place she was such a valuable asset to the Republican party that they would not leave her alone; and, second, she was filled with ideas and anxieties about the state of the world that she simply had to express. So, as she went about the country lecturing and gathering such honors as a Doctorate of Letters from Colby College; a Doctorate of Law, *honoris causa,* from Creighton University; and the Newman Club Award, she kept making "nonpolitical" speeches that were very political indeed.

One, however, was genuinely nonpolitical, and a very gracious gesture toward the wife of an old enemy. That was the speech she made at a dinner honoring Mrs. Franklin D. Roosevelt at the Waldorf. In her speech Clare said, "Mrs. Roosevelt has done more good deeds on a bigger scale, for a longer time than any woman who ever appeared on our public scene.

"No woman has ever so comforted the distressed, or so distressed the comfortable."

All of which was Clare's way of recognizing greathearted public service wherever it might be, and did not in the least mean that her opposition to the Democrats was softening.

When the Republicans asked her to address the National Convention of 1948 in Philadelphia, she came out with a razzle-dazzle attack in which, after somewhat prematurely describing President Truman as "a gone goose," she characterized the Democratic party as "less a party than a podge . . . mishmash of die-hard, warring factions.

"Take the extreme Right or Jim Crow Wing of the party," she continued, "led by lynch-loving Bourbons [it is] anti-Semitic, anti-Catholic, anti-foreign. In short, antediluvian. . . .

"Then there is the Left or Moscow Wing of the party. This is currently being master-minded by Stalin's Mortimer Snerd, Henry Wallace. . . ."

Finally she came to "the Center, or Pendergast Wing. This is run by the wampum and boodle boys, the same big city bosses who gave us Harry Truman in one of their more pixilated moments. . . ."

Certainly the razor tongue had not lost its edge.

But though she thoroughly enjoyed such forays into politics, they were in the nature of commando raids rather than a sustained come-back campaign. In 1950 she could have had the Republican nomination for United States Senator from Connecticut on a charger. Al Morano begged her: "Tell them you're a candidate." When she refused, emotional Al burst into tears.

However, 1952 was different. Ever since 1950 Clare had been shouting—and praying, too—that Eisenhower must be nominated, and Harry Luce had backed him with all he had, which was plenty. In the preconvention campaign she helped to lead Connecticut into Ike's column, and went to the Republican convention in Chicago as a delegate at large from her state.

At the convention she worked, with the fury of a woman possessed, on a twenty-hour-a-day schedule to promote Ike's cause, talking with every delegate she could collar, persuading with logic or cozening with a beautiful woman's wiles, as each case required.

After the triumphant climax she flew home to Ridgefield and rushed upstairs to bathe and change. Dorothy Holloran, to whom she had lent the cottage for the summer, was waiting for her in the library when she came down. "She had changed into a gingham dress and done her pale gold hair in two long braids," says Dorothy. "Though she had had virtually no sleep for a week, she looked as dewy as a Castle girl."

A few days after the convention Clare took off for Hollywood to revise the final script of *Pilate's Wife*. Al Morano came to her at the Beverly Hills Hotel when he arrived in Los Angeles with Eisenhower for the opening speech of the campaign. "You've got to come back, Sis," he said. "The death of Senator McMahon has thrown the Senate race wide open."

"What about John Lodge?" Clare asked.

"Look it, dear," Al said earnestly, "call him up. See what he's going to do. If he doesn't want it, you tell him you do."

Lodge told Clare to get into the race. Eisenhower, too, indicated that he wanted her to run. With Connecticut seesawing between the parties the Republicans needed a strong candidate. So Clare left *Pilate's Wife*—that lady is still patiently waiting—and flew home to fight for the senatorship she could have had by lifting her right eyebrow in 1950.

Some very peculiar things happened in Connecticut that summer, of which not the least strange was the working of John Lodge's mind. In a sense he was governor of Connecticut by courtesy of Clare, for she had persuaded Al Morano not to run for her vacant seat in 1946, and thrown her support to Lodge. His election to Congress had given him his first real start in politics, and he had risen rapidly to become governor of Connecticut in 1950.

The death of Senator Brien McMahon had made two senatorships available in 1952. Lodge could have settled the whole thing by appointing Clare to serve in McMahon's place until election. Instead he sweet-talked her into announcing her candidacy, and then appointed William A. Purtell. The truth was that Lodge had a hankering to be senator himself; but the fact that the Democratic lieutenant governor would succeed him if he resigned made it high treason to the Republican party to do so. What he wanted, according to the experts, was to get Clare and Prescott Bush into a fight for one of the nominations—Purtell was sure of the other—in the hope that the state convention would get deadlocked and turn to him.

Several times Clare said to him, "John, if you want it, I'll get out."

"No," said John. "Stay in."

Finally, when the pot was really boiling, he told Clare flatly that he would not support her for the nomination.

That put Clare behind the gubernatorial eight ball. She went to Hartford to fight an uphill battle. Harry Luce went with her, and Harry was fighting mad. He threw everything he had into the battle. Clare never gave up. She made a speech that for a moment seemed to sway the convention, and she spent the whole night at the Hotel Bond, going from smoky room to smoky room pleading with delegates.

It was no use. The machine politicians had decided on Bush, and Bush it was.

They all admitted Clare lost like a gentleman. When she finished her speech conceding the nomination to Bush by saying, "I know we all want to walk out of here as friends and comrades in a great crusade," the delegates gave her a roaring ovation that topped the applause for the winning candidate.

Harry Luce had the final word. As he stood beside his wife, a reporter asked him what he thought. "I'm proud of her today, as I always have been proud of her," he answered.

On the way back to the hotel he quirked his eyebrows at her and said, "Just think of all the money we saved."

It was Bernard Baruch who told Clare the story of how Claude Swanson after a political defeat said, "But I didn't lay down on that political ice. I got right up and began skating around."

"You're a little champ," Bernie added to Clare. "You'll never stay down."

And the very next day she was skating around. At the district convention in Bridgeport she helped Al Morano get his life's ambition, the Republican nomination for Congress. Then she went all out for Eisenhower. In seven weeks she raced all over the country making over a hundred speeches for the Republican candidate.

When the great night came, Clare was with the President-elect at the Commodore Hotel as the votes came in. And the fact that Prescott Bush was running far behind the national ticket did not exactly spoil her evening.

However, she really did not give it much thought. There were too many things to do now that after twenty desert years a Republican was President.

CHAPTER TWENTY-ONE

ROME

THE STORY OF CLARE'S APPOINTMENT AS AMBASSADOR TO ITALY has been told in Chapter One. The news of it began to get around when Clare sat with Ike and Mamie in the President's little pseudo-Colonial reviewing stand at the Inaugural Parade. Such marked attention must mean something.

That night at the Inaugural Ball Clare was so radiant with excitement that her enemies considered her radioactive. She wore a superb dress of pink satin with a bodice embroidered with glittering stones and a wide, cunningly draped skirt. Around her shoulders was a great raspberry-red stole that clashed with the color of her gown in the calculated dissonance of a Gershwin rhapsody.

Some days before, when the dress was delivered in New York, Clare had tried it on, as excited as a teen-ager with her first formal. Her mirror confirmed her highest hopes. Swaying with the exaggerated walk of a model, she went into the library to show it to her husband. He was so deep in work that he did not hear her come in.

"Look, Harry! How do you like this dress?"

Harry looked. "I like it," he said with great conviction. "It's always been my favorite dress."

Rumor was rife at the end of January. Little squibs even began to appear in the Italian papers, and Roman society shivered incredulously. On February 8 the news was official. Rome reeled as it had not since Lars Porsena of Clusium swore by the nine gods.

Ambassador Ellsworth Bunker, making his farewell official rounds in Rome, encountered a blast of criticism about Clare. He had made some friends among the aristocratic families who still clung to their gloomy cinquecento palaces. Now one of them gave a farewell cocktail party and all the guests ganged up on him.

"This is the greatest insult Italy has ever been offered," they babbled. "We are not Luxembourg or Lichtenstein but a great power, still. A woman! This they cannot do to us. You must do something! Tell the President Ike we are a proud people. Use your influence. Stop it somehow!" Even some members of the embassy joined the flap, startled and frightened by the idea of a Lady Boss.

Bunker tried to soothe all of them. "I can't do anything," he said, "and would not if I could. Mrs. Luce is a wonderful person with the interests of Italy at heart. She is, perhaps, the most brilliant woman in America."

"But a *woman!*" they groaned.

The Italian Foreign Office was in the wildest flap of all. How to deal with a woman? They pictured illogic piled upon caprice. Only wise old Alcide de Gasperi, President of the Council of State and Minister of Foreign Affairs, refused to panic. Sitting at the long cabinet table in the Palazzo Spade under a ceiling on which a sixteenth-century master had depicted Cupid sporting with the gods, he spoke calmly to his ministers. "Looked at properly, this appointment represents a great opportunity for us," he said. "I knew Mrs. Luce in Washington. She is a woman of the highest ability and understanding. I know I can work with her."

Then he added apparently inconsequentially, "I understand that the combined circulation of *Life, Time* and *Fortune* is now approximately ten million."

American reaction was hardly less turbulent. People had a persistent misconception about Clare Luce. As she says herself, "Every public figure becomes a myth. Once the myth gets going it feeds on itself. Some people like their myths, like Marlon Brando, who is reputed to have a terrible temper and is careful to make a lot of rows in public. I don't like mine. It got started in the early days and was built by other people. Part of it is that I have no women friends. This is nonsense. I have had many women friends, I've kept them from girlhood. Another part is that I talk too much. I really don't say very much, but I'm widely misquoted."

The Clare Luce myth was dusted off and held up to public view in all the papers. In addition, all the Roman arguments against a woman ambassador were brought out by people "who knew Italy." Finally, right in line with Clare's prophecy to Eisenhower, the Catholic question popped up. When the President sent her name to the Senate, Senator Olin D. Johnson of South Carolina arose to protest. He said that he had received many letters from Protestants who feared the influence of a Catholic—and a convert at that—in Rome. His objection produced no more than a slight delay. On March 2, 1953, the Senate unanimously confirmed Mrs. Luce's appointment as Ambassador to Italy.

When Clare had been in Italy a few weeks, she received a letter from Senator Johnson asking her to arrange a private audience with the Pope for some valued constituents. She took great pleasure in answering, "My dear Senator: This embassy has no official relations with the Vatican."

Nor has it any private ones. So scrupulous has Clare been to avoid criticism that she did not have a private audience with the Holy Father until July, 1955.

Although she took the oath on March 5 before Chief Justice Fred Vinson, with John Foster Dulles beaming at her, Clare did not start for Italy for nearly six weeks. She used the interval for intensive study of Italian affairs, political and economic. As she told the President in their final interview, she was convinced that the most important thing for the Italians was to settle the dispute between Yugoslavia and Italy over the great Adriatic port of Trieste, which was then divided into two zones: Zone A held by an Anglo-American Army and Zone B held by the Yugoslavs. Until Italy's historic claim to the city, which was in Zone A, was recognized, she believed that it would be impossible for any Italian government to function freely in the field of foreign affairs.

On April 14 Clare Luce sailed for Naples on the *Andrea Doria*. She chose the flagship of the Italian line rather than an American ship or plane as a compliment to the people of Italy. Harry Luce went along to see her through the first difficult days.

The voyage was serene. Aside from writing her arrival speech with the help of some Italians aboard, Clare got a complete rest—her last. There are pictures of her and Harry sitting tranquilly in deck chairs, and of Clare chattering with the bumboat men at Gibraltar like any tourist. Meanwhile the Italian pot was boiling.

The advent of Ambassador Luce brought on the wildest burst of personal publicity in the annals of the Italian press. Big headlines in all the papers of all the cities described each day of the voyage. The Italian picture magazines had a field day. The stories were mostly favorable though often erroneous.

The United States Information Service put out a biographical sketch of the new Ambassador, which ended with the almost frantic injunction:

> Will you kindly note for your files or morgue the correct spelling of her [Mrs. Luce's] name:
>
> | MRS. | CLARE | BOOTHE | LUCE |
> |------|-------|--------|------|
> | (Not Miss) | (No i) | (ends in e) | |
>
> When Mrs. Luce's name is incorrectly spelled she is sometimes wrongly identified as *Miss Claire Luce,* the professional stage and television actress.

In addition, Clare says, "I picked out my most schoolmarmish-looking picture for the official photograph."

Despite all this, one Italian picture magazine ran a photograph of Miss Claire Luce as Cleopatra being passionately embraced by Antony with the title: *"The New American Ambassador."*

Meanwhile Minister Counselor Durbrow, who became chargé d'affaires when Ambassador Bunker left, was worrying about protocol. A lady Ambassador presented all kinds of innovations in a code of etiquette that had solidified in the eighteenth century. He and his staff wrote to all the places where women had been chiefs of mission—Norway, Denmark, Luxembourg—they even wrote to Moscow to find out how India had handled Madame Pandit.

They got lots of good advice, but on the question of what to do about Harry Luce they were on their own. The protocol of seating state dinners was most difficult. Since Luce had to sit *somewhere* they decided to give him the simulated rank of minister—that is, they said to the Italian Foreign Office, "Let's make believe he is a minister."

Then with considerable forebodings, Durbrow led a little motorcade of high officials and their wives down to Naples to welcome his new chief.

The *Andrea Doria* sailed into the Bay of Naples on a superb spring morning. Clare was on deck early to see the enchanted isle of Capri wrap a veil of opal mist around its modern defacements. Off Ischia a launch cut a white slash in the blue water. The steamer stopped to pick up her pilot, and likewise Clare's pilots, Minister Durbrow and the embassy press secretary, John McKnight. Clare took them to her cabin immediately for a quick conference. Durbrow was stocky and solid-seeming—a man you could depend on. He was very correctly dressed in a pin-stripe dark blue suit and a gray necktie. McKnight had the lank casualness of a former newspaperman.

The conference was pretty stiff. Both Durbrow and McKnight were deferential and extremely correct. It was Mrs. Ambassador this and Mrs. Ambassador that, which is how the State Department had decreed Clare must be addressed. They went over the draft of her speech and made tentative suggestions. Finally formality brought on a sort of impasse. McKnight broke the freeze with a question: "Mrs. Ambassador, are you as scared as we are?"

Clare laughed with relief. "I'm twice as scared!"

As soon as the *Andrea Doria* docked, there was a press conference —at least that is what they called it. Nearly three hundred Italian journalists were crammed into the main saloon. As Clare came in they surged forward babbling questions in broken English and voluble Italian. The result was indescribable confusion.

But it was nothing to the scene on the dockside. Durbrow, knowing Neopolitan ebullience, had asked the royalist mayor of Naples to call out the *carabinieri*. These picturesque characters in blue uniforms, cocked hats, and broad white belts supporting clanking sabers, formed a cordon across the pier. Being just as anxious to see the lady Ambassador as a hundred thousand other Italians, they forgot to hold the line and the crowd surged through. It was a first-class riot in the happy-go-lucky Neopolitan way. Half the crowd had brought flowers to present to Clara Luché, as they called her. From above, it looked like a rose garden in a hurricane. Clare was at once nervous and immensely touched.

She made her graceful little speech in halting Italian, which nobody heard. Then Durbrow, Harry, and the other Americans formed a flying wedge and rushed her through the beaming, cheering, pushing mob to the big black embassy Chrysler.

The coastal road to Rome is shorter, but Clare wanted to go by Monte Cassino, so they drove across the rugged ridges that stand astride the Italian peninsula like gigantic frozen breakers. A thousand marble crosses of the cemetery at Monte Cassino were like the white blaze of a titanic ax on the dark hillside. Clare paid her respects to the dead comrades of the men she had known in the mud and ice of Christmas, 1944. Then they pushed on.

Harry rode in front, as he always liked to do, Clare and her Minister-Counselor in the back seat. During the four-hour drive, Durbrow briefed her on the immediate problems she would have to face. Each time he said, "Now this material is classified," Clare touched the switch that raised a window excluding Harry. This has been her considered policy throughout, not only to ward off criticism of herself but for her husband's sake. Both agreed that his magazines must have no secret source of information not available to all.

Conversely, Luce long ago established the policy of never mentioning his wife in his publications unless it was absolutely essential to reporting the news. He has sometimes carried the policy to a point that irks Clare considerably. For example, during the war she took the only color pictures of the Flying Tigers in Burma. *Life* published them without a credit line. Clare stormed at her husband, "Harry, this is carrying reticence too damn far!"

In the late afternoon the embassy car rolled through the circle of the hills that hold the golden cup of the Campagna. Amber sunshine lighted the fields of spring. An aqueduct ambled across the level plain, and Clare recognized an iridescent bubble floating on the horizon as the dome of Saint Peter's. She continued to talk to Durbrow in her slow, liquid voice, but her blood seemed to be boiling. Rome!

The Villa Taverna, official residence of the American Ambassador, stands in a seven-acre garden of tall ilex and cypress, cropped lawns, marble statues, and flowers, enclosed by an ancient wall. As the car swung through the gate, Clare found herself looking down a long tunnel of interlaced olive trees. At the end, dramatic as a stage set under amber spots, the formal garden glowed in the afternoon sunshine. No matter how familiar it became, Clare's heart always quickened to the beauty of that scene.

The interior of the sixteenth-century villa was less inspiring. Stripped to the bare essentials of furnishing, its marble magnificence was as cozy as a half-filled mausoleum. "We'll have to do something about this," she noted, "and fast!"

The following morning she went down to the embassy in the Palazzo Margherita. The former residence of the late Queen Mother, with its courtyards and marble staircases, its huge salons and long corridors with vaulted ornate ceilings, is crammed with the offices of the great diplomatic machine that Clare now headed. Indeed the activities of the embassy and its alphabetical auxiliaries such as FAO, USIS, and so forth, spills over into half a dozen other buildings and employs some fifteen hundred people. At least three hundred of them work directly in the embassy.

That first morning Clare, wearing a trim black suit with the red rose in its tiny crystal vase in her lapel which is her personal symbol, went through the whole building floor by floor, meeting virtually everyone of her staff. She knew quite well that she must win their loyalty if she were to function efficiently. There were three strikes against her. First, she was a Republican and after twenty years of Democratic administrations many of the Foreign Service people were obviously Democrats. Second, any change of administration sends a current of fear through people who hold government jobs, even those who are protected by civil service, and nothing breeds animosity so fast as fear. Finally, there was the Clare Luce myth to live down—even here.

That afternoon she gave a party for them all, from ministers to messenger boys, at the Villa Taverna—it was the first time many of them had seen it. The party was an immense, confused success. In the first twenty minutes the hastily assembled supply of soft drinks, food, and whisky gave out. Councilors, ministers, attachés, and consuls leaped into their cars and went scouring through Rome to restock the place, and came back laden like Saint Bernards.

From then on everybody relaxed, forgetting, for the moment, both fear and prejudice, while Clare and Harry circulated through the crowd, charging the gathering with the effervescence of their sparkling personalities.

The next day Clare got to work. By nine o'clock she was at her desk in the Ambassador's office, which was the dining room of the late queen. It is a huge, square salon decorated in light cream and gold, with decorative maps of the world in pale blue set in panels on the walls. From the carved and gilded ceiling hangs an enormous chandelier of delicate Venetian glass, and the grandfather of all oriental rugs covers the entire floor. At the far end of the room is the long table for staff meetings. In front of tall windows looking on the Via Veneto is a graceful eighteenth-century table desk. Clare's first act was to place on it a framed copy of the prayer said by Lord Astley before the Battle of Edge Hill:

> Lord, thou knowest I shall be verie busie this day.
> I may forget thee—
> Do not thou forget me.

Behind the Ambassador's chair to her right is the American flag. To her left is her own ambassadorial flag—forty-eight stars on a blue field. But that second morning it was not yet there.

According to diplomatic protocol an ambassador is not an ambassador until he—or she—presents his credentials to the head of the state. It happened that President Luigi Einaudi of Italy was in France on a state visit, so Clare could not officially function. However, to speed the process, it was decided that her courtesy call on de Gasperi would be considered as giving her temporary status.

In his capacity as foreign minister, de Gasperi received her at the Foreign Office in the Palazzo Chigi. Long-nosed and lantern-jawed, he wore the pin-stripe blue suit and gray tie that has virtually superseded striped pants as the uniform of diplomacy. As she came in, he beamed on her through his big, round spectacles. Clare was genuinely fond of the rugged old statesman, who had steered Italy successfully all through the storm-wracked years since the war. This was no cold official call but a meeting of old friends.

Clare's official presentation to President Einaudi was far more formal. The President's car drove her into the great barracks-like courtyard of the Quirinale Palace between saluting *Bersegliere* in their cock-plumed helmets. Chief of Protocol Barone Scammacca received her at the great double doors and conducted her up broad marble stairs and through long marble corridors lined by the Cuirassiers of the Guard in silver breastplates, tall horsetailed helmets, tight white breeches, and jack boots, flashing their sabers in salute. In the stately salon of the kings, President Einaudi waited to receive her. In the middle of this royal pomp, leaning heavily on his thick cane, peering anxiously through rimless spectacles, this simple gentleman seemed a symbol of democracy come at last to Italy.

When Clare entered the door of the room, the chief of protocol announced, "Signora Clare Boothe Luce, Ambassador Extraordinary and Plenipotentiary of the United States."

As Clare moved forward, she murmured to herself, "Extraordinary, *yes*, but plenipotentiary—*no*."

From the beginning she had no illusions about what any diplomat could do, and she knew it was going to be harder for her than for others, for the reasons she had already given Ike. But she did not know how hard.

The rush of work into which Clare plunged was multiplied by the press of social functions. With curiosity reinforcing official courtesy, everybody wanted to entertain the new American Ambassador. It sounds silly to let social functions interfere with work, but that is one feature of diplomacy that has not changed since Tallyrand wearily bent his gouty knee at the functions of the Congress of Vienna. To refuse the invitations of the representatives of sovereign powers is virtually impossible. Harry Luce's analytical mind figured that with some sixty embassies and legations in Rome there were at least 300 *must* cocktail parties a year and half as many dinners. Ordinarily the Ambassadress carries a lot of the social load, but Clare was her own Ambassadress. Even now she averages fourteen functions a week.

Harry tried to spare her. As he said, "If Clare can't go, she can, of course, send Durbrow. But it's a little more of a compliment if I appear as well, so I do what I can."

Incidentally, Harry Luce at a cocktail party in New York is as rare a bird as a prothonotary warbler in Central Park.

At the Villa Taverna he also did what he could. "I'm the hostess around here, you know."

Clare's first state dinner—and her first boner—took place at the Spanish Embassy. In a city of late dining the Spaniards sit down last of all. Dinner began at ten, ended at eleven-thirty. As the guests gathered in the drawing room, Clare wondered how soon she could leave. "State" had briefed her about the protocol. "Quite simple. No one leaves before the guest of honor."

So Clare watched British Ambassador, Sir Victor Mallet, Senior Ambassador of the diplomatic corps.

Time crept slowly but relentlessly by. Sir Victor, big-nosed, gray-haired, the very picture of an English diplomat, chatted urbanely and endlessly on. Twelve-thirty. One. One-thirty. Clare felt like putting matchsticks under her eyelids. Finally she whispered desperately to the Spanish Ambassadress, "What time does Sir Victor usually go home?"

"When the guest of honor leaves," was the frigid reply.

"But who is the guest of honor?"

The Señora's eyes were like black ice as she answered, "You are!"

It took the Luces forty-five seconds flat to make their adieux and get out of there. Afterward Clare learned that, as the only woman Ambassador in Rome, she often automatically sat on her host's right and when this happened she was therefore considered the guest of honor.

CHAPTER TWENTY-TWO

LEARNING THE HARD WAY

It DID NOT TAKE CLARE LONG TO MASTER THE BASIC TECHNIQUES of her job. Her mind illumines the objects on which it is turned with brilliant clarity. This concentrated beam of attention engraves the subject indelibly in the grooves of her brain. Speaking of her memory, Counselor Francis Williamson, head of the political section of the embassy, said: "Mrs. Luce can repeat to us an hour-long conversation with, say, the Prime Minister, with the fidelity of a tape recorder."

Durbrow noted: "She does her homework thoroughly; she thinks things through using a lawyer's logical method. Say there are four courses of action open, she evaluates them with clear logic plus thorough understanding and decisively chooses the best."

Staff meetings were held at the embassy every Wednesday. Clare encouraged everybody to speak up, she much preferred a clash of ideas to no ideas at all. John Deneen, Chief Information Officer, U.S.I.S., said that these discussions had the outspoken character of an argument in a man's club. The Ambassador was quite capable of holding her own. As Deneen put it, "Her mind has a diamond edge."

If the discussion got too warm, she eased the strain with a joke or an impromptu limerick.

Members of the Ambassador's staff were surprised to find their memos to the "Amb," as they sometimes affectionately called her, were answered immediately and decisively. Clare usually took care of them between midnight and two o'clock in the morning.

If the Americans were amazed by her mentality, the Italians were flabbergasted. Indro Montanelli of the influential *Corriere della Sera*, amusingly describes their consternation: "Our politicians expected an easy time. They thought her Ingrid looking for her Rossellini, and being Italian, everybody thought himself a Rossellini. They were very disappointed when they found no Ingrid, she. It took them quite a while to adjust to the mind of a man clothed in fragile femininity."

It was fortunate that Clare was a quick study, for events crowded her. She had been in Italy a scant week when Defense Secretary Charles E. Wilson arrived on April 30, for top-level conferences with Italian Minister of Defense Rudolfo Pacciardi. Clare's experience on the House Military Affairs Committee during her four years as a congresswoman enabled her to take an intelligent part in the discussions. In fact, Harry Luce, who does not hand out accolades to his wife carelessly, says that she has a genuine sense of strategy.

The discussions of Italy's contribution to NATO went on all day. That night Pacciardi gave a state dinner for Wilson at the beautiful Villa Madama, where the Italian government entertains distinguished foreigners. The official pictures show the American Ambassador, ethereal in pale blue satin with a Juliet cap on her pale blonde hair, while statesmen, diplomats and generals swirl around her, their thoughts quite evidently far from war. Outside the crowds were shouting, "La Lucé! La Lucé!"

Clare rightly considers herself Ambassador to all Italy, not just to Rome. She has visited every large city in the peninsula, a practice she began, shortly after she arrived, with a trip to Genoa. The hotel clerk there was probably the only person in Italy who did not recognize her. As she came up to the desk he asked, "What name, please?"

Clare grinned at him and said, "Why not look on my luggage."

The clerk obliged and wrote in the register, "Raw Cowhide."

As Clare had feared, the State Department's ukase that she must be called Mrs. Ambassador caused all sorts of trouble in the Italian language. In Turin the Italian introducing her got so mixed in his genders that he called her Signore [Mr.] Luce. A waiter got the giggles and all the people at the lunch wore broad grins.

Clare countered by telling them an anecdote of the principal of the Castle School. Miss Cassidy Mason was an ardent feminist and told her girls that they could do everything a man could do. Sixteen-year-old Clare asked, "Everything, Miss Mason?"

"Everything," said the head mistress firmly. "All you need is faith in yourself and faith in God, because *She* will protect you."

The Ambassador's visit to Genoa was followed on May 5 by a trip to Milan to make her first major speech—to the Milanese Chamber of Commerce at a dinner in the Hotel Continental. The signs of the zodiac must have been sadly askew, for it was a star-crossed occasion. One little sentence that she spoke started a row which reverberated from Sicily to San Francisco.

A brief look at Italian politics is necessary to understand the explosion. A general election was to be held within two weeks under a new election law which de Gasperi had jammed through the Chamber for the sake of government stability. This law automatically gave any party gaining 50.01 of the votes a large working majority in the parliament. Confident of victory, de Gasperi had staked his government on the result. Electioneering was at its peak, and the electorate was seething.

However, there were no indications of trouble that night in Milan. Colonel James Angleton gracefully introduced the American Ambassador, and she rose to speak. In a severe black evening gown and the horn-rimmed glasses she needed to read her speech, Clare, for once, looked almost "schoolmarmish." Her words were all honey at first, for she was able to announce a further American contribution of twenty-two million dollars to bolster the Italian economy. She went on to say, "In Italy's thrilling forward progress along the ancient highways of her natural greatness, she can count confidently on America's intimate and warm cooperation."

Then came the fatal sentence. Clare spoke it slowly, solemnly: "But if—I am required in all honesty to say this—but if—though this cannot happen—the Italian people should fall the unhappy victims of totalitarianism, totalitarianism of the right or of the left, there would follow, logically and tragically, grave consequences for this intimate and warm cooperation we now enjoy."

This sounds innocent enough, and certainly it was true. Most important, it was U. S. official policy toward Italy since the end of the war. The Ambassador's staff, which had prepared the speech for her, had insisted on putting in the sentence. Mr. Durbrow thought it would help to combat ugly rumors that the United States would look with favor on a neo-Fascist victory. Nor was there any adverse reaction at the dinner. When Clare sat down the applause, according to her husband, was "thunderous."

First reports in the government papers were favorable. Nor were the Communists upset. Oddly enough the first howl of wounded pride came from the neo-Fascist and Monarchist press. The Communists then saw their chance and opened up with intense indignation over "The American Ambassador's attempt to interfere in the internal affairs of Italy." Giovanni Guareschi, creator of the gentle Don Camillo, was the most vindictive of all. He had been unsympathetic toward Clare from the first. To greet her arrival his monarchist paper, *Candido,* had published a cartoon of the American Embassy flying an American flag edged with lace. Now he fairly frothed at the typewriter. One editorial implied that the American Ambassador was mentally deranged.

Clare pretended to ignore the burst of adverse publicity, as she always does. Actually she was hurt and bewildered, as she always is.

The final blow came when de Gasperi's party lost the election by only fifty-seven thousand votes. Worse still, the Communists polled thirty-six per cent of the vote. That was when the American press picked up the bludgeon. They said that Mrs. Luce's speech had tipped the scales against de Gasperi.

Did it? A careful evaluation of Italian opinion indicates that it did not. The real reasons for de Gasperi's defeat appear to have been overconfidence; the unpopularity of his election law—"the trick law" they called it—and the distrust of the great Italian industrialists of the Prime Minister.

Minister, now Ambassador, Alberico Casardi says, "The speech did not change a single vote—well, maybe one."

Other Italian statesmen and independent journalists agree that its effect was neglible. The American State Department backed Clare up, as indeed they should, since her speech followed Secretary of State John Foster Dulles' tough new look in foreign relations, which he shortly made clear by his remark that if France did not accept the European Defense Community, America would be forced to "an agonizing reappraisal" of its position in Europe.

Clare herself says, "You'd think that I invented the Communist party in Italy."

One further fact was conveniently ignored both by Clare's critics in America and in Italy: the fact of the one million, two hundred and fifty thousand "invalid" or uncounted ballots. A recount of these ballots some months after the election showed that Mr. de Gasperi *had* won. But, having conceded the election on the advice of some of his ministers, it was too late for Mr. de Gasperi to do anything about it. The knowledge that he had been cheated of his victory by the bad advice of a few Cabinet Ministers certainly hastened Mr. de Gasperi's death.

In any event, the Milan speech marked the beginning of a long and difficult period for Clare. No longer did the crowds yell for "La Lucé!" American papers published rumors of her recall. These were eagerly picked up by the Italian Communist press, which boldly announced that "the Old Woman with the Evil Eye" was going to be sent home.

Furthermore, Clare's conduct of official business was made infinitely more difficult by the fact that there was no Italian government with which to conduct it. In June de Gasperi resigned and then attempted to form a new government. He was voted down. Amintore Fanfani and Attilio Piccione likewise failed to command a majority in the parliament. It was August before Giuseppe Pella finally won a vote of confidence as Premier. Even then, Italians regarded his tenure of office as so transitory that they called it "The Beach Government," because it was only expected to last until people got back from the beaches.

Actually, Pella, a big, hearty man with a beak of a nose and a forthright manner, managed so well and gained such popularity that his government lasted until December, when Mario Scelba and Fanfani combined to cut his political throat.

To the difficulties of the Ambassador's official relations was added the exasperation of silly social stings. The Roman nobility were miffed by the fact that she had so little time for nonofficial functions. On that first ride from Naples to Rome, Durbrow had advised the new Ambassador not to become too deeply involved with the sterile round of Roman society. She would have to see some of them, he said, because while they played no real part in the political life of Italy, they had a certain nuisance value.

Certainly Clare, who had served her apprenticeship in the social whirl in Newport long ago, never intended to slight these ancient Romans; it was just that other things were more important. Elsa Maxwell, arriving for a visit in Rome, says that she found Prince Torlonia (who is married to the Infanta Beatrice, daughter of the late King of Spain) in a lather. It seems that the Torlonia visiting cards, left at the Villa Taverna, had not been acknowledged. "Who does this woman think she is to insult the daughter of a King?" he demanded.

"You can't blame her. She may not have seen your cards, may have lost them," Elsa soothed him.

This was in fact the case, and Torlonia's honor was satisfied by two neatly engraved pieces of pasteboard.

However, the whispering campaign in the Palazzos had repercussions in similar but more influential circles in America, and re-echoed back to the Villa Taverna.

Two more events added to the ambassadorial distress. Harry Luce had to return to America to look after his great journalistic enterprises. At state dinners and receptions, cocktail parties and vast public gatherings, Clare had felt comfortably secure with her husband, big, shaggy, and distinguished, always close at hand. And every night, even the latest ones, he read her to sleep. Clare found it a wonderful way to forget the irritations of the day. She missed Harry sadly.

Miss Margaret Case, her friend since the days when they were both on *Vogue,* came to stay at the Villa. On the rare happy nights when there was no dinner to go to, the two of them had supper served on trays in Clare's bedroom and talked of old times. Then, at nine or nine-thirty, a Marine guard would arrive with a dispatch case and Clare would go to work on her vast correspondence (one thousand letters a week) and the mass of papers that represented the business of what is one of the two or three busiest embassies in the world, while the Marine stood by, waiting to return any official papers to the embassy at midnight.

The final blow that hit Clare was definitely below the belt. She succumbed to a horrid affliction which strikes down nine out of ten Americans in Italy, known as "Roman tummy." It is caused by the richness of food cooked in olive oil and highly flavored, combined, perhaps, with germs to which Italians are immune, but Americans, used to our antiseptic diet, are an easy prey. Nothing makes one feel more miserable. The brilliant Roman sky goes gray before lackluster eyes, and each sufferer feels like that Spartan boy as the fox gnawed his vitals.

Clare suffered from this malady off and on for six months, during which time the multicourse meals of Italian hospitality were sheer martyrdom. Now that her system has adjusted, she can go through a Roman banquet from caviar to the chocolate-and-whipped-cream dessert without a quaver.

CHAPTER TWENTY-THREE

THE ARMS OF THE CITY OF TRIESTE

THE PEAK OF CLARE'S TRAVAIL AND THE NADIR OF HER POPULARITY was reached in July, 1953, though nobody realized she had passed it until long afterward. The improvement began with her personal staff. She had arrived without any personal entourage at all. In May, Miss Letitia Baldrige came over to be her social secretary, on the recommendation of Allen Grover, vice-president of Time, Inc.

Tish Baldrige is a big, handsome girl, filled with warmth, energy, and enthusiasm. But she arrived in a somber mood. It seems that the night before she left, she had attended a dinner party at which the Clare Luce myth was the specter at the feast. At least half the guests had heard something about Tish's new boss, "on the very best authority."

"They told such awful stories," Tish later explained, "that my father said, 'If you can't stand it after three weeks I'll cable you your fare home!'"

"So I came in terror," she concluded, "and remained to adore. Behind the scenes of the apparent formality here, there's constant confusion and turmoil. And laughter."

Once, soon after Tish's arrival, Clare said to her, "Would you be a darling and bring me my mink coat, the silver-blue one."

A shadow of envy crossed the girl's face. "I'd give anything," she said, "to get a husband who could give me a blue mink." "Listen, darling," Clare said, "many a girl has married for a mink, only to discover that what she really had got was a skunk."

Tish says, "I never thought working for an ambassador could be such fun."

Tish had served with Ambassador David K. L. Bruce in Paris and knew how to walk the tightrope of protocol and to juggle potentates, princes, and politicians at the dinner table—she could even spell the names of the dishes in French. When she took hold, a lot of social snarls got untangled. Those that did not were laughed away.

The arrival of her personal secretary, Dorothy Farmer, in June, was even more helpful to Clare. Dorothy is a round, dynamic little woman who is utterly devoted to The Boss. Besides being extremely efficient at her job, Dorothy spends her life guarding Clare from unnecessary intrusions. Though she is amiable and gregarious by nature, she can be as fierce as a terrier protecting its sleeping master. "I'm the antisocial secretary," she says.

Somehow in the middle of all her official business, Clare also found time to do something about the Villa Taverna. The great vaulted hall, bare as a car barn when she came, was warmed with thick green carpets, and flower boxes in the windows. She changed the décor of the small drawing room from muddy chocolate to soft gold brocade. Other rooms were rearranged and Clare found many lovely old pieces in the cellar that could be refurbished and used. Most important of all, she filled the house with the beauty of great art.

The Luces own one of the finest private collections of modern art in the world. Clare ordered the famous pictures stripped from the walls of their apartment in New York and their country place at Ridgefield and brought over to lend graciousness to the Villa Taverna. The genius of Monet, Rouault, Delacroix, Fragonard, Renoir, Dufy, Segonzac, Pissarro, Sisley, Chagall, Goya, and a dozen more of the modern masters served to lift the spirit of the American Ambassador's guests. And all the rooms were made gay with the flowers that are so plentiful in Rome. Thus the Villa Taverna became not an official residence but a home, warm and welcoming. Welcoming, certainly. The guest book at the Villa Taverna shows that over eight thousand Italians and Americans have come there for dinners, luncheons, and receptions.

Harry Luce came back to Rome late in July. He took one look at his wife and said, "You need a rest."

Then he went out and hired a yacht.

The *Niki* was one of those graceful, frivolous vessels that have sailed into the present from the age of elegance. It required eighteen crewmen and three officers to man her, and she was as anachronistic in these utilitarian times as a clipper ship or the Queen of England. And as lovely.

The Luces joined the *Niki* at Civitavecchia. With them were Miss Margaret Case, Sir Victor and Lady Mallet, and their little, golden-haired boy, who looked like A. A. Milne's incarnation of British childhood, Christopher Robin. Clare was devoted to the little boy and would have been if he had not been half so beautiful. For a child—almost any child—seems temporarily to fill the void left by her own lost daughter.

The yacht sailed to Capri and went on to cruise the silken Tyrrhenian Sea. Harry snoozed in shorts on the forward deck, looking a little like a hibernating bear. Clare, who can never quite relax, read, and talked, and ordered the yacht to heave to while she did graceful swan dives off the fantail stern.

The cruise was not quite as restful as Harry had hoped. His wife kept dashing back to Rome by plane to keep official engagements, and fresh relays of guests joined and left the yacht at every port.

One of these was Grillo of the Italian Foreign Office. Because of the part he played in great events, he deserves more than casual mention. Romigio is his given name, but no one ever calls him anything but Grillo, which means cricket in Italian and seems to suit him because of his dark liveliness. This is no disparagement. No one who knows the Italian Foreign Office underrates him. However, an American hostess, who tried to be the Perle Mesta of Rome, once did. Grillo likes to tell the story on himself.

It seems that the lady decided to give a huge party for all the shiniest dukes, princes, exiled kings, and tycoons in Rome. She telephoned Grillo whom she had never met.

"Marchese del Grillo?" she asked.

"This is Grillo."

"I've never met you, but I've heard so much about you," she

babbled, never letting him get in a word. "They say you're young and handsome, you dance divinely and, of course, your family is one of the noblest in Rome. You must come to my party next Wednesday."

"*Un momento!*" said Grillo. "You have been sadly misinformed. I am not young. Even my best friends do not think me handsome. I do not dance at all. I am not Marchese del Grillo, nor am I related to any noble Romans. I am just plain Grillo of the Foreign Office."

"Oh! There's been some dreadful mistake," the lady gasped. "Well, I'm so sorry. No doubt we'll get together sometime. Well, good-by."

That lady will never be a Perle Mesta anywhere.

Actually, Grillo comes from a low-income, middle-class family. In his youth he took part in the March on Rome. "The greatest bluff ever," he says. "We had no supplies. If they'd kept us out another two days we'd have gotten hungry and gone home."

"Fascism was not political then," he adds. "We were just anti-Communist."

Like so many young idealists who teeter temporarily toward totalitarianism, Grillo was soon disillusioned. Now he hates fascism so much that he will not eat at the Palazzi Restaurant, the most delightful luncheon spot in Rome, because it is housed in the luxurious modernistic villa that Mussolini built for his girl friend.

By hard work, ability, and that even rarer attribute in Italian politics, integrity, Grillo has worked his way up to the rank of minister, heading the all-important American Section of the Italian Foreign Office.

He describes the cruise on the *Niki:* "I did not know Mrs. Luce well, until one day she called me up and invited me to go on the yacht with her. 'Join us Monday and stay until Wednesday,' she said, which is your American way of preparing a graceful exit in case you turn out badly."

Grillo says he cut a poor figure at first: he got seasick. Lean and saturnine, his face must have looked frightful with its greenish pallor. Even his old-fashioned white flannels seemed odd in contrast with Harry Luce's shorts and wild sport shirts.

But he recovered, and his brilliant mind illuminated many an obscure corridor in Italian politics for Clare. Grillo, too, was enchanted. "We had some wonderful talks," he says. "I was surprised by her personality. On Wednesday I was all packed up to go, but she said, 'You're crazy. You are going on with us.' So I went all the way to Portofino.

"When I got back I made a point of trying to convince these fool Italians that it made no difference whether the Ambassador was a man or a woman. She was intelligent and had great influence with the President and, through her husband, with the American people. I had a difficult time. It got so they pointed the finger at me—I became known as Mrs. Luce's man.

"You don't know how to play the Luce card, I told them.

"They all said, 'She won't last long. Let's wait for her successor.'

"They have changed since then," he adds.

When Clare won Grillo's confidence aboard the *Niki*, she won an important skirmish in her battle against Italian prejudice and one of the best of many firm allies in the storm that was about to break on the summer calm of the Italian scene.

Portofino. The *Niki* lay in the narrow harbor that is a mere slit between the rocky cliffs on which the pastel villas cling and riotous gardens hang. It was so serene that the flawless water repeated all the colors of the sky and cliffs and foliage and faithfully mirrored the white grace of the yacht. Sprawled on the round cushioned seat at the stern Clare was almost ready to say, "Let this moment stay!"

The smiling wireless operator who came forward with his daily message from the Rome Embassy looked hardly like a messenger of Mars. Clare read it idly. As she read all languor left her; she vibrated with excitement.

"Have cars at the dock. Wire the embassy to send the plane to the nearest airport," she commanded. "My vacation is ended."

The news contained in the message was bad. Yugoslavia had announced that it was about to annex Zone B of the Trieste enclave. The Italian government countered by moving troops to the frontier. Peace in Europe once again hung precariously on the judgment of a few overwrought men. War could come from the nervous reflex of some young Italian or Yugoslavian recruit's finger on a trigger.

The only thing sudden about this development was the bomb-shell announcement from Belgrade. Tension between the two countries had been building ever since the end of World War II. Throughout the summer it had almost imperceptibly increased. Minister Casardi says, "We had been having secret discussions with the Yugoslavs ever since June of '51. They were very tough. They controlled Zone B, while the Allies held Zone A. We held nothing and so were in a very weak position to bargain. After the fall of de Gasperi's government, Tito got more truculent. He went back to his project of leaving the actual city of Trieste to Italy, but keeping so much of the harbor he could strangle the port."

That, in effect, was what the struggle was about, only twelve hundred yards of land, but strategically placed so that the country which held them controlled the greatest port on the eastern side of the Adriatic.

Clare had been aware of this situation from the moment of her appointment. She said to Eisenhower before she left, "Don't under-estimate the danger of Trieste. We supported the Italian position on the Free Territory of Trieste in 1948 in order to help them win their elections against the Commies. There is great resentment about what they see as our unfulfilled promises."

In Rome she had found that this was, if anything, an under-statement. She had tried all summer "to convince our own people that it was the key log in the Italian foreign policy jam." Now it looked as though the logjam might be blasted by the Yugoslavs and the Italians with their own cannons.

When the American Ambassador reached Rome from Portofino, the newspapers were howling for war in black banner headlines, and the Italian Cabinet was oscillating on the verge of drastic ac-tion, as angry notes flew from Belgrade to the Chigi Palace and back. Clare's first job was to persuade Pella to proceed with pru-dence. To this end she attended a meeting between him, British Ambassador Sir Victor Mallet, and French Ambassador Jacques Fouques Duparc. Since Pella spoke no English, Minister Casardi acted as interpreter. According to him Clare carried the ball at the historic meeting.

This was only the first of many conferences between the American Ambassador and the Prime Minister, at which Casardi interpreted. It appears that for once the Ambassador's irrepressible femininity was no disadvantage.

"Pella is a man of great personal magnetism who likes a lovely lady," Casardi says. "They got on well together from the first. A lady has an advantage when speaking of something that others dislike. There is still a certain courtesy left, even among politicians, and if they have something unpleasant to say, they will say it less unpleasantly to a woman than a man."

The Labor Day weekend of 1953 was a horror. No one knew if war would come the next day or even hour. The entire staff— everyone—of the American Embassy remained on duty. Many of them, including the Ambassador, worked all night. Five great capitals, London, Paris, Belgrade, Rome, and Washington, were vitally involved. The exchange of top-secret messages was tremendous. Each had to be encoded and decoded by the little group of men and women in the cypher room.

At one point when war seemed highly probable, Clare's forked wit sizzled like lightening against the somber clouds. "At least," she said bitterly, "if Italy and Yugoslavia go to war, we'll find out what American tanks can do against—American tanks."

The reference was to the fact that we had sent arms to both countries, which made her task of convincing the Italians of our good will doubly difficult.

Throughout September crisis followed crisis, and conference piled on conference. General Alfred Gruenther, Supreme Commander of SHAPE, flew in. Clare conferred with him, Pella, and General Efisio Marras, Italian Chief of Staff. After that conference Pella said, "Molto saddisfacente."

On September 21 she made a flying trip to headquarters of the European Command at Frankfort for more military briefing.

Through it all the heavy social schedule continued. Now, if ever, the American Ambassador had to appear at diplomatic functions apparently serene and carefree. Night after night she would leave some state dinner at midnight and go alone to the darkened embassy to read the latest cables and prepare her replies.

Somehow the peace was kept. Italian statesmen and Americans alike say that Clare played a vital role. Meanwhile, negotiations among France, England, and America, in which Clare persistently pressed the Italian cause, resulted in a joint declaration on October 8, stating in effect that Yugoslavia could have Zone B, but that the Allies would move out of Zone A and permit the Italians to take over. Thus, at last, they would have an equal bargaining position.

Now it was Tito's turn to rage. He threatened to attack the Italians if they moved into Zone A. So the decision was never implemented. A complete stalemate resulted.

Immediately after the declaration of October 8 Italian flags broke out all over the city of Trieste. British General Winterton, commanding the Allied forces there, fearing trouble, ordered them removed from local government buildings. In the months that followed in Trieste a number of Italians were killed. Never was the U. S. more unpopular in Italy. The rioting spread to Rome.

On the morning of October 10 Elbridge Durbrow was sitting in his office conferring with a visitor. Across the Via Veneto a mob of students held in check by a thin line of police were hurling insults and anything else they could lay hands on at the embassy. Reinforcements were arriving for both sides, and things looked pretty stormy. Suddenly Francis Williamson shot through the door, his face white, eyes glittering behind his spectacles. "For God's sake, go down and get The Boss off the street! She's out there alone!" he gasped.

Clare had been returning from an early conference with Sir Victor Mallet, when her driver found the Via Veneto blocked by police lines. He turned around and tried to reach the embassy by a side street. That, too, was closed off.

"I'll get out and walk," Clare decided.

Gino, the old embassy chauffeur, was horrified. "No! No! Excellency!"

Clare said gaily, "I'll be all right," and disappeared into the crowd, walking toward the entrance of the embassy, where she found a group of American journalists who were there to report what would happen if the rioters reached the tall, wrought-iron gates.

By the time Durbrow reached her, pandemonium was breaking loose across the street not twenty yards away—tear-gas bombs bursting, fire engines pumping colored water through high-pressure hoses, jeep sirens screeching, and five thousand people yelling and howling. Durbrow admits he was scared stiff.

"Come in quick, Boss," he begged, "it's not right to take this risk."

Clare's cheeks were as red as the rose on her lapel, her eyes shooting blue fires of excitement. "I'm sorry. It's like being a war correspondent again. Brings out the old journalist war horse in you."

One of the correspondents broke in, "The riot was started by a group of students who want to give you a petition. The chief of police says they can't see you."

"Then that makes this part of the Ambassador's job," Clare answered. She said to Durbrow, "Go find the chief of police and ask him to talk to me."

Durbrow succeeded in locating the officer and bringing him to Clare.

"Go in!" he ordered in Italian. "You are in danger."

By now Clare knew enough of the language to make herself understood. Speaking slowly as always when she is excited, she said, "No! You go tell these people that if any of them want to talk to me, I'll receive any small delegation they agree on in my office. Plainly I can't receive a thousand people."

The police chief left, saying he would pass on the message if he could.

Clare waited on the street for about twenty minutes. Somehow her message had spread through the crowd. Things began to calm down, and Clare retired to the safety of the embassy. She never saw the chief of police again. He was wounded shortly after by a Communist or Fascist rioter. The reporters who had heard her give the message played it up big in the evening papers. Never since then has there been an unfriendly demonstration against our embassy in Rome. But there have been, especially at the time of the Trieste settlement, many friendly ones.

Throughout the next two months Yugoslavia and Italy remained with locked horns. The Italians had announced that they would not negotiate until they had occupied Trieste. Tito stood by his ultimatum of war if they moved in. Clare became very discouraged.

"I've been here nine months," she confided to Durbrow, "and what's happened? The election was lost. The government spends its time fighting itself. Nothing has been accomplished."

"You have not been here long enough to realize why diplomacy creeps so slowly," Durbrow said. "I don't know why myself, but you just cannot force it. There are so many factors that slow things up—ancient mores and local prides that can only gradually be overcome."

"In other words, I must take for my motto that old Italian saying, *Pazienza e coraggio*," said Clare. Patience and courage. And, she added, "*Silencio*."

A break came in December. Pella discreetly suggested a way out of the impasse to the American Ambassador. She flew to Washington and proposed it to the President. It was that the Allies conduct secret negotiations with the Yugoslavs to discover on what terms Tito would permit the Italians to move into Trieste. Clare agreed, but added her own suggestion—that the negotiations should be conducted neither in the overheated capitals of Rome or Belgrade but quietly in some other friendly capital.

The actual negotiations were carried on in London by Llewellyn Thompson, American Ambassador to Austria; Geoffrey Harrison, Assistant Secretary of State for Foreign Affairs for Britain; and two Yugoslavian diplomats. They began on February 2, 1954, and tentative agreement was reached on May 30.

Meanwhile Pella's government had been replaced by one headed by Mario Scelba, with Attilio Piccione and, later, Gaetano Martino, as Foreign Minister.

"In June and July," according to Francis Williamson, "we negotiated with the Italians. Through August and September we negotiated with both, but we never let them meet."

Clare took no part in the actual negotiations, but she had a very great part in urging patience, courage, and, above all, silence, on the Italians and in sending from Rome suggestions of ways out of particular difficulties which the negotiators had encountered in London. When the negotiations virtually broke down late in

August, Clare, who was in the United States, went again to President Eisenhower and proposed that he secretly send veteran diplomat Robert Murphy to make his views known to Scelba and Tito. Murphy was starting on an inspection trip anyhow and he could be detoured inconspicuously to Belgrade and Rome.

Minister Casardi says, "Murphy broke the deadlock."

The Trieste agreement was announced on October 6, 1954. By it Italy was given Trieste free of the danger of interference. The Yugoslavs also seemed satisfied with the provisions made for their security in the settlement. All Europe breathed a little easier as a trouble spot, with the explosive potential of the Polish Corridor, where World War II began, was erased.

On the night of October 6 Clare gave a very select little party at the Villa Taverna. It consisted of the Durbrows, the Williamsons, James O'Sullivan, a young officer of the embassy, who had been the Trieste problem specialist, and the young men and women from the code room, who had worked so long and devotedly, days, nights, and Sundays, to get the messages through.

These few people were the only ones who knew the full story. They, in turn, presented Clare with a plumed *Bersagliere* helmet as a souvenir of the final settlement of the long and dangerous Trieste question. Few other questions had ever engendered such a flood of messages from so many capitals.

The reaction in Italy to the Trieste settlement was spontaneous and tremendous. The Italian papers outdid themselves in praise of the American Ambassador. Even independent old Guareschi admitted he had been wrong. Americans were suddenly the most popular people in Italy, and when the Ambassador drove out the crowds again yelled, "La Lucé! La Lucé!"

The Italian government showed its appreciation in a charming gesture typical of its imaginative courtesy. The head of the Foreign Office, Count Zoppi, gave an official luncheon at the Villa Madama for all the Americans who had taken part in the negotiations. Speeches were made; toasts were drunk. Clare was radiantly happy.

At the end Zoppi, at the head of the long table, turned smiling to the lovely lady beside him. "Mrs. Luce," he said, "the last time you were at the Foreign Office you forgot a personal belonging. I take pleasure in returning it to you."

He produced a golden cigarette case that Clare always carried, on which were little charms, symbolizing high points in her career, from Vanity Fair to the Capitol at Washington. She knew she had not left it anywhere. Why, Tish had told her it needed repairing!

As she looked at it, she saw that something had been added. It was a new little charm in rubies and brilliants, of the arms of the City of Trieste. So this was what they really thought . . .

The American Ambassador burst into tears. The head of the Foreign Office of Italy wiped his eyes, and Minister Counselor Durbrow and all the other guests blew their noses happily. Nobody said anything for several long seconds.

Then Zoppi took the case again: "There is space for one more emblem on it," he observed.

"Yes," Clare said faintly. "What do you suggest?"

"I should like to see there a charm to commemorate the occasion of your becoming Senior Ambassador of the Diplomatic Corps," Zoppi answered.

Which meant that he hoped Clare, a very junior diplomat now, would remain for years in Rome.

CHAPTER TWENTY-FOUR

A VALIANT WOMAN

IT MIGHT BE SUPPOSED THAT THE HAPPY SOLUTION TO THE TRIESTE crisis would give Clare a respite from pressure. It did—for a couple of weeks.

By this time the Villa Taverna was running as sweetly as a carefully broken-in-Cadillac. The staff of twelve servants functioned smoothly under the generalship of Maître d'Hôtel Mario Capitano, who knew the diplomatic ropes as well as the Doyen of the Corps Diplomatique. However, the fact that they were efficient does not imply servility. They were, in fact, a merry lot, who waited on you with what can only be described as respectful camaraderie.

The whole atmosphere of the house was gay. Clare's dogs, a pair of poodles diplomatically dubbed Scusi and Prego, scampered around, and there was a general atmosphere of pleasant confusion. To the beauty of the fine paintings and Harry's collection of ancient Chinese ceramics and jade which gave interest to the rooms, Clare had added a collection of conversation pieces in the hall. There were a miniaturelike painting of Portofino by Noel Coward, a brick-dust Moroccan landscape by Winston Churchill, and a stiff Grant Woodish portrait of Lincoln which was the work of President Eisenhower. They were, of course, presents from these gifted doodlers in oils.

Clare's own most neglected talent was drawing. When she was a girl she had done vaguely promising pen-and-ink sketches. She continued all through her life to be a doodler—it took the form of caricatures of prominent figures. But painting she never dared try.

Then Winston Churchill presented her with a box of oil paints when she visited him in Sicily in the Spring of 1955 and gave her some tips on painting. Her presently announced ambition is to find leisure to do some "serious amateur daubing." She observed that if she could only persuade Eisenhower to give her a few hints on painting figures—which she, like Ike, prefers to landscapes—she would have the distinction of being the pupil of the two most illustrious amateur artists in the world.

Though they have no pretensions to artistic or technical excellence, her oils and water colors painted after only a month of practice have a naïve delight and some feeling for design and color. They might be described as modern primitives, possibly because Clare's uncontrollable sense of humor somehow sneaks in. The series of scenes of her early life which she painted in June, 1955, are hilariously funny and have the underlying pathos that is the essence of real humor.

Pleasant as the Villa Taverna is, it has certain drawbacks. For instance, there is a zoo just back of it, and sometimes the lions roar so loudly at night that you picture them leaping over the wall and stalking their prey among the flowerbeds and fountains. Another thing is the ancient catacombs under the garden, which reputedly lead away for a mile under Rome to the ancient Church of St. Agnes. Clare remarked, laughingly, "Fortunately, they don't lead to the Vatican, or there would be a Congressional investigation."

Actually, her only official acts of a religious nature have been to intervene on several occasions with the Italian government in behalf of certain Protestant missionaries who had been in trouble with the police authorities for excessive zeal in proselytizing. Clare persuaded the Italians to let numbers of these missionaries continue their work. On July 29, 1955, she finally had an audience with the Pope to pay her homages, as thousands of American public officials and ambassadors, Catholic and Protestant, have done as private citizens, to the man who has labored so long in the cause of world peace.

Hospitality was the keynote at the Villa. From the moment a guest arrived he felt a welcoming warmth, an atmosphere that the popular legends do not always associate with the stiffness and formality of embassies. Mrs. Grover, who was Clare's house guest part of that autumn of 1954, commented, "The Villa is one of the happiest houses I've ever stayed in."

People of all nationalities poured through there. Of course, hospitality is part of an ambassador's business, but the brand offered by the Luces had none of the forced air of many official functions.

Such openhanded entertaining cannot be done for peanuts. The Ambassador's salary and entertainment allowances covered just about one third of the cost of the establishment. Clare footed the bills for the remainder—she would not let Harry help her there, though she was eternally grateful for his help as a genial host.

Luce had now established his own office in Rome, quite apart from Time, Inc.'s premises. It was distinctly different from the famous thirty-third floor. Its ancient elevator operated with typically Italian parsimony of electricity. You had to put a *jettoni*— a slug—in a slot in order to make it work. Harry's staff, in addition to the *Time* bureau itself, consisted of an extremely intelligent Italian woman, the Duchessa Lante della Rovere, and two girl secretaries. From there he kept a firm hand on the pulse of *Time* around the world.

Though Clare did not take her husband's financial help in running her embassy, she loved the handsome presents he gave her. Sometimes she even conveyed a hint to him through Dorothy Farmer. Shortly before Clare's birthday, April 10, 1954, Dorothy tackled such a mission. This time Harry laughed at her: "What would I do without my little helper? But I have made other arrangements."

On the morning of Clare's birthday, she awoke as usual at seven-thirty and Tish Baldrige brought in a great stack of mail and telegrams. The Ambassador scrambled through them, looking for a message from her husband, who had been obliged to return to America. "Isn't there anything from Harry?" she demanded.

"There is a cable," Tish said, producing it.

Clare tore it open and read: *"Happy Birthday to my Madonna of the Roses."*

"That's certainly pretty, but I don't know what he means by *that*," she wondered aloud, "unless he's sent me lots of roses for my birthday."

"If you come downstairs you'll see what he means," laughed Tish.

Clare grabbed a robe and raced down the great staircase. Tish guided her to the small salon. As she reached the doorway, Clare stopped in wonder and awe.

Hanging on the wall, subtly spotlighted to enhance its superb colors, was one of the most beautiful paintings of the Madonna and Child she had ever seen. She instantly recognized it as being of the Florentine School of the late fifteenth century. Although it was nearly five hundred years old, the pearly flesh tints of the Child were as fresh as this morning's dew, and the gold of Mary's halo gleamed mint-new. Though the figures were stylized in the manner of the time, they were not stiff, but alive with the transcendent beauty of their divinity. The background was a trellised vine with glossy leaves and dark red roses.

Dorothy Farmer told the Ambassador that the painting was by Pier Francesco Fiorentina and was called the Madonna of the Roses. Clare blinked back tears. Roses were her most loved flower. If Harry had searched the world—but of course he had—he could have found no more perfect birthday gift.

Undaunted by the spate of official parties, Clare occasionally gave one just for fun. Such was a spur-of-the-moment supper in honor of John Steinbeck, attended by this biographer, in October, 1954. Steinbeck, with his ivory-knobbed cane and an air of fleshy high living, seemed a long way from Cannery Row, but there was no denying his rather heavy brilliance. Mrs. Steinbeck, slim, dark and outgiving, was the perfect wife for a man of letters.

In the gray-and-gold dining room, enlivened by colorful paintings by Monet, Segonzac, and Pissarro, the Ambassador sat at the head of the table. In the golden candlelight, her profile was as pure as a Grecian marble, but her eyes were full of the excitement of good talk. In fact, all of the ten people present seemed to be raised to the *nth* power of their personalities by the stimulus of politely clashing minds.

John Steinbeck developed an extremely interesting theory of the new semantics needed to pierce the Iron Curtain. "It is no use using the old words," he said; "their meaning has been corrupted. For example, in Russia peace now means war until communism has conquered the world. Democracy equals Soviet dictatorship;

and liberty is the right to obey. So we must speak only of small, concrete things, using a coinage of words that cannot be debased."

The conversation then ranged from American propaganda methods and techniques around the world to the influence of the American novel on the writers of modern Italy, from the sort of cultural exhibits that would best represent America abroad to the possibility of war in the Formosa Strait over Quemoy and Matsu.

After dinner, as we sat in the small salon of the Villa, Clare spoke happily of the evening. "This is what I always missed most in politics," she said, "the stimulus of searching minds like Steinbeck's, the joy of hearing brilliant talkers exchange ideas with no axes to grind. Believe me, when I have finished this job I hope to retire from politics to my dear Connecticut hilltop."

Then she laughed and added, "I say this in spite of what Al Smith once told me: 'In politics, never say good-by, just "au revoyer." ' "

One could not doubt that she meant it. And yet one wondered if anyone so aware of the problems and urgencies of the times and, quite rightly, conscious of her ability to do something about them, could settle for a hilltop, however beautiful. On our way home John Steinbeck agreed that three weeks among the white birches of Sugar Hill would change "good-by to 'au revoyer.' "

Clare said herself she was charged with three tasks as Ambassador to Italy. The first was to further, by every means possible, Italian and American friendship, and to aid Italy to play its great new role in the Western Alliance. The second was to help settle the Trieste problem so that Italian diplomacy could enter more vigorously into the international scene. The third, and not the least important, was to aid by every proper means the young democratic republic of Italy to fight the malignant growth of communism in the Italian body politic.

In the first two years of her mission the Trieste question was solved. And Italy joined the Western European Union. As to the third, she has had the satisfaction of seeing the Italian government slowly but surely breaking the strength of the Communist party—especially the strength of the Communist labor unions.

Though her popularity with the Italians after the Trieste settlement probably set an all-time high for American ambassador, she was still an object of controversy. As one British correspondent put it: "If Mrs. Luce says it looks like rain, a lot of people will indignantly deny it; others will say she should stop interfering with the Italian weather; and a large minority will suggest that she stop talking and *do* something about it."

Clare was completely determined to do all that could be done to aid the democratic government in Italy.

The Italian attitude toward communism is quite different from that of America. In the first place there is no opprobrium attached to being a Communist—how could there be when one third of the electorate votes that way. Actually, as Indro Montanelli of the *Corriere della Sera* pointed out, there were a lot of material advantages to be gained by calling oneself a Communist. For one thing, it was a lot safer.

Montanelli says, "American kindness is very dangerous. The common Italian will say, 'If I am a registered Communist I have nothing to fear. If Russia wins I have nothing to fear, I'll be on the winning side and guard the prisoners. On the other hand, if the U. S. wins, I have nothing to fear, for they don't know who their enemies are. *They* don't keep lists.' If he is an intellectual he may add, 'Besides I may win a literary prize, because the Communists always win the prizes.'

"Also it is very difficult to be anti-Communist here, because you are accused of being Fascist. Thus we are the prisoners of words. The Americans are also the prisoners of words—justice, liberty, democracy. They just don't work with Communists."

Another good reason for being a Communist in Italy is the fact that many labor unions are Communist-dominated, and the great industrialists play ball with them to avoid strikes. Many factory owners actually contribute to the party funds. The workers' point of view is that if you vote right (that is, left) you are assured of your seniority and promotion.

Clare agrees with the Italian statesmen who say that such people are "bread-and-butter Communists." She believes that a very small percentage of the Italian voters really want communism. The rest are protest voters.

Clare expressed her feelings about the Italian Communists in a speech at Faneuil Hall in Boston on July 4, 1955. "These [Communist] Italians," she said, "want the wrong thing . . . when they want communism. But, may God bless them and guide them still, they want it for the right reason. They want to be free of the old economic tyrannies that denied them equality of opportunity with others in their society."

She added that "the shining fact is that Italy is emerging as a vibrant and dynamic nation . . . firm in the framework of the great Western Alliance."

However, Clare's logic cut right through the pleasant fantasy that Italian communism, if it got control, would be "different." No matter how different the Italian people might be from the Russians, communism in power would be the same ruthless tyranny that it was in Russia and everywhere else. To treat it in a *dolce far niente* manner was playing into the hands of the real Reds. Many influential Italians—even members of the government—believed that nothing could arrest the drift toward communism. It seems that Clare thought otherwise. But she kept her thoughts strictly to herself.

From the muddle over the Milano speech she had learned that public comments on Italian politics were apt to boomerang; but in private conversation with all the leaders of Italian thought, with politicians, industrialists, and intellectuals, she tactfully but plainly voiced the policy of her government: that it would never support an Italian Communist state, subservient to the Kremlin. "She tells us the truth," exclaimed one wondering cabinet minister. "It may be unpleasant truth, but it is an agreeable novelty to know exactly where one stands."

Nor did Clare fail to carry out Washington policies in questions of aid. She closely followed her instructions which said that the money of the United States taxpayer should not be used to support the Communist party in Italy. Owing to the complex labor situation in Italy, that is what had been happening in a backhand sort of way. We were giving large offshore contracts to Italian firms for military supplies for Italian defense. Some of the money thus spent went into the pockets of Italian workers who were being forced by the Communist unions to kick back part of their wages to the party.

What Clare did to counteract this situation is succinctly described in an AP dispatch that Congressman Albert P. Morano read into the *Congressional Record* of January 6, 1955, which he described as "an article which underscores graphically the splendid, realistic job that United States Ambassador to Italy, Clare Boothe Luce, is doing to help swing the balance against Communist inroads [in Italy]."

The article stated in part:

"ROME, December 26—A United States policy of no aid contracts for factories dominated by Red workers is hitting Italian communism where it hurts.

"More and more the men at the benches are voting for non-Communist representatives in shop elections. They want work—and Uncle Sam is handing out no offshore procurement contracts where the Communist-controlled Italian Federation of Labor is in the saddle.

"United States Ambassador Clare Boothe Luce pioneered this get-tough policy 4 months ago. She ordered an $18-million ammunition contract canceled after Communists gained strength among workers of the Officina Vittorio Meccanica, near Milan.

"Two months later, to prove that the United States meant business, a second contract was withdrawn at Palermo, Sicily. For $7,528,000, this order would have provided Italy with a new 1,500-ton destroyer escort at American expense. Cancellation came after factory workers increased the Communist majority on the factory committee even after the United States Order. . . .

"Now the workers know there will be no offshore procurement orders for factories whose workers vote these Communist commissions and union officials into office.

"United States officials report that since Mrs. Luce's crackdown factory elections have been running strongly anti-Communist. Anti-Communists have won even in many former Communist strongholds, they say. . . .

"Behind the scenes, the United States is quietly trying to assist this shift by persuading Italian employers that improved treatment of workers, as well as more workers' benefits, will bring increased production and cut Communist strength.

"Italian industry is notorious in Europe for backward labor practices, although there are such bright spots as the Olivetti company. In the last 2 years, under quiet American pressure, such firms as Fiat have stepped up workers' benefits and improved labor relations.

"Mrs. Luce also authored this affirmative policy. Firms with good labor relations and practices are more likely to get United States aid contracts than others. Knowing this, the smart industrialists are getting their labor practices into line.

"The results in employee good will is beginning to show gradually—and that, too, means fewer Communist workers in Italy."

When American contracts with companies dominated by Communist unions were canceled, there was a howl of rage from the Communist and fellow-traveling Italian press, who charged "intervention by the U. S. in Italian internal affairs." But Clare went on serenely carrying out American policy. The Italian government and the Italian industrialists stood equally firm in their long fight against Communist domination.

The payoff came in December, 1954, in Fiat's big Avio factory in Turin, where the Communists lost their long-held control by a vote among the workers of 1,920 against the Communists and only 77 for them.

And in Washington, Democratic Senator Stuart Symington reporting to the Senate on these events concluded: "The senior Senator from New Hampshire [Styles Bridges] and I are glad to make this report to the Senate and to commend the actions of Ambassador Luce in the matter herewith presented."

Nor was the trend away from communism confined to factory workers, but became evident in politics. True, Scelba's government fell shortly after his triumphant tour of the United States in the spring of 1955. But this was only because the Italian politicians were getting tired of one man holding the spotlight for eighteen months. Scelba's successors were just as anti-Communist and pro-West. The real answer lies in the Sicilian election held in June, 1955, when the Communist vote was cut from 35 to 20 per cent of the total.

Even in moments of comparative serenity such as the autumn of 1954, Clare's schedule remained ferocious. From her awakening at seven-thirty to bedtime, long past midnight, Clare never stopped for an instant. The forces of nature also conspired to keep her

from a life of ease. Early in November, 1954, the village of Salerno, of fearful memory to Americans, was almost wiped out by a
flash flood following a tempest. Over a hundred people were killed
and several thousand were left homeless.

Writing in the *Il Progresso Italo-Americano*, Mario Palladini said
that the other ambassadors acted as expected. They sent "the proper
expressions of regret" or even went so far as to make a personal
diplomatic call. At most they "subscribed a few *dinaros* to the fund
for succoring the victims."

The moment the news reached the American Embassy, Clare
went into action and appealed to Washington for instructions to
let the U. S. aid the flood sufferers. Within a matter of a few days
a long caravan of U. S. Army trucks were carrying American supplies of food and necessities to the victims; and she pledged American money—and her own—to the relief fund.

But, as she remarked to her Air Attaché, General Cassady,
"Largesse without good will is useless."

So she flew to Naples herself. For two days she tramped in mud
and rain through the wreckage of Salerno, visiting the victims in
hospitals and in the ruins of their homes, bringing them her personal assurance that help was coming.

Another calamity and another supremely tactful gesture helped
strengthen Clare's popularity in Italy. Just before she left for the
United States in January, 1955, an Italian airliner crashed at
Idlewild Airport in New York with great loss of life. Clare immediately canceled her reservations on an American airline and flew
to America on an Italian line plane.

In chronicling the success of Clare's mission to Italy, it is not
intended to imply that she alone was responsible for the fortunate
developments there. Nobody with any sense would believe that
unaided she brought about the Trieste settlement. Incidentally,
Clare's comment on that is simply, "It was done by a brilliant team
of negotiators. Perhaps my only contribution was the pigheaded
interest I displayed from the beginning in getting a settlement."

In any event, the fact remains that Trieste was settled and the
tide has turned—temporarily at least, against communism in Italy.

The rising standard of living, especially in the industrial north, where almost every worker now has his Topolino—his little mouse Fiat—or at least a motor scooter; and the government economic reform efforts in the depressed areas of the south, Clare says, are the most important factors.

And yet Clare was Ambassador when these things happened. Had they gone wrong, who would have been held responsible? But they went right. As they say in racing, "You pay off the way the numbers go up."

The American people have generally realized what has happened in Italy. The flop-over of public opinion has been interesting to watch. Up to the summer of 1954 any mention of Ambassador Clare Boothe Luce brought the comment, "Isn't it awful the way she has messed things up!" In 1955 mention of her name produced a knowing nod of the head and the comment, "I hear she is doing an excellent job."

More concrete recognition has come to her in the praise of her superiors in the State Department and the White House, and the award of honors by universities and civic associations. On January 17, 1955, the Poor Richard Club of Philadelphia conferred on her its Gold Medal of Achievement, which had previously been awarded to such men as President Eisenhower, General Mac-Arthur, and Will Rogers, but never before given to a woman.

In March, Georgetown University conferred on Clare the degree of Doctor of Laws, *Honoris Causa*. The citation began: "Georgetown University rejoices today in honoring one to whom Solomon's salute, rarely merited, is given with all appropriateness—a 'Valiant Woman' . . . Her first and enduring hatred has been for sham and pretension . . . and she has exposed evil with luminous clarity. But always her purpose has been to heal, not to wound. Always her gifted intelligence has striven to serve the heart's dearest cause, which is love."

There has also been instituted a considerable move to nominate Clare Luce for Vice-President on the Republican ticket in 1956. What will come of that nobody knows, but it is worth quoting a comment made by Clare when a reporter asked her what she thought of the idea: Said Clare, "We will not see a woman Vice-President in my lifetime."

Perhaps a greater tribute than public honors is the private opinion of her colleagues in the American Embassy in Rome. In the beginning they were almost as upset as the Roman aristocracy. In fact so much twittering talk went on that the then-Ambassador, Ellsworth Bunker, called a staff meeting and ordered them to stop it.

Now they are completely loyal to The Boss. Elbridge Durbrow summed up their feelings when he said, "I admire her for three things in particular. One, she is intelligent. Two, she seeks advice and takes it with an open mind—you can say exactly what you think to her. Then she makes up her own mind. And three—her sense of humor. As an old careerist, I could ask for no better boss."

Clare is equally cognizant of her debt to her staff—from Durbrow right down to the young men and women in the code room. In a speech before the Cleveland Council on World Affairs in March, 1955, she said, "No ambassador, however experienced, however hard-working, however wise, can do any better job than his team will let him do. The ambassador must lean heavily on the men on his team, on his political officers, his economic officers, his information officers, and all his other advisers in their various fields. If they are a good team, as I believe mine in Rome is, then his job will be well done. . . . The hard core, the backbone, of any diplomatic mission must be and must remain the Foreign Service professionals . . ."

A book about a person like Clare Boothe Luce, who is rising toward the peak of achievement, cannot end. It just stops. Her achievements cannot be properly evaluated while the heat of controversy is still on. Neither can her complex character, with its combination of logic and mysticism, of decisiveness and compassion, be clearly understood, since it, too, is evolving.

As to her ability as America's first woman ambassador to a major power, let not her friends have the final word, since such quotes are always suspect. Adversaries usually speak the salty truth, so let that word come from Senator Stuart Symington, Democrat, who has fought Clare's ideas from hell to breakfast. Senator Symington, who had made an inspection tour of American embassies in Europe, said, "Without question, Clare's embassy was the best organized of those I visited in Europe. She put on an excellent briefing for us with her staff, giving us very accurate information, and Clare contributing most of all. She has a rare capacity for getting facts. An operator!

"In fact, she is one of those people who, when you think they're not quite following you, ask a question that shows they're 'way ahead of you."

Then the Senator grinned. "You can believe what I say," he added, "because I'm against her politically. The fact is that when Clare acts like a woman, she's better than most women; and when she acts like a man, she's better than most men."

As to her character, Georgetown University hit the bull's-eye when they called her a "Valiant Woman." Solomon's verses do seem to fit:

> *Who shall find a valiant woman? Far and from the uttermost coasts is the price of her.*
>
> *The heart of her husband trusteth in her, and he shall have no need of spoils.*
>
> *She will render him good and not evil all the days of her life. . . .*
>
> *She is like the merchant's ship, she bringeth her bread from afar. . . .*
>
> *She hath considered a field and bought it: with the fruit of her hands she hath planted a vineyard.*
>
> *She hath girded her loins with strength, and hath strengthened her arms. . . .*
>
> *She hath opened her hand to the needy, and stretched out her hands to the poor.*
>
> *She shall not fear for her house in the cold of snow: for all her domestics are clothed in double garments.*
>
> *She hath made for herself clothing of tapestry: fine linen and purple is her covering.*
>
> *Her husband is honorable in the gates when he sitteth among the Senators of the land. . . .*
>
> *Strength and beauty are her clothing and she shall laugh in the latter day.*

She hath opened her mouth to wisdom, and the law of clemency is on her tongue. . . .

Favor is deceitful, and beauty is vain; the woman that feareth the Lord, she shall be praised.

Give her of the fruit of her hands: and let her works praise her in the gates.

INDEX